Charles Taylor

SIX JOURNEYS:
A CANADIAN PATTERN

Brigadier James Sutherland Brown

Bishop William White

James Houston

Herbert Norman

Emily Carr

Scott Symons

ANANSI   TORONTO

Published with the assistance of the Ontario Arts Council and the Canada Council.

House of Anansi Press Limited
35 Britain Street
Toronto, Canada   M5A 1R7

Cover Design: Grant Design/John Grant
Made in Canada

77 78 79 80 81 82   6 5 4 3 2 1

Canadian Cataloguing in Publication Data

Taylor, Charles, 1935—
    Six journeys

Bibliography: p.
ISBN 0-88784-057-4 bd.   ISBN 0-88784-056-6 pa.

1. Canada — Biography.   I. Title.

FC25.T38   920'.071   C77-001114-4
F1005.T38

ACKNOWLEDGEMENTS

House of Anansi Press would like to thank the following people for their kind permission to reproduce photographs of subjects: *Brigadier James Sutherland Brown*: Atholl Sutherland Brown; *Bishop William White*: Dr. Gordon B. White; *James Houston*: James Houston; *Herbert Norman*: Dr. Howard Norman; *Emily Carr*: Provincial Archives, Victoria, B.C.; *Scott Symons*: Scott Symons.

Excerpts from *Place d'Armes* and *Heritage: A Romantic Look at Early Canadian Furniture* by Scott Symons reprinted by permission of The Canadian Publishers, McClelland and Stewart Limited, Toronto.

Excerpts from *Ghost Fox* by James Houston reprinted by permission of The Canadian Publishers, McClelland and Stewart Limited, Toronto.

To my Mother and Father

CONTENTS

INTRODUCTION   I

Brigadier James Sutherland Brown   1

Bishop William White   39

James Houston   73

Herbert Norman   105

Emily Carr   153

Scott Symons   189

NOTES   245

In this era when the homogenising power of technology is almost unlimited, I do regret the disappearance of indigenous traditions, including my own. It is true that no particularism can adequately incarnate the good. But is it not also true that only through some particular roots, however partial, can human beings first grasp what is good and it is the juice of such roots which for most men sustain their partaking in a more universal good?

George Grant, *Technology and Empire*

INTRODUCTION

Canadians do not like heroes, and so they do not have them. They do not even have great men in the accepted sense of the word.

George Woodcock

If Canada does not often produce great artists, scientists and professional men, it is not because the material is not amongst us, but because we do not know how to handle it. The characteristics of genius too often arouse our suspicion and distrust, whence it comes that our prophets are so often without honour in their own country.

B. K. Sandwell

More than most peoples, Canadians are prejudiced in favour of the ordinary: it is a function of our history, our climate and our geography. In a harsh land, we still honour all those pioneering virtues which impose restraint and engender mediocrity. If the work ethic has become less compelling, if a variety of immigrants has weakened the grip of our residual Calvinist rigidity, we are nevertheless the creatures of our historic experience. Revolutions produce heroes: it is one reason why the Americans have such an abundance of exemplary figures. But we lack a revolution, and our rebellions are notable mainly for their ineptitude. As Hugh Hood has pointed out, we have never succumbed to the twin cults of Byronism and Bonapartism, the personal and public versions of the Romantic Hero. Even our constitution enshrines the resolutely unheroic goals of peace, order and good government.

We are so uncertain in our response to greatness that an outside opinion can sway our judgment. It took the Chinese to make a hero out of Norman Bethune, and many Canadians accepted this verdict only when it was pointed out that our wheat sales might increase. Yet not even a Nobel Peace Prize could do the same for Lester Pearson, since Pearson was too much like the rest of us, with a basic Canadian diffidence. We found this reassuring: it seems we take a perverse pleasure in trivializing our public figures. When we look to the past, we need to see our heroes flawed: a drunken Macdonald or a lunatic Riel. This makes them less demanding, even dismissable. When a potential great man — a Diefenbaker perhaps — emerges among us, we are quick to cut him down to size, and to rejoice in his blunders. As Woodcock has also written, Canadians "suspect the sheer gigantic irrationalism of the heroic, for we like to consider ourselves a reasonable people." It might almost be said that something in us hates a hero.

Despite this reluctance to acknowledge greatness in our midst, it is nevertheless clear that we have produced some remarkable people whose qualities often verge on the heroic. With a moment's reflection, any reader could suggest several Canadians, living or dead, whose attributes place them far above the ordinary run of their compatriots. It was never my intention to produce such a list, but for a long time the six subjects of this book have grappled my imagination. Apart from their specific virtues — especially their courage and panache — there was a tone or style to each life which struck me as quintessentially Canadian. At first it was hard to understand why this was so, since there was such an obvious diversity among them. But as I explored these lives, a curious pattern began to emerge.

At the start I could see one common link: my six characters represented British pioneer stock, rather than the contemporary mosaic. And while I chose them for themselves, and not to illustrate some sociological theory, this congruence seemed more appropriate than accidental. It has become fashionable in recent years to deplore our British heritage, but even this steady denigration of our traditions is a back-handed tribute to their potency. It is not only that British pioneers and their descendents were largely responsible for the creation of Canada, and are still dominant in our public affairs. It is also that British patterns became ingrained in our culture and have largely determined, for better or worse, the texture of our lives. Anyone who seeks to explore the deeper recesses of the Canadian spirit must eventually confront its basic Britishness.

Despite this British background, however, I soon realized there was no political or philosophical or religious persuasion which was common to all six characters. Indeed, there was apparently a world of difference between — for example — the Tory patriot, Sutherland Brown, and the liberal internationalist, Herbert Norman. In a similar way, some were Anglican, while others were Calvinist or Methodist: this was not merely a matter of church attendance, since it involved the essence of their sensibilities. Nor did they even belong to the same era: Bishop White and Emily Carr were fundamentally Victorian, while James Houston and Scott Symons are still among us.

Clearly there was no common tradition, yet the more I delved into each life, the more I discovered common themes. Despite the diversity of dates, each of my characters was in some manner a Victorian. Each had that exuberant spirit which animated the General Gordons, the Richard Burtons, the Hester Stanhopes and all those other Victorians who seem to have been born with a passion for the exotic, and with an appetite for more than their society had to offer them. Together with this craving for experience, each had some of that driving energy which impelled the Victorians to their best achievements. In a Canadian context, one thinks of the men who built the railway and opened up the West. Whatever their faults, these were men of substance; as we apprehend them in old photographs, they have a forceful presence which is rarely seen today. (Compare their portraits to those of any contemporary Canadian cabinet or board of directors.) Since Canada became a nation in the Victorian era, it is perhaps more than coincidental that this sort of energy and style has continued to prevail among the best of us.

Like the most exemplary of the Victorians, the subjects of this book felt a need to serve a larger cause. In their different ways, they appear as missionaries for something that is greater than themselves, something that transcends the narrow secularity of their time. Each was seeking a nobler and more spiritual way of being human than their Canadian society encouraged or even tolerated. They were believers and even visionaries; their lives were directed by an impulse which was basically religious, although hardly constrained by mere orthodoxy. Instead, some can be said to have created their own particular faiths, finding their inspiration in entities as remote as ancient Chinese temple paintings or the pre-historic Caves of Lascaux.

This religious impulse also made them conservative — not in a narrow political sense, but in the deeper sense of trying to enact traditions which are rooted in faith, and which rebuke the corroding cynicism of recent decades. Each was opposed to modernity, to what George Grant has called "the central fact of the North American dream — progress through technology". They steadfastly resisted the bland new world of the technocrats, although each chose a different form of opposition. There were those who wore masks: Herbert Norman guarding his sensitivity with the urbane guise of the scholar-diplomat; Bishop White exercising his spiritual intensity behind the facade of an extraverted man-of-affairs. And there were those, like Carr and Symons, who were much more blatant in confronting their compatriots, and who mounted their challenge with a showman's style. Their fortunes have been just as varied: in some cases there was compromise, in others an adamant refusal to capitulate. We are dealing, among other aspects, with four very particular deaths, and two lives whose outcomes are still in doubt.

Their society seldom heeded them. Sometimes it opposed them, although the opposition was almost always underhand. It was not so much a case of destroying these disturbing visionaries, as making them seem irrelevant. When Sutherland Brown began to embarrass his political and military masters, they avoided an open confrontation, and dispatched him with a flurry of memos. Perhaps this technique is particularly Canadian in its furtiveness: the only sustained example of overt opposition in this book is Norman's persecution by Americans.

More often, however, these six Canadians met with a bland acceptance which rarely hid a fundamental indifference. Carr was almost suffocated by a tolerance which ignored the deeper meaning of her work. We are pleased to have White's Chinese treasures in the Royal Ontario Museum, and we regard the Eskimo art which Houston fostered as part of our culture — but we hardly allow either to touch our lives. If Symons is also tolerated — and even subsidized by a government which once sent foreign police to hunt him down — the heritage he champions is still officially and systematically denigrated. If Norman is honoured, it is mainly as a victim of the McCarthy era, while the real implications of his suicide are conveniently overlooked. With each life there is a sense of enormous waste: how much *more* there might have been, if only their compatriots had been less fearful and begrudging. But our indifference to our prophets is also essentially Canadian: we seem incapable of using them.

Faced with such a strange mixture of opposition and indifference, each of these Canadians was forced into a life of loneliness and isolation. They felt compelled to escape their Canadian society, and to sharpen the edges of their identities in different forms of exile. For it was not only that each had a deeper, richer vision which demanded to be lived, and which Canada-as-modernity denied. It was also that to live that vision, each sought fulfillment in the older values of another civilization. This seems the most striking of their common traits: more than derivatively Victorian, it suggests a pattern which could be quintessentially Canadian.

In some cases (Brown, Houston, Symons), the "alien" culture was an authentic Canadian tradition which had been betrayed by the proponents of modernity, and thus made unnaturally foreign. In other cases (Carr and Houston again), it was our native peoples who offered the fuller vision — just as they themselves were being so strenuously modernized. For Bishop White, it was a matter of finding sustenance in the rich heritage of Chinese art and thought — at a time when his own Christian traditions had long been perverted, and when even those Chinese traditions were giving way to modernity in the form of Communism. With Norman, there was a reliance on another Oriental culture, and a stubborn adherence to an

older humanism which had been debased by its modern fol-
lowers. Going beyond his immediate Canadian and European
background, Symons finds his life-giving vision in the incarnational worlds of Mexico and Morocco.

This is not to state that Canadians can achieve
authenticity only by undertaking odysseys to distant lands, by
going native, or by losing themselves in a foreign creed. But it
is to suggest that to flourish as Canadians we need to be more
than contemporary Canadians: good technocrats and complacent taxpayers, mere victims or survivors. All the subjects of
this book explored the life-enhancing insights which older cultures have embodied so emphatically and which comprise our
human heritage. They journeyed into spiritual realms which
modern Canada ignores or denigrates, yet none was an escap-
ist: each was concerned to formulate a vision which could
work in Canada, for Canadians.

Brigadier James Sutherland Brown

In early July of 1922, Colonel James Sutherland ("Buster") Brown, DSO, CMG, set out by motor car from Ottawa on a trip to New York State. At the age of forty-one, he was Director of Military Operations and Intelligence in the Department of National Defence — in other words, he was in charge of Canada's military planning. Four other officers were with him in the car: the Assistant Director of Signals, Lt Col E. Forde, DSO, and the General Staff Officers of Military Districts Three, Four and Five: Lt Col F. O. Hodgins, DSO, Lt Col R. O. Alexander, DSO, and Lt Col J. M. Prower, DSO.

All five soldiers were in mufti, but snapshots they took of each other along the route indicate they could hardly have been mistaken for ordinary tourists. All wear dark suits, white shirts and what appear to be regimental ties. Despite the formality of dress, however, there is something boyish and carefree about the men in these photographs, something in their faces and their stance that suggests a glorious lark. Sutherland Brown took most of the photographs: in the only one in which he appears, we see a man of average height with a firm chin and a prominent, assertive nose. It is a strong face, with nothing tentative about it, but the humour in the deep-set eyes belies the fierceness of the military moustache. A swashbuckler, you might think, with a trace of the sensualist. Even something of a rogue.

The five Canadians crossed the American border at Ogdensburg. For nearly a week, they made a thorough tour of the northern regions of New York. By the time they returned to Ottawa, they had travelled 1,119 miles. Their subsequent Secret Report (which is signed by Sutherland Brown) covers 66 foolscap pages, with 56 photographs neatly pasted beside the text. There are also appendices which are largely road maps of the state, presumably acquired at gas stations.

Aside from the snapshots they took of themselves, the travellers pointed their cameras at views which were hardly the normal tourist attractions. Most of the photographs in the Secret Report show road and railway junctions, as well as arsenals, bridges and canals. Most of the prose concerns topography, geography and communications. A typical paragraph states that

> The GRASS RIVER which flows through CANTON and proceeds in a north-easterly direction entering the St. Lawrence near CORNWALL provides an obstacle against lateral advance south of the St. Lawrence. In its upper reaches it is fordable by Infantry, but the destruction of road and railway bridges would prevent any transport crossing, until rebridged.

Venturing into the larger cities, the travellers found that Albany, the state capital

> is situated on the right bank of the Hudson and is practically a focus for all the communications for New York State, as well as routes both highway and rail, leading from Massachusetts and Vermont. The capture of ALBANY would therefore block all communications to Northern and Western New York and to a certain extent into Vermont.

Vermont was another area of particular interest to Sutherland Brown. In the following July, he was again on the road, this time with Col Forde who was at the wheel of a McLaughlin Six. In the course of five days, they covered 703 miles inside Vermont; on their return, Sutherland Brown produced another Secret Report with 59 foolscap pages and as many photographs.

Once again the travellers concentrated on towns which focused highway, railroad and canal routes. Their photographs again show bridges and armouries, as well as passes through the Green Mountains. Their report has sections on the geography, communications and industry of the state, and such typical comments as:

> RUTLAND, population about 15,000, is a place of great
> strategic importance. . . a Force operating along the Lake
> Champlain line would have to protect its flanks by hold-
> ing the Rutland passes.

Like northern New York, Vermont is seen primarily in
military terms — in this case, as an obstacle between the Canadian border and the rest of New England: "If the passes of
the Green Mountains were held, there could be no direct communication between armies trying to advance up the Cham-
plain Valley and those trying to advance farther east between
Maine and New Hampshire."

Not all the observations are contemporary, however. In
both New York and Vermont, Sutherland Brown visited
historic battle sites, and then refought the engagements in the
pages of his reports. He is sharply critical of British general-
ship during the American Revolution, and concludes that if a
concerted attack had been launched from Canada, the revolutionaries might have been defeated. At the very least, he
argues, the present boundaries of Canada would run along the
Mohawk and Hudson Rivers. He is just as scathing about
some of the British generals during the War of 1812, especially
the "spineless" Sir George Prevost. If Prevost had only taken
the initiative after crossing the border in 1814, "no doubt
there would have been a very different situation in North
America today. Vermont, New Hampshire and Maine might
have been British possessions."

Nor is Sutherland Brown reluctant to make political
and social observations. He describes Saratoga as "a spa, filled
with hotels and Jews. I saw more Jews in a few minutes passing through Saratoga Springs than I have seen in one place in
my life before." In Vermont, he is critical of the many bill-
boards and the lack of good hotels, as well as the attitude and
appearance of the people. ("If they are not actually lazy they
have a deliberate way of working and apparently believe in
frequent rests and gossip. The women throughout the rural
districts appear to be a heavy and not very comely lot.") Most
of all, he casts a scornful eye on every sign of American chau-
vinism:

> Nearly all the inscriptions on historical sites were rather

braggadocial in character, referring to the prowess of American arms in "the fight for liberty". If these statements were not altogether untruthful they are misleading. All along our journey the American flag "Old Glory" was flying everywhere. This continual flag flying and distorted descriptions of historical occurrences are apparently all part of the American plan to weld their nation together and to Americanize a large number of foreigners they have admitted to their country annually for the past one hundred years.

But these are sidelights. To Sutherland Brown, in charge of Canada's military planning, the sole purpose of his reconnaissance of New York and Vermont was to pinpoint the canals, the mountain passes and the road and rail junctions that would have to be captured in the event of war. His Secret Reports are nothing less than a blueprint for a Canadian invasion of the United States.

What is going on here? How can we possibly explain the enormity of these Secret Reports? Can it all be some monstrous joke? After all, this was the early nineteen-twenties, a period of general prosperity and good relations between Canada and the United States. Both nations had fought as allies in the First World War: evocations of 1812 were hardly prevalent in the rhetoric of politicians on either side of the border. Since that earlier war, there had been times when Britain had cause to be concerned about the southern defences of its Canadian dominion, but in 1919, Admiral of the Fleet Viscount Jellicoe, heading a naval mission to Canada, indicated that war between the British Empire and the United States was so unlikely a contingency as scarcely to affect future Canadian defence plans. Two years later, Admiral David Beatty told the Canadian Club of Toronto:

> When you look at the map and you see a great frontier line, stretching over 3,600 miles, and you scratch your head and say, "Well, what is defending it?" Nothing but the sound common sense, the sound good-will of two practical nations.

This was certainly the belief of most Canadian leaders. Mackenzie King became Prime Minister for the first time in 1921; some years earlier, he had already begun praising the unprotected frontier, maintaining in a speech: "We have substituted for competitive arming a system of international conciliation and arbitration, as a means of settling international differences."

Clearly this was the voice of "sound common sense" — liberal, practical and progressive. As Canada and the United States advanced toward a shared future of continental prosperity, it was ludicrous to consider conflict across the border as anything more than a quaint memory of earlier and less enlightened times.

Yet here we have — in 1922 and again in 1923 — the Director of Military Operations and Intelligence, the man in charge of Canada's military planning, putting on civilian clothes, loading up his camera, slipping across the border . . . and spying. Then returning to Canada and drawing up Secret Reports which describe the best way for Canadian forces to invade the United States.

It should not be presumed that Sutherland Brown was acting out some private fantasy. It is no small matter for a senior officer to engage in espionage against a powerful neighbour. (Suppose he had been caught, camera in hand, pointed at some arsenal. . . .) Yet Sutherland Brown made his clandestine trips with the approval of his superiors; moreover, the records of the Department of National Defence contain references to similar missions. Writing to the Chief of the General Staff from St. John, New Brunswick, in May 1921, Brig-Gen A. H. Macdonnell, commanding Military District Seven, requested "permission to hire a motor car and proceed into the United States *incognito* twice during the early summer with my General Staff Officer, in order to make a personal reconnaissance of four roads to Portland (Maine)."

So these were far from unofficial endeavours. In fact, each spying expedition was based on a Top Secret document locked in the safe of every Military District commander from British Columbia to the Maritimes. This document — Defence Scheme No. 1 — was Canada's official strategic plan throughout the nineteen-twenties. It had two major premises:

(1) the only immediate military danger to Canada was from the United States, and (2) in the event of war, the best defence would be an offensive thrust across the border in several key sectors. To prepare for such an invasion, senior staff officers were specifically urged by the Scheme to make "advance reconnaissances" within the United States.

Had the whole Canadian General Staff gone out of its collective mind? Or can we identify an individual culprit: a single officer who had taken advantage of his position to impose his remarkable views on his compliant colleagues? If so, he would have to be the author of Defence Scheme No. 1: the same Colonel (later Brigadier) James Sutherland Brown whom we have seen setting out so blithely and so resolutely on his spying expeditions.

Yet Sutherland Brown was far from an eccentric misfit. One of the most highly regarded staff officers in the Canadian army, he had earned his post on merit, and was soon to be marked for further advancement. Moreover, his strategic and political views were shared at that time by nearly all his senior colleagues — often with considerable enthusiasm. If those views seem remarkable to us today, it is not because Sutherland Brown was mad, or even notably misguided. Rather, it is because we have debased an authentic tradition which lies at the heart of our history, and which Sutherland Brown embodied so proudly and emphatically.

James Sutherland Brown was born on a farm outside Simcoe, Ontario, on 28 June 1881. Not much is known about his childhood except that he often devised elaborate games in which British and Canadian forces, led by himself, were given the task of repelling American invaders. His playmates mocked his obsession with the Yankees, but he was strong-willed, and they never could persuade him to let them become cowboys and Indians.

Simcoe is not far from Queenston Heights. So it seems likely that young Jimmy (the "Buster" came later) was stirred by tales of Sir Isaac Brock and the great battle of 1812 in which the British general lost his life, but repelled the Americans and saved the day for Canada. Another influence was

The Captain, a beautifully printed English schoolboy magazine which Jimmy read avidly for its patriotic stories, and which was a forerunner of those boys' weeklies later attacked by Orwell for implanting reactionary ideas in impressionable minds.

Yet the knowledge was already in his blood. Both parents were the descendents of Scottish immigrants. A great-grandfather, McArthur Brown, probably of Kilfinan, went to America about 1750, settled in Massachusetts and moved to Upper Canada after the American Revolution. For James Sutherland Brown, his United Empire Loyalist lineage was more than a source of pride. It was the foundation of his deepest convictions. Years later he wrote that

> One hundred thousand of the best blood of the Thirteen Colonies migrated from the United States during and immediately after the war. Many others came later. Many were killed and brow-beaten into submission. Many did not have the wherewithall to get away. Those that came to the north formed the backbone of British Canada. Their descendents today are a safeguard for all time to come.

Historians have dispelled the myth that the Loyalists were all upper class Tories and fervent Anglophiles. They were a disparate group, and many had mixed motives for moving north, and remaining under the British Crown. Yet in their new home, removed from the overpowering influence of American liberalism and republicanism, the Loyalists took the lead in shaping a political culture which was significantly different from the more clamorous, less restrained society emerging south of the border. They were seeking a way of being American *and* British: a way of living together in the New World without denying the vision of civilization which animated Europe. Above all, they differed with the American revolutionaries over what it meant to be a human being. They refused to accept the American doctrine of essential freedom: a doctrine which sees the land, the native peoples, other nations, even one's own body — everything except one's will — as raw material to be subjugated and used according to one's desires. This is the doctrine which George Grant has described as the foundation of our modern technological civilization; while the Loyalists could not predict the full flowering of the American Empire, while they were often inarticulate in their forebodings, they sensed that there was more to human existence than "life, liberty and the pursuit of happiness" — that there was, in fact, a natural law which constrained man's freedom, which demanded and permitted both reverence and contemplation, and which offered a deeper, richer vision of man's spiritual potential.

It was something felt as much as it was ever stated. In the War of 1812, it caused most of the Loyalists to join Brock and the British in repulsing the American invaders who burned their farm houses and even their parliament at York. Allegiance to the idea of a British Canada was further fed by more American attacks after the 1837 rebellion and by the Fenian raids of 1866. To help keep these memories alive, there was always the arrogant talk of politicians in Washington. As late as 1889, when Brown was eight years old, US Secretary of State James G. Blaine proclaimed that "Canada is like an apple on a tree just beyond our reach. We may strive to grasp it, but the bough recedes from our hold just in proportion to our effort to catch it. Let it alone and in due time it will fall into our hands." Ten years later, when Brown was a young soldier, Lord Minto, the Governor-General, wrote to his brother in England that "There is a general dislike of the Yankees here and I do not wonder at it ... What the Canadian sees and hears is constant Yankee bluff and swagger and that eventually he means to possess Canada for himself."

Little wonder that Jimmy Brown grew up with visions of Redcoats in his head. Little wonder that he imagined the US Cavalry surging down the road, and dreamed up schemes to send them reeling back. For he was bred and raised in the proud tradition which caused another Scottish-Canadian to assert: "A British subject I was born — a British subject I will die."

It seems likely that these feelings were strongly echoed in the family home, although this is only conjecture. Surviving records tell little about his father, Frank Augustus Brown, except that he was a farmer (hardly rich but definitely gentry), that he married Anna MacIntosh Horne in 1879, and that he died in 1915, aged sixty-six or sixty-seven, when his son was serving overseas. There were also two younger daughters: one died without issue and the other was burned to death when she was sixteen. Such, at any rate, was the family tree which James Sutherland Brown set down in later years in an urgent, flowing hand. Yet legend persists that he had, in fact, a brother (or possibly a brother-in-law): a member of the militia who offended Brown by foresaking the military for a banking career at the time of the First World War, and who was *never mentioned again,* not even when Brown drew up his genealogy.

So there was temper here, as well as pride: a stern, unforgiving nature directed against all those who failed to match Brown's own high standards. There was also, as we shall see, warmth and humour and compassion, but in the fullness of his wrath, Brown was a formidable figure, almost an Old Testament patriarch.

In later years, Brown said little about his father, leading to another family legend that the two had quarreled early on. If so, this would be only the first of many occasions when Brown took dead aim at Higher Authority. Although he was a firm believer in rank, discipline and all the military virtues, he could never resist opposing superiors when he thought they were mixing tyranny with folly.

Whatever the source of Brown's dispute with his father, it can be surmised that his mother exercised a restraining influence. Certainly it was Anna who talked him out of running away to join the British against the Boers when he was only eighteen. Instead he finished his secondary schooling in Simcoe, and then spent two years studying law at the University of Toronto. But he had long been determined on a military career, and had joined the 39th Regiment of the Norfolk Rifles in the autumn of 1896 when he was only fifteen. Every summer after that he attended military camp; he also earned a Staff Certificate from the Kingston Military College, passing at the head of his class. On 25 June 1906, three days short of his twenty-fifth birthday, James Sutherland Brown was commissioned as a lieutenant in the Royal Canadian Regiment. His career was underway.

With the turn of the century, Canadian-American relations seemed set on a happier course. The border raids and diplomatic disputes of previous decades had hardly been forgotten or forgiven, but the possibility of an Anglo-American war involving Canada had certainly receded. As late as 1910, Maj-Gen. C. W. Robinson, a Canadian in the Imperial Army, stated in his book *Canada and Canadian Defence* that defence against the United States was still Canada's major military problem, but he also regarded actual hostilities as highly unlikely. When Lord Dundonald came out from Britain to command the Militia, he was assured by Prime Minister Laurier: "You must not take the Militia seriously, for though it is useful for suppressing internal disturbances, it will not be required for the defence of the country, as the Monroe Doctrine protects us against enemy aggression."

Not all Canadians shared Sir Wilfred's rosy view of American benevolence. During the Reciprocity Election of 1911, they paid more heed to President Taft's boast that reciprocity would "make Canada only an adjunct of the United States." They also took note when Champ Clark, Speaker of the House of Representatives, said "we are preparing to annex Canada", and he hoped he would see the day "when the American flag will float over every square foot of the British North American possessions, clear to the North Pole." Laurier's opponents made good use of such inflammatory statements: under the slogan "No Truck Nor Trade With The Yankees" they trounced Sir Wilfred at the polls.

Despite these excitements, Brown was given little reason during his early years in the Permanent Force to believe that his childhood games would ever be played in earnest. Some of his first assignments, in fact, involved those "internal disturbances" which had aroused Laurier's concern. In 1907, he was sent to Nova Scotia to help keep order during an especially bitter strike of coal miners at Glace Bay; in 1910 and 1911, he was involved in similar duties in Cape Breton. Many years later, when he was strapping on his ceremonial sword, Brown was asked by one of his young sons if he had ever used it to kill any Germans. Brown, who loved soldiering but hated war, seemed glad to reply he had never killed anyone, in any manner. Searching for some deed which might impress his son, he finally recalled that he had once hit a miner in the face with the hilt of the sword, in order to stop a riot.

As we shall see, Brown had a strong suspicion of trade unions, as well as a staunch Tory belief in law and order. While he was never heard to regret his role in helping to suppress the strikers, however, this was hardly soldiering as he had studied it. So he was more than happy to be selected for a two-year staff course at Camberley in England — not only because this showed he had been singled out as a promising officer, but also because it took him for the first time to a country which had always loomed so large in his imagination. Although he never adopted an English accent, he was already beginning to favour the slang — sometimes pungent, sometimes sentimental — which was used by British schoolboys and soldiers of that time and which he must have first encountered in *The Captain.* "Cad" and "rotter" were among his favourite epithets, England was often "Blighty", and when his memory for names began to fail in later years, he would frequently splutter: "You know who I mean . . . Old Blood-and-Guts!" "Buster", of course, was a standard English nickname for anyone named Brown.

Brown spent only one year at Camberley before the Great War intervened. Summoned home to Canada, he returned to Europe with the initial Canadian contingent in time to take part in the second battle of Ypres. That he killed no Germans in this or any other battle is explained by the fact that he had been marked as a skillful staff officer with a sound grasp of strategy and a flair for organization. Promoted to major, he advanced quickly to the post of Assistant Quartermaster General of the Canadian Army Corps.

In 1916 there were two diversions from the war: one pleasant, the other painful. For several years Brown had been courting Clare Temple Corsan of Toronto and Hamilton — often from a distance. At his request she joined him in England where they were married on June 27. With his bride ensconced in a house in Wimbledon, Brown returned to France where he contracted in rapid succession bouts of dysentery, tonsillitis and rheumatic fever. The fever was to recur throughout his life: in a later statement he traced its origins to the fact that "instead of living in more or less comfortable billets, I was quartered in deep dugouts." After several months of hospitalization and sick leave, Brown returned to action in early 1917, ending the war as Assistant Adjutant and Quartermaster-General of the First Canadian Division.

He was awarded his DSO in 1915, with his CMG to follow in 1918, and he was five times mentioned in despatches. It had been a good war — solid if not spectacular — and his superiors were clearly pleased with him. Raised to the rank of Brevet Colonel in 1919, Brown returned to Ottawa with every expectation of further advancement.

By now he was thirty-eight and the cast of his character had set. Proud and pugnacious, he was never reluctant to reveal his basic principles. A few years later, he was to outline some of those principles in a crusty letter to W. J. Neale, headmaster of the Model School in Ottawa. It was 1925 and there was another strike among the Cape Breton coal miners. Buster and Clare's first-born, Malcolm, was a pupil at the school; he returned one day to tell his father that a collection had been taken to aid the strikers. Sutherland Brown (he was now using both barrels) was aghast, and wrote to Neale that the collection was absolutely wrong. Recalling his own experience in Cape Breton, and asserting that the trouble had been brought into the area by the United Mine Workers of America, he went on:

> I stand four-square for the British Empire. I don't believe in Bolshevism, Labourism, Socialism, or any other "isms" that stand for the disruption of society or the pulling down of our present institutions. At the same time, I hold no brief for the British Empire Steel Company which is dominated by a Montreal Jew by the name of Wolvin. They undoubtedly have not dealt with their labour in the proper way, but, nevertheless, most of the trouble in Cape Breton has been caused by one McLaughlin and others of his ilk, who have never done an honest day's work in their lives and sucked their substance from people who were foolish enough to listen to

them or cowed into a state of non-resistance.

Here it all is — the love of Britain and British ways, the deep suspicion of American interference, a suggestion of anti-Semitism and a firm adherence to conservative politics, including a belief in the virtues of honest toil and a defence of the working class in the face of liberal-capitalist greed. In one great surge of feeling directed at the hapless headmaster, Sutherland Brown had nailed his colours to the mast.

These beliefs derived not only from his Loyalist background, but also from a later and closely related tradition. By the last decades of the nineteenth century, loyalist and patriotic impulses, bolstered by proud memories of 1776 and 1812, and fed by every annexationist statement from American politicians, reached their zenith in the Canadian Imperialist movement. In more recent times, "imperialism" has taken on a distinctly odious connotation, suggesting Soviet tanks in Prague, and American bombers over Hanoi. But in Canada, it embodied one of the deepest emotions in our public life: the determination to avoid assimilation by the United States through preserving and strengthening the links with Britain. The Canadian Imperialists were formidable orators, writers and propagandists who included in their ranks such stalwart figures as the teacher and scholar George Parkin, the economist and humourist Stephen Leacock, the university principal George M. Grant and the dashing cavalry officer Col. George T. Denison, who threatened to meet all annexationists on horseback with his sword.

To the Imperialists, annexation by the United States was the most immediate and pressing threat to Canadian independence and their cherished traditions. In terms that would not be far out of place in the nineteen-seventies, they viewed with dismay the Americans' inability to maintain law and order in their cities, the corruption that seemed endemic to their politics, and their growing racial problems. Just as a later generation of Canadians would be profoundly troubled by the American intervention in Vietnam, so the Imperialists mistrusted a bellicose republic which contrived a war with Spain, seized islands in both the Atlantic and Pacific, wiped out whole towns in suppressing the Philippine rebellion, and dominated the Caribbean under the menacing reach of Teddy

Roosevelt's "big stick". To suggest — as did Goldwin Smith and others — that Canada had nothing to fear from its southern neighbour struck the Imperialists as disastrous folly.

The struggle between the Imperialists and their opponents was a major theme in Canadian life in the thirty years before the First World War, and the conflict was bitter and divisive. Their opponents held that Imperialism was incompatible with Canadian dignity, unity and self-government. To the Imperialists, however, there was nothing paradoxical about their intense awareness of Canadian nationality and their desire for a stronger and more cohesive Empire. In their view, complete independence from the Mother Country would be self-defeating, even if desirable or attainable: left on its own Canada could hardly avoid annexation by the thrusting Yankees. But within the Empire, Canada would not only continue to enjoy the protection of British arms, it could also achieve a position of equality and even domination, as well as a growing voice in the great international issues of war and peace. This was very much in the dominant Canadian tradition: a direct development of Sir John A. Macdonald's policy which held that the Anglo-Canadian connection was the foundation of Canadian freedom.

"I . . . am an Imperialist," said Leacock, "because I will not be a Colonial." In short, Canadian Imperialism was a genuine form of Canadian patriotism. Patriotism is a more accurate word here than nationalism, which has also taken on a pejorative tone. As Orwell noted, nationalism has an aggressive and exclusive connotation, since it involves "identifying oneself with a single nation or other unit, placing it beyond good and evil and recognizing no other duty than that of advancing its interests." Patriotism, on the other hand, implies "a devotion to a particular place and a particular way of life, which one believes to be the best in the world but has no wish to force upon other people. Patriotism is by its nature defensive, both militarily and culturally." In this sense, while Sutherland Brown can loosely be called a nationalist, he is really a patriot.

Aside from Col. Denison's theatrics, there was always a strong military aspect to the Imperialist movement. At the heart of the Loyalist tradition was the legend (often exaggerated in the telling) that it was the ordinary Canadian people, grouped in their Militia, which had done at least as much as British soldiers to repulse the Americans in 1812. The Imperialists were fully aware that Canadian independence did depend ultimately on the Royal Navy, and on British willingness to spring to Canada's defence. But they argued that national dignity — and Canadian influence within the Empire — required a greater fighting capacity. This led them to press for a strengthened Militia and military drill in the schools, as well as Canadian participation in the Boer War. When young James Brown tried to run away from Simcoe to join the British in that war, it was an early sign of his allegiance to a tradition which was to dominate his life.

By 1920, his fortieth year, Sutherland Brown was able to give practical expression to his beliefs and loyalties. This was when he became Director of Military Operations and Intelligence: the one man in the whole military establishment whose job was to formulate strategic plans. Since there was no Canadian intelligence service, and no Canadian embassies or legations in other countries, and since Sutherland Brown had practically no staff, he had to compile all his own information. "No one can occupy my post satisfactorily unless he is a glutton for reading," he wrote, citing newspapers and periodicals, military publications, accounts of other nations' policies and a huge quantity of files relating to disarmament and the League of Nations. "I find," he added at the end of his tenure, "that I can never get away from professional thoughts and I have not read more than three novels in the last six years."

The most dramatic product of his labours was a 190-page document which took four months to prepare and which was sent to the commanders of all Military Districts on 12 April 1921. This was Defence Scheme No. 1. For more than a decade, it was to represent official strategic policy for the Canadian armed forces. At the top of the first page, under the heading VERY SECRET, Sutherland Brown implanted a stern warning that the existence of the Scheme was to be unknown to anybody in each District except the Commanding Officer: "Only such parts as are necessary will be communicated, either verbally or by very secret letter to the members of your Staff and Heads of Services and Departments, that are necessary to help you mature your plans."

In developing his major thesis — that the main threat to Canada was invasion from the United States — Sutherland Brown·relied on assessments of the world situation by the Imperial General Staff which included the possibility of a war between the Empire and America. He did not deny that Canada might be threatened from farther afield, but he noted that the British Cabinet had concluded that another major European war was not likely to occur during the next five or ten years, and so he devoted his initial attention to the threat from the south.

Analysing the problems faced by Canada — including its long frontier with the United States, and vulnerable railways and waterways — he quickly concluded that "THE FIRST THING APPARENT THEN IN THE DEFENCE OF CANADA IS THAT WE LACK DEPTH." He went on to develop his boldest concept: that Canada could only defend itself by invading the enemy.

Sutherland Brown had no illusions that the Canadians could sweep down through the United States, gaining heroic victories and even re-enacting the burning of Washington. Instead he favoured a limited offensive which would tie up American forces at several places along the border, diverting them from any concerted drive into the Toronto-Montreal-Ottawa heartland. He hoped that such spirited action would convince the Americans that the conquest of Canada would once again prove too difficult. If not, it would buy time until the British could join the action.

Time would be gained by advance reconnaissance of strategic objectives, speedier mobilization and — above all — taking the initiative. In the event of hostilities, Canada would strike first by sending Flying Columns across the border. The Flying Columns would contain Cavalry, Cyclists, Machine Gun Units and Mobile Infantry. Their objectives were described in detail:

> *Pacific Command.* The field troops of Pacific Command to advance into and occupy the strategic points including Spokane, Seattle, and Portland, Oregon, bounded by the

Columbia River . . .

Prairie Command . . . should converge towards Fargo in North Dakota . . . and then continue a general advance in the direction of Minneapolis and St. Paul . . .

Great Lakes Command . . . will, generally speaking, remain on the defensive, but rapid and well organized raids should be made across the Niagara Frontier, the St. Clair Frontier, the Detroit Frontier and the St. Mary's Frontier, with sufficient troops to establish bridgeheads . . .

Quebec Command . . . will take the offensive on both sides of the Adirondack Mountains with a view of converging . . . in the vicinity of Albany, N.Y. . . .

Maritime Command . . . will make an offensive into the State of Maine. . . .

With his Scheme completed, Sutherland Brown travelled across the country to rally the District Commanders around his strategy. Most were swept up by the sheer daring of his planning. One District Commander mildly pointed out that Defence Scheme No. 1 had been drawn up for "forces which are to a certain extent non-existent." (At the time, the Permanent Force had fewer than 4,000 members, while the United States had 175,000 men under arms.) But none disputed the central thesis, and many were soon adding refinements for their own regions, and proposing their own reconnaissances. A future Defence Minister, Maj.-Gen. George R. Pearkes, VC, was then General Staff Officer in the Calgary Command: later he recalled that Brown had personally explained the Scheme to him. "It was a fantastic, desperate plan, but it just might have worked," Pearkes maintained. "The Americans had very few troops close to the border. We might have been able to divert their forces to the flanks, and to hold them out of central Canada until Britain intervened, or second thoughts prevailed in Washington."

Back in Ottawa, Sutherland Brown threw himself into the task of expanding the planning upon which the Scheme would depend for its success. In a Secret Report on the Defence of Quebec and the Lower St. Lawrence, he argued that the Gulf of St. Lawrence between Nova Scotia and

Newfoundland was the proper place for basing the Royal Navy's Grand Fleet in case of hostilities between the Empire and the United States. Like Defence Scheme No. 1, this was a detailed and closely reasoned document, but it, too, was less a mechanical exercise than something which was deeply felt. Sustained by his traditions, Sutherland Brown clearly approached his task with a certain relish. Nor was he an arm chair strategist: the boy who routed make-believe Yankees from his Simcoe farm had become a soldier who personally scouted the invasion routes in New York and Vermont. This was certainly foolhardy: on these trips, we see Buster Brown in all his quixotic extravagance. He seems to have enjoyed himself enormously.

But he was hampered by lack of funds. In 1927, the last year in which he held the post of DMO&I, he complained in a memorandum to the Chief of the General Staff that his intelligence budget was only $1,500. He proposed that this sum be raised to $5,000, and that the money be used

> to buy maps, pamphlets, books, etc. concerning the United States; to provide paper for printing Intelligence maps; for distributing a small amount to each Military District for the purpose of subscribing for United States papers and Service journals, etc. etc., and also to provide for any special reconnaissance that may be undertaken from time to time by special officers.

One remembers how Sutherland Brown was quick to pick up road maps from gas stations on his New York and Vermont reconnaissances — and then attach them to his Secret Reports. This, it seems, was practical necessity: there is not very much intelligence that can be purchased for $1,500 a year. But if the DMO&I was hampered by a paltry budget, this reflected the financial constraints on the whole Canadian military establishment throughout this period: it was no indication of Sutherland Brown's personal standing. Indeed, he became a Brigadier in 1928, and was named to attend the Imperial Defence College in London. Traditionally, this posting was a firm indication of eventual high command.

There is also little doubt that many of his fellow officers still shared Sutherland Brown's political and strategic views. On the eve of his departure for London, he received a letter from Maj.-Gen. J. H. Elmsley, commanding Military District Three at Kingston:

> I am very glad indeed that you have been selected for the War College; because with your intimate knowledge of our Canadian and Empire affairs you will be a useful man to represent our interests. Furthermore you are what I call an Imperialist (for want of a better word) and opposed, as every straight-minded Canadian, to American influence in our Canadian and Empire policies, and also to their claim to dominate the affairs of the whole world.
>
> Always be moderate in what you say; nevertheless, never lose the opportunity of advancing the advisability of:–
>
> (a) An Empire defensive scheme not subject to the whims of changing administrations, and,
>
> (b) A European Entente to fight American policies, both military, naval and economic and their vast publicity agencies.

Sutherland Brown must have been gratified by this brusque statement of support; he may also have had reason to fear that officers with different views were coming to the fore. One of his last acts before leaving Ottawa was to write another memorandum to the CGS which defended the political assumptions upon which he had based Defence Scheme No. 1. In this memorandum, he conceded that many people would argue that war between the United States and the British Empire was unthinkable. But, he added, "I have studied the United States and the United States' citizens since I was a youth and I flatter myself that I know something about them . . . The day may come when the United States may think she is strong enough to bluff the British with a threat of war. It is necessary then for the Empire to be in a strong position to meet this threat." Perhaps sensing that not all his superiors would share his perceptions, he went on to argue that a strategy which provided for the defence of the frontiers would cover, with only slight variations, any military problem with which Canada might be faced. He also urged that his Scheme should be brought up to date, and that the Militia should be organized for the primary duty of home defence.

This advice was never acted upon: nothing was done to keep the Scheme in line with changing conditions. There then appeared on the scene Maj.-Gen. A. G. L. McNaughton, a brilliant and outspoken officer who was to prove Sutherland Brown's sternest adversary in later years, and the agent of his downfall. From the time that McNaughton became CGS at the end of 1928, Defence Scheme No. 1 was doomed. By 1931, McNaughton had drawn up the first new assessment of Canada's military situation in a decade. This noted the growing harmony in strategic matters between Britain and the United States, adding that "Politically, Canada's position *vis-a-vis* the United States has been immensely stabilized," and that Sutherland Brown's assumptions and conclusions should not continue as the basis for Canadian military planning. In May 1931, Defence Scheme No. 1 was officially cancelled. In October 1933, the District Commanders were ordered to burn all documents relating to the Scheme. Only a few months earlier, Sutherland Brown had retired as officer commanding Military District Eleven; it was a small mercy that he was spared the task of personally throwing his most notable achievement to the flames.

It is hardly surprising that Defence Scheme No. 1 was burned: by that time, both the author and his views had become heretical. Ironically, Sutherland Brown drew up his plan in 1921, the year in which Mackenzie King became Prime Minister. Most likely King was never made aware of the document; at that time, military matters were hardly his major concern. If he had seen the Scheme, it would have had a much shorter life, for King could hardly have countenanced its assumptions, preoccupied as he soon became with detaching Canada from the imperial system and enmeshing her destiny with that of the new Romans across the border. His efforts were soon enshrined in the Authorized Version of Canadian history: that stirring chronicle which charts our progress from colony to nation, from the shackles of British rule to the lucrative alliance with our friendly neighbours to the south.

By daring to affirm that the Americans might actually be a threat to Canada, Sutherland Brown sinned mightily against the Authorized Version and all of its proponents. He has been made to pay for his transgression: to the limited extent that Defence Scheme No. 1 has been considered by Canadian historians, it has not been treated kindly. According to James Eayrs (writing in 1964), the 1922 Washington Conference ended Anglo-American naval rivalry and the last possibility of an Anglo-American war: only the isolation and lethargy of the Canadian military kept Defence Scheme No. 1 in operation for nearly another decade. To Eayrs, Sutherland Brown was guilty of "strategists' cramp", which he defines as the occupational disease of military planners, involving "a kind of creeping paralysis of the imagination when it comes to assessing the influences of a changing political and technological environment upon the fortunes of his country."

Yet this is hindsight, the occupational disease of historians. It certainly over-simplifies a complex situation. Despite the Treaty of Washington, there were still important differences between the United States and Britain, especially economic issues. At the end of the nineteen-twenties, there was also deep concern in Canada about the nation's vulnerability to American pressures. A Canadian ship had been sunk by US guns on the high seas, after which Ottawa had cravenly complied with US demands to partake in the farce of prohibition by banning liquor exports; Washington had also adopted new tariffs which seriously hurt Canadian industry. As late as March 1930, the distinguished Canadian journalist B. K. Sandwell wrote an article for *Saturday Night* under the heading "Anglo-American War Possibilities" which discussed the prospects for an American invasion.

As it later turned out, this surmise was far from fanciful. In 1974, another historian, Richard A. Preston, revealed that just as Sutherland Brown was preparing for an attack from the United States, American defence planners were, in fact, plotting such an invasion. American majors and colonels had been putting on civilian clothes, loading up their cameras, and making their own spying trips inside Canada; at the American War College, they then compiled a series of invasion scenarios. In 1926, one such plan envisaged operations in the Great Lakes area, leading to a notable victory: "The United States mobilizes an immediate offensive into Canada to prevent the junction of British and Canadian forces, drives Great Britain from the western hemisphere, and defends all national territory." As late as 1930, a U.S. War Department plan gave priority to the capture of Halifax in the event of American-British hostilities; it also envisaged attacks across the Great Lakes, on Winnipeg and along the Pacific coast.

This was the exact threat which Defence Scheme No. 1 had been drafted to counter. It is true, of course, that the formation of military plans does not always signify the likelihood of actual hostilities. But there are few certainties in international relations, and it was the job of Sutherland Brown and his American counterparts to anticipate contingencies.

Despite the disclosure of the American invasion scenarios, Sutherland Brown has not been officially rehabilitated. Although it was Canada's strategic plan for a decade, Defence Scheme No. 1 is still a non-event in Ottawa. Not only was it burned; apparently it never even existed. In late 1975, an American scholar revealed yet another invasion scenario. (One begins to suspect there is no end to them.) This dated back to 1919, when the US Army devised a battle plan for the conquest of Saskatchewan, either by tanks or cavalry, with the support of huge cannon mounted on railway cars. A Toronto newspaper took up the story:

> When informed of the plan's existence last week, a spokesman for the Canadian defence department paused several seconds in startled silence. "I can categorically assure you," he said finally, "that we have never had any plans to invade the US. Furthermore, I'm pretty sure we've never prepared for an attack from the US side."

Mercifully unaware of the oblivion which would befall his great work, Sutherland Brown sailed for England in 1928. With his posting to the Imperial Defence College, he seemed to have been picked by his superiors for high command. By the time he returned to Ottawa in early 1929, however, his prospects looked much less promising. This was only partly because Defence Scheme No. 1 had fallen into disfavour during his absence, and its author's political views were clearly contrary to those of the King Government. There was also something deeper at work: a clash of personalities which foreshadowed a basic philosophical dispute between Sutherland Brown's conservatism and the liberal technocracy which was taking over the political and military establishment.

This was evident when he reported to McNaughton, the new CGS. "I saw at once that his former attitude of more or less friendliness towards me had changed to one of severe coldness," he later wrote. "Having assumed office over the heads of better qualified men he at once became a cold-blooded administrator." There may have been some jealousy in this assessment. Six years younger than Sutherland Brown, Andy McNaughton had been appointed a brigadier at thirty-one, commanding an artillery brigade in France during the First World War. Since then he had never looked back, becoming Deputy Chief of Staff during the early nineteen-twenties, and preceding Sutherland Brown by two years at the Imperial Defence College. Before his appointment as CGS, he had commanded Military District Eleven in British Columbia, the very post to which Sutherland Brown was now on his way.

It is quite possible that the general and the brigadier saw themselves as rivals; certainly their temperaments were opposite. McNaughton was an engineer and intellectual who delighted in technical subjects. To Sutherland Brown, he always seemed callous and vindictive. "General McNaughton sniped at me for four and one-half years," he later wrote. "Some four years ago he took advantage of a personal and confidential letter I sent him. This is unforgivable and nobody but a cad would do such a trick."

When the two men met in Ottawa, it was the opening round in a conflict which would eventually destroy Sutherland Brown's career. Despite his premonitions, however, he took up his new job with considerable enthusiasm. With responsibility for the defence of the Pacific coast, Military District Eleven was a prized posting. The Sutherland Browns were also delighted to be moving to Victoria, a comfortable and complacent town which offered an ideal environment in which to raise their three young sons. Victoria was solidly

British: its schools, clubs and churches were steeped in Sutherland Brown's own Anglo-Canadian traditions. Although he was raised as a Presbyterian, the Brigadier had by now become an Anglican. This was partly because Clare was staunch in that faith, and partly because Anglicanism was the religion of the armed forces. While he was not especially a religious man, there may have been a deeper motivation. With an approach to life that was both romantic and reverential, Sutherland Brown was Anglican by temperament, and greatly different from those prudent and puritanical Scottish Calvinists of southwestern Ontario whom John Galbraith has depicted.

Sutherland Brown also had an actual command for the first time in his career. Again, he seems to have enjoyed himself enormously, especially when he led his Militia on manoeuvres. Whether riding with them at full gallop across the open country, swimming with them in the buff, or camping with them in bivouac, he stayed close to his men, and shared their discomforts. As Pearkes, then serving as his General Staff Officer, recalled: "He worked the Militia hard, but unlike some commanding officers, he also really cared for them. They all loved him, and their morale was never higher."

A photograph from this period shows Sutherland Brown on manoeuvres in the Okanagan Valley. He sits on a horse, with a troop of mounted soldiers in the background. It is a romantic scene, and Sutherland Brown confronts the camera with a fierce pride. One thinks of those youthful games in Simcoe, and wonders what was passing through his head. But if Sutherland Brown was dreaming of 1812, he was also preparing for 1939. There was nothing outdated about his manoeuvres: on more than one occasion, he virtually commandeered visiting British warships, and used them to despatch his Militia against the beaches of Vancouver Island in combined assaults that were forerunners of the seaborne landings of the Second World War.

Aside from training the Militia, Sutherland Brown launched an active recruitment campaign, personally seeking out promising prospects. This was his attempt to make the best out of a very bad situation. In his view — and it was shared by other senior officers — the Canadian armed forces,

starved of both men and money, were woefully ill-prepared to
fight any sort of war. As early as 1924, he had published an
article in *The Canadian Defence Quarterly* in which he strongly
criticized the haphazard mobilization in 1914, and maintained that there were still no coherent policies for either the
Permanent Force or the Reserve Militia. "The Government of
every other civilized country in the world has taken its military problem in hand and put its military house in order.
Canada has not yet done so. The Canadian Government
should give early and concentrated attention to the military
problems of Canada." Otherwise, he warned, "we will suffer
that most terrible thing in war — the loss of the initiative."
Successive governments ignored all such warnings. When war
broke out in September 1939, Canada had no troops ready for
immediate action.

Such views — especially when expressed so trenchantly
and so openly — hardly endeared Sutherland Brown to his
superiors. In May 1933, he was rebuked in a confidential
memo from the Adjutant-General, Maj-Gen A.H. Bell:

> Information has been received at National Defence
> Headquarters from responsible sources that you have on
> occasions given voice to public criticism of senior officers
> at Defence Headquarters. While the reports received are
> sufficiently indefinite as not to require action, I would
> remind you that senior officers holding prominent posi-
> tions cannot be too careful in expressing their opinion on
> these matters.

Sutherland Brown retorted that he had never criticized
his superiors — at least in public — and that he regarded loyalty as his very best quality. But he never believed that loyalty
should be stretched to the point of tolerating foolish or
inhumane policies. As he later wrote:

> I am no time server. Ever since I was able to form reason-
> able opinions I have acted upon certain principles. I have
> stood up for my subordinates when it was necessary for
> me to do so. I have expressed my opinions as a Comman-
> der should be allowed to do so.

Yet his opinions were increasingly out of kilter with the

policies of Ottawa; furthermore, his outspoken advocacy of them was to cause the final break with McNaughton and the end of his career. Significantly, the dispute had nothing to do with military strategy. The cancellation of Defence Scheme No. 1 had cast a shadow on its author, but this was not the point at issue. Rather, it was the administration of the Work Camps which had been established as a partial answer to the Depression, and which were run by the Department of National Defence.

The camps were McNaughton's idea. Perhaps the most important assignment carried out by the military between the two world wars, they provided food, shelter and clothing to any man who was single, able-bodied, homeless and unemployed. (By 1932, nearly one-quarter of the labour force was out of work.) Each man entered a camp at his own request, to work on airports, highways and other public projects.

From the start, Sutherland Brown kept a close watch on the BC camps. As the local military commander, he was responsible for aiding the civilian authorities in the event of serious riots. When a strike broke out in the Princeton Camp in January 1933, he was quick to inform Ottawa that it was the work of Communist agitators. But he added that many of the men's complaints (about rations, clothing and working conditions) were fully justified. After inspecting the camps, he came back aroused and angry. In a torrent of outspoken memos, he harangued his superiors about the squalid living conditions, and the delays in providing tools and other equipment to get the men working. There was further disagreement over money. Each inmate in the camps received twenty cents a day for his work. McNaughton ruled that this pitiful allowance should be given as credit in the camp stores; Sutherland Brown replied that the men should be paid in cash, so that the transaction could have at least some semblance of dignity.

There was more to this dispute than administrative details. Above all, it showed how deeply Sutherland Brown's most enduring human qualities were uncongenial to a political and military establishment which was increasingly stressing the liberal standards of efficiency and expediency. To Ottawa, the Work Camps were a pragmatic approach to an overwhelming problem; McNaughton and his civilian superiors clearly regarded Sutherland Brown's concern for the dignity of the inmates as an annoying irrelevance.

But this concern sprang from the heart of Sutherland Brown's conservative creed. Two decades earlier, he had helped suppress strikers in the Nova Scotia coal mines; in singling out Communist agitators in the BC camps, he was again acting as a firm opponent of "Bolshevism, Labourism, Socialism, or any other 'isms' which stand for the disruption of society." Yet he was far from an ally of Big Business, or an enemy of the working man. In Nova Scotia, he had seen how the workers were exploited through the notorious company stores; now he felt the same approach was being followed in the Work Camps. Privately he complained that McNaughton was herding the unemployed into the camps like animals, and treating them like prisoners. As a conservative, Sutherland Brown believed that human society was an organic entity in which every member had responsibilities to his fellow citizens. So he held that the unemployed should be treated with dignity, compassion and as much generosity as circumstances would permit.

These differences were aggravated by the growing animosity between Sutherland Brown and McNaughton. The CGS was already being widely and publicly accused of using the Work Camps to exploit slave labour. It was bad enough to be criticized by socialists and other leftwingers; to be attacked even privately by one of his senior commanders must have seemed a much graver affront. The angry exchanges between Ottawa and Victoria continued throughout the spring of 1933; later Sutherland Brown wrote that "the main torrent of abuse and impractical orders were mainly levied at me. As I had the confidence of most everyone in British Columbia I can only take it that the Chief of the General Staff was trying to drive me into a corner where I should resign."

Sutherland Brown had already been given grounds for this suspicion. In May, he had received notice of his next assignment — to command the Military District in Winnipeg. Although theoretically equal to Victoria, this was not so prestigious a post. To Sutherland Brown it smacked of demotion, since he had been hoping to return to Ottawa as either

Adjutant-General or Quartermaster-General. So this was further confirmation of how badly he had fallen out of favour.

By now he was again ill with the rheumatic fever he had contracted in France, and also wracked with over-work and worry. After a long talk with Clare, and after thinking it over for several days, he submitted his resignation on his birthday, June 28. At the age of fifty-two, James Sutherland Brown had lost his occupation.

For the rest of his life — another eighteen years — Sutherland Brown was to be a spiritual exile from a Canada which became even more hostile to his conservative principles, his loyalist traditions and his staunch patriotism. He made his exile in Victoria: with its own British traditions, the city was less susceptible than most Canadian communities to this systematic denigration of his deepest beliefs. It became the garrison from which Sutherland Brown confronted — with anger and amazement — a nation which seemed to have lost all sense of its own history, all feeling for its roots, all awareness of the real threat to its independence.

Although he seldom allowed himself to become bitter, his anger was never appeased. He had proclaimed loyalty to be among his greatest virtues; in the aftermath of his resignation, he proved this point by moving decisively to discourage widespread resignations on the part of his sympathetic subordinates in BC. But he never forgave the senior officers whom he felt had conspired to ensure his downfall. He found further cause for resentment in the fact that he was not promoted to major-general on his retirement, even though such promotions were common practice. In the future, it would be a problem for Victoria hostesses whenever McNaughton came to town, since they soon learned it was not wise to bring the two men together in the same living room.

Always a fighter, Sutherland Brown refused to concede that his beliefs had suffered lasting defeat. So he ran as a Conservative candidate in federal and provincial elections, impelled by a passionate distrust of Mackenzie King, whom he called a sly fox, and an urge to rally Canadians against the menace of socialism. Clare opposed these ventures, stating that only unpleasant people went into politics; her husband retorted that unless good people had a try, the situation would never be improved. As hard as he tried, however, he never won a seat. While he had a common touch, and was widely admired and even loved by his soldiers, he found it difficult to speak from a platform to large and diverse audiences. Too often he was stiff and awkward, with too much of the aura of an old soldier.

Once again, his abhorrence of socialism did not imply any enthusiasm for the business world. With three growing sons, a mortgage on his house, few savings and a pension that was hardly lavish, Sutherland Brown was pressed for funds throughout the Depression. While he always managed to employ a maid or nanny, he could never afford a car. Although he refused to stint on the education of his sons, he was forced to make other economies, such as resigning from his club, and he even gave up sending Christmas cards. Shortly after his retirement, he became a junior partner in a stockbrokers firm. But he soon discovered that business practices were too sharp and slick for a man of his temperament. He quit after six months, abandoning his small investment, and maintaining that stockbroking was more than a little unethical, and certainly no proper profession for a gentleman.

This was his last attempt to earn money. The army had been his life since he was little more than a boy: through the long years of his retirement, he never found a satisfactory substitute. Yet he was far from idle, becoming active in both the Canadian Legion and especially the Army, Navy and Airforce Veterans in Canada, building up their local organizations and helping soldiers who had fallen on hard times. At the other end of the social scale, he served as *aide-de-camp* to successive Lieutenant-Governors of British Columbia, often representing them on official occasions.

Both activities were in character. Buster was anything but a snob. There was nothing he liked better than to stand in the mess or veterans' club, drinking beer with his "old sweats" and swapping earthy anecdotes. But he was just as happy to report for duty at Government House where he revelled in the ceremony and the protocol. Above all, he rejoiced in the chance to wear his uniform again. An official photograph

shows him taking the salute at a Remembrance Day ceremony. Buster stands in profile, his uniform immaculate, his
moustache bristling fiercely. He has developed a splendid cor-
poration, but the back is ram-rod straight.

In fact, Sutherland Brown long persisted in the hope
that he would again become a soldier. The library in his home
was lined with books, including rare and important works on
military strategy. Night after night, he would sit up late,
under etchings of the Indian and South African wars, studying the campaigns of Marlborough, Napoleon and Wellington. Despite his passion for history, this was more than
tranquil contemplation. As the news from Europe became
increasingly ominous, Buster was preparing his return to
arms. Several of his books were on the American Civil War, so
it seems likely he was stirred by the story of Grant, patiently
biding his time during all those long years of obscurity in
Galena, waiting for the summons to leadership and glory
which he knew must come.

For Sutherland Brown, the summons never came. This
was the greatest blow of all. When war broke out in 1939, he
was only fifty-eight: he felt certain he would soon be offered a
command. As the months went by, he was first astonished and
then anguished when Ottawa failed to call him. Having long
foreseen it, he was all too aware of the army's lack of combat
readiness. Surely there must be something he could do to
help? Surely they hadn't forgotten him entirely?

No, they hadn't. Defence Scheme No. 1 may have long
been relegated to the flames, but its author had spoken out too
often and made too many enemies. "Personalities," said Gen
Pearkes. "That was why they never used him. It was a tremendous shame they never gave him a command. He was a great
leader of men, but he never had the chance to show what he
could do."

Buster was deeply, terribly hurt. Pride seems to have
prevented him from initiating an approach to Ottawa.
Instead he did the best he could: visiting the BC camps to bol-
ster the morale of the recruits (there was some indication that
Ottawa frowned on even this), greeting the ship that brought
back the Canadian survivors from the debacle of Hong Kong,
helping out in the canteens. It was a sad war, and one image

sums it up: Buster in his library, with large maps of Europe, the Middle East and Asia on the walls, listening every evening to the BBC reports, and marking the progress of each campaign with pins and flags.

For Buster and Clare, there was yet another blow. In 1941, their second son, Ian, died in an air training accident. But their eldest, Malcolm, a career soldier and a graduate of the Royal Military College, served with distinction in Europe, rising to the rank of Lieutenant Colonel, and earning the DSO. Their youngest, Atholl, joined the RCAF and won the DFC for gallantry in action in the India-Burma theatre.

Once again, Sutherland Brown refused to become bitter or despondent. Above all, his pride and energy sustained him. To keep down the grocery bills during the Depression, he had developed a huge garden, about half the size of a football field, where he worked hard and happily for hours on end, humming snatches of Gilbert and Sullivan, and raising enormous cabbages and other vegetables. He had a green thumb, and his favourite plant was a camellia tree, which provided flowers for his button-hole. These were tokens of his pride: even after the war, he was still unable to afford a car, but whether walking or taking the bus, he always dressed as a perfect gentleman. Something of a dandy, he had taken advantage of his London posting to have a prodigious number of uniforms and suits made for him by Hawkes Bros of Saville Row. These wore well, and always looked well on him, with his camellia as the finishing touch. He also had beautiful boots and shoes, and was meticulous in washing and drying his feet. As he told his sons, an infantryman always takes good care of his feet.

His pride was based on implacable convictions. Just before the war, Sutherland Brown gave the fullest account of his beliefs in a letter to his eldest son, written after Malcolm had left Victoria for RMC:

> You will remember our conversation before you left. May I put down a few thoughts for your guidance —
>
> 1. First of all always act the part of a gentleman; decent people will like you and others will respect you.
>
> 2. Do not forget the Church of England. It is something

more than a religious body; the whole splendour of the British Race is reflected in it. It stands for the Monarchy.

3. Listen well and be careful of what you say. If you are careless in your speech you will not be listened to. Be accurate in what you say. Withhold biting remarks and sarcasm; they have their value at times but should be used sparingly. A kind word, a thoughtful expression, a little sympathy may make you a friend for life.

4. Be extremely careful of money matters; learn the value of the dollar. Do not be stingy, but be careful. Thrift beats prodigality by a great distance. In fact, prodigality is hardly in the race at all.

5. In sports, play the game, but do not ruin your health and prospects in life by a burst of excessive zeal. Do not be selfish to win laurels; co-operative team play is the thing. You have done very well so far, Malcolm!

6. Always be a British Subject loyal and staunch, a good Canadian. (Frown on this "native son" stuff.) Do not forget your Scottish background. It is solid and material. Politics are out of your sphere at present but do not be carried away by any socialistic nonsense; it is not founded on human understanding. Stick to conservative principles. They always win in the end. They stand for order and dignity, a reasonable amount of discipline in natural life, with the minimum interference with the liberty of the citizen, the thorough investigation of new thoughts and ideas before adoption. Conservative principles rise above a Conservative party and a Conservative party above a Conservative Government — yet we Conservatives believe in strenuous leadership.

7. Be kind and respectful to all servants and those of inferior position: be polite and open with all superiors, but do not be a toady or a sycophant, nor arouse their displeasure by being cheeky or forward.

8. Gain popularity by decent methods. Remember you can soon be found out if you are a hypocrite. The fall from a pedestal is painful and you may never again

recover. Be a "square shooter". Learn to be a leader. You must be human, kind and sympathetic, yet firm. A cold-blooded fish is one of the most despicable of human creations.

9. Read history carefully. Learn the development of your race and the Empire. Cultivate the habit of good conversation and take every opportunity of speaking without making yourself a bore, nuisance or joke. A cultured man is an asset in any community. Be smart and clean in your person, avoid little offensive habits. Remember it is not "the coat you wear but the way you put it on." Avoid sloppiness in everything but do not overdress. Some little habits of dress may be characteristic and useful.

This is the essential Sutherland Brown. It is easy to smile at some of his precepts, but only a cynic would mock at them. There is prejudice here, and calculation. There is also pride, honour, a basic humanity and powerful feelings which are all the stronger for being circumscribed by a firm sense of social duty.

These conservative beliefs sustained Sutherland Brown throughout his remaining years. He was always active, and not even a heart attack slowed him down for long. With his strong Biblical sense, however, he often said he knew his span would be three score years and ten. In the spring of 1951, he took ill again, entered hospital and died soon after, just weeks short of his seventieth birthday. The *Daily Colonist* had a front page headline: "Victoria is the poorer by the passing of Brig Sutherland Brown." He was buried with full military honours: a major-general, five brigadiers and two colonels were among his pallbearers; the congregation was packed with other ranks, especially his "old sweats".

Since his death, Sutherland Brown's name and reputation have suffered a curious fate. As we have seen, scholars and government officials have either ignored him or else dismissed him with amazement. But in the surge of nationalism that followed our Centennial and amidst the revulsion over Vietnam,

Buster began to re-emerge as a genuine folk hero. There was something about him that began to nag at us, something that refused to be forgotten. Within two decades of his death, it was evident that he simply would not disappear.

Some of these manifestations were bizarre. In 1968, a group of Saskatchewan radicals banded together to protest the use of Canadian land and air space for training purposes by bombers of the US Strategic Air Command. They called themselves The Colonel J. Sutherland Brown Volunteer Brigade. Then *Last Post,* a leftwing magazine, published an article called "The Great Unfinished Task of Col J. Sutherland Brown", with an updated version of Defence Scheme No. 1. (Instead of striking south across the border, Canadian forces would occupy or destroy hydro-electric installations, uranium fields and other industrial and resource complexes *within* Canada, thus striking a lethal blow at the American economy.) A Toronto author, Juan Butler, wrote an inventive novel called *Canadian Healing Oil* which was partly concerned with the evils of imperialism, and which had excerpts from Defence Scheme No. 1 as a preface. Radio and television programs which explored the limitations on Canadian independence treated Buster with affectionate humour, as a patriarch of the nationalist cause.

There is one obvious reason for Sutherland Brown's apotheosis: events have proved him right. It is not only that historians have discovered the Americans did, in fact, have numerous plans for the invasion of Canada. Even if there was never much likelihood that these scenarios would be pulled from dusty files and applied to real hostilities, they betokened a much more dangerous and pervasive threat. Put bluntly, the Americans were instinctively bent on the political and economic domination of Canada, as part of that messianic drive which an earlier generation had called their Manifest Destiny. With his Loyalist and Imperialist background, Sutherland Brown had always recognized this danger. Nor did he envisage it entirely in military terms: in lectures and official papers throughout the nineteen-twenties, he warned repeatedly that Canada's vast natural resources might be coveted by the United States, citing hydro-electric power, asbestos and the forest industries. He persisted in such warnings throughout the years when Mackenzie King and his allies shifted Canadian political allegiances from London to Washington, and fostered the transformation of Canada into an economic satellite of the United States.

American domination was achieved without specific military threats. Given the supine policies of Canadian leaders, such threats would have been superfluous. Sutherland Brown's was a military mind: having perceived the danger, he sought to meet it in terms of his own profession and his specific responsibilities. Yet the Flying Columns which he would have sent across the border were a soldier's answer to a threat which was no less real for not having ultimately to be expressed in military terms: a patriot's response to an acutely apprehended challenge. Canadians are less free today because too few of our politicians, civil servants, businessmen, labour leaders and academics shared his forebodings. At no time were they prepared to view the United States as a threatening imperial power. This would have meant too many hard choices; it was so much easier, so much more profitable, simply to sell out.

We should not be surprised by our present fate. Canadian liberals share, with their American counterparts, a belief that man is essentially free to shape his world according to his own desires. Through sheer will, the liberal strives to dominate his environment; his major weapon is a modern technology which, by its very nature, tends to turn us into ciphers, the raw material of our giant computers. For all its noble rhetoric, the liberal doctrine seeks to create a world in which mere progress and material welfare are enshrined as the ultimate good. In such a world, independence is both illogical and irrelevant. Whether Americans or Canadians, we must all become citizens of the new universal empire of technology.

Sutherland Brown instinctively opposed such a fate. In 1928, just before he left for London, he articulated a patriotism which went far beyond his emotional attachment to Great Britain. As he wrote in a farewell memo to his superiors: "Canada is slowly, but surely, moulding a national feeling which stands for looking after her own interests and she will show a strong front to any demands from the United States." This is the real basis of Defence Scheme No. 1. It establishes

Sutherland Brown as a key link in the evolution of Canadian sensibility from its Loyalist and Imperialist traditions to the resurgent nationalism which began to flourish about the time of our Centennial in 1967, and which then became increasingly militant.

This, in turn, is the deeper reason for Sutherland Brown's re-emergence as a pop hero for the nationalists. It is not only that events have proved him right; he also reminds us of our strongest roots. No longer, in fact, do intelligent radicals follow Frank Underhill in a continentalist identification of Canadian progressivism with its American counterpart. Increasingly they are turning to conservative intellectuals such as George Grant, Donald Creighton and Harold Innis for an alternative view of an organic society which was based on British traditions and an explicit rejection of liberal republicanism. Only in this tradition can they find any hope for both independence and social change.

Although a traditionalist, Sutherland Brown was ahead of his time, and not only in his patriotism. In the nineteen-thirties, he began to worry that there were already too many people in the world, and that Canada had begun to squander its natural resources. He warned that it was folly to seek to match the Americans in their high standard of living: Canadians would do better to limit their population growth, curb their immigration, husband their resources, and abandon the chimera of economic expansion to preserve the quality of their existence.

It is not because of these concerns that we remember Buster Brown. Instead, we recall him as the quixotic warrior — a cavalier in an age of roundheads — who dared to plan a Canadian invasion of the United States. It is easy to mock him for his spying expeditions in New York and Vermont. While we may laugh at him, however, his emergence as a folk hero suggests that we recognize a deeper importance to his life. Perhaps unconsciously, we sense there is something to Buster which is authentically Canadian, something which we have largely lost in our rush to emulate our American cousins. A personal style, a very individual panache, it goes beyond politics and military strategy since it is finally a matter of sensibility and faith.

Bishop William White

William Charles White was born in 1873 and died in 1960. This is a remarkable span, stretching from the heyday of the Victorians through two world wars and well into the nuclear age. As a young man, White attended the funeral of Sir John A. Macdonald; he survived to witness the rivalries of Pearson and Diefenbaker. When he arrived in China as a youthful missionary, the Manchus still ruled from the Dragon Throne; by the time of his death, the Communists had been in power for more than a decade. In the shadow of such changes, White himself was transformed to an extent that was equally dramatic. Starting as a zealot who burned to bring heathen souls to Christ, he became an energetic bishop whose greatest achievements were administrative rather than evangelical. In turn, the bishop became an assiduous curator who all but abandoned his ecclesiastical activities to create one of the world's major collections of Chinese art. On the face of it, White's religious impulses were overtaken and superceded by his immense practical gifts: the spiritual pilgrim became a hard-headed executive. It would almost seem that White was a Victorian seeker who turned himself into an archetypal twentieth-century man, and killed his spiritual intensity for the sake of pragmatic success.

Yet there is a deeper pattern to White's unusual odyssey. It was something that the Chinese sensed, with their customary astuteness, when he arrived among them. For they called him Huai Li-kuan which can be translated as "One who searches for the light" or "One who diffuses enlightenment". Then he was given a second name which meant "One who searches for the rare, the wonderful, the mysterious".

From an early age, Will White instinctively sought some greater challenge than was offered by his immediate Canadian surroundings. Yet it was Africa — not China — which first stirred his imagination. In 1893, his twentieth year, he began to keep a diary. The initial entries are filled with Africa and the torment which thoughts of a missionary life aroused in him:

> [I] have felt a burden of Africa on my soul today, as I never felt it before . . . I broke down completely and wept till long after I got in bed. The spirit seemed to be striving for me to give up myself for Africa, on the other hand, I counted up all the sufferings I would have to undergo, but I thought of Christ dying for me, so I offered myself as ready to die in Africa for Christ.

There are few hints in White's background as to the source of these strong feelings. The family came from Devonshire, where Will was born and where he spent his first seven or eight years. His father, Henry James White, was a mason-contractor-builder who emigrated to Ontario and eventually established his family in Norwood, a country town near Peterborough. There were ten children, of whom Will was the eldest. They lived comfortably, in a solid brick house which Henry White had built as a proud example of his craftsman's skills. Unlike his younger brothers and sisters, Will never established a close relationship with his father; much more often he turned to his mother for advice and consolation. Since Henry was often working far from home, it was mainly Mrs. White who ran the household and raised the children. Neither parent was especially religious, and they made only ritual appearances at the local Church of England. But they insisted that their children attend each Sunday, and say their prayers each night. All this was normal and conventional — again we can only wonder at the source of young Will's early fervour.

Yet the times were certainly propitious for the evangelical zeal which White was soon to manifest. It was a confident, prosperous, assertive age. Canada was a young and lusty nation; under Macdonald (whom the Whites revered) it was busy thrusting its railroad to the Pacific and filling the

Western prairies with flocks of immigrants. At the same time, Canadians rejoiced and shared in the splendour of the British Empire. In 1887, when Will was fourteen, Queen Victoria's Jubilee marked a half-century of her rule; there seemed no reason to doubt that all those red patches on the map would last forever. One of Will's younger brothers was to fight in the Boer War; like James Brown in Simcoe, Will grew up in a home that was imbued with conservative and British traditions.

Something else was in the air: a surge of religious feeling which infused these secular concerns with a divine justification. Toward the end of the century, a doctrine of imperialism was developed in Europe and North America which stressed the self-evident superiority of the white race and its moral duties toward the so-called lesser races. In 1887, Joseph Chamberlain, then a rising young British politician, lectured a Toronto audience about "the greatness and importance of the destiny which is reserved for the Anglo-Saxon race . . . infallibly predestined to be the predominating force in the future history and civilization of the world."

In Norwood, such views must have been greeted as plain common sense. Just about everyone in the small town was British by origin, and the settler days were fresh in many memories. As they regarded the prosperous farms which they or their immediate ancestors had carved out of the stubborn forests, the citizens could only feel that some special virtue was inherent in their race, and that they were part of a larger, pioneering movement which was spreading Christian civilization throughout the heathen world. These views were propounded from the pulpits of the churches — Methodist and Presbyterian and Baptist as well as Anglican — which dominated life in the community, and which fostered standards of hard work, simple piety and social responsibility. There is no indication from White's early diaries that he had encountered the work of Darwin, Marx, Spencer or any other radical Victorian thinker who might have tempered his youthful fervour with a certain scepticism. If he differed from his contemporaries in Norwood, it was only in his determination to find a larger world in which to test his restless energies.

In 1893, the year of those first diary entries, White had just moved to Ottawa to take the post of assistant secretary of the YMCA. After finishing high school, he had already served for two years with the Y in Kingston. It was a career which seemed ideally suited to some of White's characteristics. Slim and wiry, he was bursting with vitality and enormous enthusiasm for any task he undertook, whether it was getting up at 5:30 am to start the fires, arranging meetings and conferences, leading camping and hiking expeditions, distributing notices or raising money. From the start he showed that he was a born organizer and a natural executive. When you add to these his robust health and his love of games and the outdoors, including a passion for bicycle hikes of more than twenty miles on country roads, you have the image of an ideal scoutmaster.

But this was only part of the picture. Apparently a no-nonsense extravert with a strong confidence in his own abilities, White also had a deep contemplative streak. His diaries are filled with introspective passages and anguished accounts of his unworthiness. At times his religious experience approaches the mystical: more than once he writes with ecstatic joy of a "meeting with Jesus", and it is clear that his communions with Christ were direct and overwhelming encounters. The diaries also indicate that White was intensely ambitious and hungry for recognition. ("I asked myself if I would be willing to go out to Africa to spend my life, without anyone knowing where I was or anyone to think of me. After a great deal of meditation, I said 'yes' to Jesus.") There was also a growing evangelical impulse: time and time again, he records how he sought out an acquaintance for "a good square talk" on spiritual matters.

It is highly doubtful that these strong and often conflicting traits could ever have been satisfied by the simple challenges of a YMCA career. Something in White was thrusting him out into the world as well as deeper into himself: something that demanded to be tested. "My life, I feel, will be a life of hardship and suffering," he told his diary. Given the temper of the times, it is no wonder that his thoughts became directed to missionary work.

If his thoughts turned first to Africa, it may have been

because the so-called Dark Continent had an unusual fascination for Victorians. The search for the source of the Nile had
taken on some aspects of a crusade; David Livingstone, who
died the year White was born, was still remembered with ven-
eration. And there was more to this than religious zeal: given
the emotional and sexual repressions of the Victorian age, it is
easy to understand the appeal of Africa, with all its primitive
and instinctive connotations. But it would be fanciful to suggest that young Will was strongly — if unconsciously —
motivated in this manner. While his diaries have references,
some of which he later inked out, to a "horrible besetting sin",
there is no evidence that he was morbidly repressed, or had
undue difficulty in sublimating these temptations.

About the time of his twentieth birthday, White's
application to the Domestic and Foreign Missionary Society
was accepted, and he was named to lead a band of lay missionaries to the Congo River. Steadily, however, the exciting
prospect dimmed, much to his frustration. First his mother
advised caution, then financial and other difficulties stemmed
the flow of missionaries to Africa. So Will turned his thoughts
to China where a few Canadian missions had already been
established. There is no indication from his diaries that he was
attracted by Chinese history and culture or, indeed, that he
knew anything about them. But he was stirred by meeting a
Canadian family, home on leave from their mission in Fukien,
and hearing them describe their work. A year later, when
news reached Canada that this family, the Stewarts, had all
been massacred, White felt compelled to take their place. Yet
he was far from happy at the prospect:

> Had serious thoughts in regard to China. Find out that
> my desire for Africa is a selfish one and worldly. God for-
> give me. I don't want to go to China, but an unaccount-
> able feeling tells me tonight that is where God is going to
> send me.

By now he had left the Y to become a scholarship
student at Wycliffe College in Toronto, one of the leading
schools for Anglicans who aspired to the ministry. He had
realized that a missionary needed more than a high school
training; perhaps the Stewarts had also told him that the

Chinese valued a good education almost more than any other attribute. Tackling his studies with his usual zest, he was soon winning first class honours in most of his subjects. Outside the college, he worked with the sick and destitute, listened to every great preacher who came to town, and preached his own first sermons. As further preparation for a missionary life, he read medical books, studied anatomy and toured hospitals and morgues. He also studied dentistry and practised on his friends with pliers: however painful for the friends, this would also prove extremely useful. Somehow he also found time for sports. Fitness had always been a prime concern: now he was playing football, basketball and lacrosse, as well as swimming, canoeing and snowshoeing.

Bursting with health, energy and confidence, White was one of those annoying young men who excel in *everything*. On the evidence of his diaries, he was also a prig and a puritan; strongly in favour of sexual continence and aghast when a friend served wine with dinner. Serious and conscientious, he seems to have had little sense of humour. Moreover, he had far from abandoned his liking for "good square talks". Some of the older students were angered by his overtures, especially since White made them feel they were less than fervent in their faith. Shortly before his death, White could still recall how a group of his seniors had lectured him on his excessive zeal, even to the point of calling him a Methodist.

This was close to the mark. With his evangelical zeal, White at this time does seem more Methodist than Anglican. It is significant that he spent several years working for the YMCA, which was largely a Methodist phenomenon. With his muscular Christianity, his love of sports and his earnest concern for the spiritual welfare of others, the young White could have stepped from the pages of a Ralph Connor novel. As we have seen, there were both Methodist and Presbyterian churches in Norwood, and the small town had something of that narrow, Calvinist, turn-of-the-century atmosphere which Connor captured in his Glengarry stories. Marked by such influences, White was an Anglican more by chance than conviction: because it was his parents' denomination.

It seems appropriate that he attended Wycliffe College which, although Anglican, was definitely Low Church, especially in contrast to the more august and pretentious Trinity College. While in Toronto, White went to Baptist, Methodist and Presbyterian services, as well as gospel and evangelical meetings. But he drew the line at the Roman Catholics: he was disturbed by their ritual and pageantry, and complained in his diary about their propensity to "idol worship".

In his early twenties, White was hardly an attractive figure. He was narrow and puritanical, and his religious zeal often seemed self-righteous. Again, however, this was only part of the picture. His tormented introspection in his diaries was evidence of an uncommon spiritual intensity, and a deep hunger for transcendence. "Oh! that I were more like Christ," he wrote at the start of 1895. "I want this year to be more like Him, more faithful, more unselfish, more loving, more on fire. No ambition for self but all ambition for the name of Christ." In Kingston and Ottawa, he had often painted, written poems and delighted in music. (He played the guitar, took singing lessons, and sang solos in church and at other functions.) These were tokens of a latent artistic sensibility; even in his troubled descriptions of the gilded Catholic cathedrals, there is a hint of fascination beneath the condemnation.

From the time he arrived in Toronto, however, White felt compelled to constrain his introspection, and suppress his sentience. His diary entries become shorter, more factual and much less introverted. Absorbed in all his activities at Wycliffe, he also had little time for painting and poetry. While he retained his intensity, this was directed to evangelical ends, with his fellow students as surrogates for the heathens he hoped that he would soon encounter. Bent on a missionary career, he seemed determined to develop all those extraverted, practical qualities that such a life demanded.

Although White's outlook and opinions would undergo drastic transformation in the years ahead, there was always one constant factor in his character: a determination that was relentless and often ruthless. Nothing would distract him from his quest — not even romance. While in Toronto, he was involved in the lengthy courtship of Annie Ray, a student at the Church of England Deaconess and Training House. There were many setbacks and much mutual soul-searching — most of which were occasioned by White's firm commitment to the missionary life, and Annie's reluctance to leave her widowed mother. White's priorities were always clear. As he wrote in early 1896:

> Nothing of worldly love, even Annie's love, could be compared to Christ's love. From now on is going to be a new era in my life. Henceforth I am dead to the world, dead to human love, if it comes in the slightest between Christ and me... If I have Annie for my wife, then alright, if not, all glory to Him.

Eventually these difficulties were resolved, and Will and Annie became engaged. "She had settled the matter herself," White wrote, "and had come to the conclusion that I was dearer to her than even her widowed and lonely mother. It awes me to see her love for me. It was so deep, so sincere. God forgive me for ever entertaining the slightest feeling against her."

But marriage had to wait. In May 1896, White was ordained as a deacon. Promised the next missionary posting, he was told by the church authorities that he would have to sail alone. He accepted this verdict without demur. And so he left for China — still a bachelor — on the 21st of January 1897.

White was only twenty-three when he sailed from Vancouver on the *Empress of Japan*. Although he was mature for his years, it was an enormous undertaking. While reading may have broadened his outlook, all his direct experience had been confined to the smug and provincial world of late nineteenth-century Ontario. To thrust oneself into the Orient is always an adventure; at the turn of the century it demanded the courage and perseverance of a pioneer. This was especially true for White since he would tarry only briefly in the relatively comfortable world of the treaty ports, where the Westerners had carved out their privileged sanctuaries, and would soon be heading into the interior of Fukien province, where he would be surrounded by millions of Chinese, with only a few fellow missionaries for occasional company. Despite his enthusiasm and self-confidence, his shipboard diary reveals a certain trepidation:

I am the only missionary on board and all seem such a worldly lot that I can have no Christian fellowship with them. I feel so lonely and downcast and realize already that even in the initial step the missionary's life is a life of difficulty and pain.

There would be danger as well as difficulty. After a busy day in the provincial capital of Foochow, White was on his way by sampan to the inland mission at Kienning. Enroute he stopped to pay homage at the graves of the Stewart family and other missionaries massacred in the previous year. It was a disturbing reminder that anti-foreign feeling was mounting in China and that missionaries in their isolated outposts were often easy targets.

For the next ten years White was to live and work in three inland Fukienese towns: Kienning, Nang Wa and Longuong. As he had feared it was a hard, lonely and frustrating life, even after Annie came out to join him. (They were married in Shanghai in October 1897.) At the end of his initial year, the young missionary summed up his first impressions in a long report to the church authorities in Toronto. His only favourable comment was on the "extreme beauty" of the countryside. (Nestling in the Dragon-Mist Mountains, Kienning was surrounded by tea plantations with sparkling brooks, clumps of bamboo and masses of rhododendrons and azaleas.) But he had nothing good to say about the Chinese themselves, noting that "it is a country in which 'every prospect pleases and only man is vile!'" He was especially struck by "the absence of any eagerness on the part of the natives to embrace Christianity." Even the few Chinese converts had faults and "at times show inconsistencies which would be thought very grave in Church members at home." With a modicum of charity, White admitted that the converts had a hard time because of the evil environment in which they lived — "on all sides is deceit, immorality, idolatry". Above all he had come to recognize that the Fukienese were stubbornly set in their ancient ways:

> From their birth up there has been nothing in their training to give them any tangible idea of anything better, and so they remain content with what their fathers and

grandfathers before them were content with, and can't imagine there is anything better, until by medical or evangelistic work, or their own unbounded curiosity, they are brought within the sound of the Gospel. Even then there has to be a long course of training and teaching before the Heathen heart can grasp this amazing fact: the wonderful love of the Heavenly Father. Truly, if a man ever needed patient and persevering faith, it is here!

Despite his initial disillusionment, White threw himself into the task. He came to realize that missionaries had a better chance of making converts through social work, rather than direct evangelism. Putting to good use the rudimentary skills he had learned in Toronto, he was soon busy pulling teeth, setting dislocated bones, and performing a host of minor operations. After the move to Longuong he established a boys' school, took charge of a leper colony, and began working with Chinese officials in the Anti-Opium League.

It was not an easy life for either Will or Annie. As White noted in his diary, travelling through the countryside was a constant exposure to mud, filth and dingy, over-crowded inns. At all their missions the Whites were subjected to thieves, indifferent workmen, unreliable servants and hostile "idol priests". At times hostility became outright menace. In 1899, feeling against the foreigners erupted in the Boxer Rebellion. More than 200 missionaries and their families were murdered in northern China, in addition to about 20,000 of their converts. As disturbances spread to the south, the Whites were forced to take refuge in Foochow.

All this began to leave its mark. When White arrived in Fukien, his appearance was so youthful that many Chinese wondered why such a mere boy was allowed to travel on his own. Several years later, he was still slim and his large blue eyes retained their look of eager expectation. But now his face was leaner and more ascetic, with a new cast of firmness and authority. "I am much harder-featured now," White noted when he came across an old photograph of himself in Ottawa. By now, too, the busy man-of-affairs had almost completely taken over from the introspective youth. During this period White's diaries become increasingly factual, increasingly less

thoughtful, until they peter out into mere listings of engagements. Something *was* hardening in the man. Frustrated by
the enormous obstacles to his work, convinced that many of
his fellow missionaries were too often complacent and ineffi-
cient, he was becoming even more stubborn and aggressive in
his views.

Again, however, this was only part of the picture. By
now he was a family man with three young children. Father-
hood seems to have tempered his severity, for he was a patient
and generous parent who could set off a whole verandah full
of firecrackers in celebration of a birthday with the same
infectious enthusiasm he brought to all his pursuits. Despite
the burden of his duties, there was always something new for
him to try, whether it was making jam from local fruits, growing flowers and vegetables, or learning to play Chinese musi-
cal instruments. Always curious and observant, White also
began to collect local stones and artifacts. This was an early
indication of the great passion which would dominate his later
years. For he was not nearly as hardened and set in his ways as
he sometimes appeared, and about this time we begin to see
signs of a striking transformation: a fundamental shift in his
response to China and everything Chinese.

When he arrived in Fukien, White was filled with the conventional notions of his day about the essential superiority of the
Anglo-Saxon race and the spiritual depravity of the lesser
breeds. These feelings were reinforced by his own intense faith
and his conviction that he had been especially chosen to bring
salvation to the heathen. From the start, he realized that he
could do his work only if he could speak the language: within
a few years he had earned the rare accolade of "the foreigner
who speaks Chinese like a Chinese." As another practical
concession he grew a queue and adopted Chinese dress (partly
so he would be less conspicuous in a crowd, partly because the
loose-fitting Chinese gowns were much more comfortable
than the stiff Western suits). But he felt it was a "great sacrifice" to wear such heathen garb, and he noted in his diary that
Annie was also greatly troubled.

Despite these concessions, White remained convinced

that since the Chinese lived in darkness, every aspect of their culture could only be benighted and inferior. He was especially upset by the "idolatry" he found on every side: this became a burning obsession. Satan — just as much as Christ — had always been a presence in his life. As a student in Toronto, he had felt the Devil's evil influence. ("Satan pressed me sorely . . . Satan told me I had a good sermon, but nobody praised me.") Now, in temples and pagodas, the young missionary saw the Prince of Darkness leering out at him from every carved and moulded figure. "There is a very strange feeling comes over me in such places," he wrote after a visit to a Confucian temple, "just as if there were a thousand pairs of fiends' eyes burning at you from every crack and corner and watching for an unguarded moment on your part to do you damage."

Whenever one of his missions gained a rare convert, White took special pleasure in the destruction of the convert's household idols. In late 1898, he described such a scene in a letter from Nang Wa:

> I shall never forget the night a little handful of us stumbled in the dark to hold a service before burning the idols! We roused out all the men in the hamlet to come — about thirty in all — and then in the flickering light of tallow dips, sang hymns and prayed . . .

> After this, we took down all the idols and idolatrous scrolls, the charms and shrines, idolatrous prayer books and paper money, and piled all in the centre of the mud floor.

> The heathen had by this time all gone out, some with frightened looks upon their faces, feeling perhaps that something dire would be sure to follow such sacrilege.

> The good man's wife too was in a fearful state, for she was not yet reconciled to the idea of putting away the idols.

> One idol in particular she wanted to keep — "It is so new and beautiful and cost such a lot; couldn't I keep it for the children to play with?" But all had to go on the pile, and then, the fire being applied, we watched the smoke

and flames with a joyful heart, feeling that it was a real
sacrifice to God, for it was no easy thing for the old man
of sixty years to break off from the old associations and to
stand alone for the cause of Truth and Christ.

Even allowing for the evangelical temper of the time,
White's glee at the burning of the idols seems excessive and
fanatical. It may well have been that he was already starting
to feel an instinctive *attraction* to the Chinese culture — an
attraction which the young missionary could only suppress
through acts of passionate destruction. In a diary entry from
the same year, he describes another conversion and its "crown-
ing event": taking down the household gods and a large "idol-
atrous scroll". This time, however, nothing was burnt. For as
White noted: "I brought home the scroll and one of the little
gilt idols and perhaps some day they may find their place in
the mission." Later — in Longuong — he began actively to
collect small works of art, to study social and religious customs, and to copy down inscriptions that he noticed on temples, inns and homes.

In fact White was changing. It was no sudden
conversion, and it implied no lessening of his Christian faith.
Yet slowly, steadily and with mounting enthusiasm, the
young missionary was tempering his dogmatic evangelism
and opening himself to the Chinese way.

The crucial period began when White moved from
Longuong to Foochow in 1907. His previous missions had all
been situated in country towns which were at least as provincial in their way as his own Norwood. Here the three great
Chinese traditions — Confucian, Taoist and Buddhist —
were to be found only in a degenerate and rudimentary
hodge-podge, and intermingled by the credulous peasants
with a host of even older superstitions. In these initial years,
White seems to have encountered few if any Chinese of the
mandarin class: sophisticated intellectuals who would have
introduced him to their culture at a higher level. An early
diary entry from Kienning describes with obvious derision the
"great person" of the town: "He is quite a swell and carries a
little dirty white comb hung on a string around his neck with
which he diligently combs the few straggling hairs on his lip."

In Foochow, however, White was soon meeting the

leading scholars and officials of the province, most notably the head of the Confucian gentry who invited the missionary to his home, and gave him a tour of the temple and school over which he presided. Since Foochow was a major city, its leading Confucian would be a man of erudition, cultivation and sensitivity. We can imagine him receiving his guest with enormous courtesy, serving a fragrant variety of the local Oolung tea in exquisite cups, explaining the subtleties of the scrolls on his walls, describing with disarming modesty his role in the affairs of the Chinese Empire, and undoubtedly discoursing on the finer points of Confucian ethics.

We can also imagine the impact on the missionary. By now White was in his mid-thirties. Always strong-willed and confident, he had gained considerable authority from his hard decade in the countryside. It was not in his nature to feel insecure or inferior in the presence of another, but it is quite likely that he felt a distinct unease. There was nothing in his background, including the best living rooms of Ottawa and Toronto, to compare with the simple elegance of the Confucian's home. It is doubtful that the conversation of his teachers at Wycliffe had ever been so learned and civilized. Certainly no one had ever spoken to White with the assurance and implicit superiority that sprang from having roots in a culture stretching over several thousand years of extraordinary excellence. It is quite possible, in short, that White began to feel a bit uncouth. At least he began to realize that a civilization could hardly be benighted if it produced leading men such as his new Confucian friends, and works of art such as he could see in all their homes.

It was not just a case of White's aesthetic sensibilities being reawakened by his exposure to Chinese scrolls and porcelain, nor was it simply that the elegance and high manners of the mandarins made his own background seem decidedly provincial. These were tokens of a deeper revelation: that the Chinese culture, far from being inferior to his own, was rich in opportunities for spiritual fulfilment.

This is not to imply that White came to doubt his Christian faith, for such would never be the case. But the simple pieties of his Norwood background, and even the more subtle theological doctrines of his Wycliffe teachers, could no longer satisfy his spiritual hunger. His personal *mélange* of Low Church Anglicanism, Methodist evangelism and Calvinist muscularity must now have struck him as being almost as rudimentary as the primitive mixture of Chinese beliefs he had encountered at his inland missions. This is surmise — since White no longer brooded on such matters in his diary — but there is evidence from this period that he was, indeed, seeking a deeper and more sophisticated expression of his religious impulses, and that this quest was closely linked to his new appreciation of the Chinese way.

His search involved a growing sense of ritual and ceremony. Shortly after moving to Foochow, White became a Freemason and was initiated into the South China District Lodge. It was to be a compelling interest for the rest of his life. In Masonry, White found not only an extension of his Christianity, but also parallels to the Chinese customs he was coming to respect. In later years, he wrote articles which linked Masonic rites to the Worship of Heaven and other ancient Chinese ceremonies. Praising the Chinese for their "sense of accuracy in the performance of ceremony and ritual", he found the source of this capacity in China's long tradition of moral philosophy, and in its symbolic wealth.

All this began to be apparent to him in Foochow. White came to believe that Christianity and Chinese doctrines, especially Confucianism, could be complementary, rather than competitive. He would always make the distinction between the "natural religion" of the Chinese and the "revealed religion" of Christ, maintaining that Christianity was different, and higher, because it was redemptive. But he was struck by the tolerance of his Chinese friends and the strong ethical base of their Confucian faith, which seemed a reflection of God's moral law.

At this stage, the ambiguity in White's Chinese name seems decidedly appropriate. As he showed a growing fascination for the Chinese way, he must indeed have struck the mandarins as "one who searches for the light". But if White had overcome his youthful bigotry, if he had begun to sense that Chinese culture had much to offer him, he was still steadfast in his missionary role. As "one who diffuses enlightenment", he had no doubt that Christianity was ordained to conquer

China. If anything, his encounters with the mandarins had increased his optimism, since he found them much more receptive and broad-minded than the Chinese in the interior. Like the Jesuit missionaries of earlier centuries, he became convinced that his evangelical work would best succeed if he concentrated on the upper classes. As with other foreigners before and since his time, White may have allowed himself to be deceived by the politeness of his hosts. There is much in Christianity that could only deeply offend an educated and ethnocentric Chinese, but to dwell on these differences would have struck the mandarins as the height of bad manners.

At any rate, White was given little chance to convert the aristocracy of Foochow. It was a time when all the churches were expanding their missionary work in China. In 1908, White was instructed to scout the prospects in Honan, a vast province in north-central China which was only slowly being opened to Western influence. Reporting on his trip, he recommended the establishment of a mission at Kaifeng, the provincial capital, to be headed by a bishop.

There was never much doubt about the candidate (although the Archbishop of Canterbury demurred for some time at appointing a Canadian bishop, to head a mission under the direct control of the Canadian Church). White's long experience in Fukien, his command of the language and his administrative abilities made him the obvious choice. Called to Toronto, he was consecrated in St. James' Cathedral on the 30th of November 1909. Only thirty-six, he was now Bishop White.

He was also on the brink of his most active period. For much of this time — about another fifteen years — the "one who searches for the light" and even the "one who diffuses enlightenment" would be subordinated to the hard-driving administrator and the energetic man-of-affairs. There was something in his temperament (it had been evident as early as his time at the Ottawa YMCA) which demanded a vigorous life of practical achievement. This had often troubled him: as a young man, he had chastised himself in his diary for his worldly ambition. He wanted to achieve great deeds in the name of Christ, but he was tormented by the thought that his real motive was a desire for recognition and fame. During his early years as a missionary, he was still distressed by his "conceited selfish spirit" — "I am so full of the ego," he wrote, "and all my castles and ambitions when I look closely at them have the object of self-glory."

Despite such scruples, White had too much energy and drive not to hunger after great achievements. But these would never satisfy his spiritual longings, and it was a fortunate chain of circumstances which took him to Honan. For when he again turned to the quest which he had begun in Foochow, he would find himself even better placed to seek enlightenment.

During his first decade in Kaifeng — where he and Annie arrived by sedan chair during a blinding dust storm in March 1910 — White reached his peak as a dynamic administrator. His achievements were all the more remarkable because even in terms of China's long and troubled history, this was a time of unusual turmoil. The Revolution of 1911 which overthrew the Manchus also launched a prolonged period of civil war. It was a time when bandits and warlords rampaged across the countryside, and foreigners could rarely feel secure. Widespread floods and famine added to the ferment of unrest.

Close to the heart of China, Honan was never immune from these disturbances. Stretching over 68,000 square miles south of the Yellow River, Bishop White's diocese embraced 35-million people. With about 300,000 inhabitants, Kaifeng itself was a crowded capital with burgeoning industries and little natural beauty. It was enclosed by an immense wall, while a few picturesque ruins were a reminder that the city had been the seat of the Sung Empire about one thousand years earlier.

From the start, White launched an energetic building campaign which resulted in residences, schools, hospitals, an orphanage and eventually a cathedral. As in Foochow, he soon established good relations with the local mandarins; again there was an emphasis on education, medical care and other social work in order to convince the practical Chinese that the Christian way was both useful and responsible. When a serious famine swept through northern China shortly after

White's arrival, he plunged into relief work. Under his direction, whole trainloads of supplies were brought into the province to feed the starving. This performance was to be repeated again and again, most notably during the disastrous famine of 1920-21. On several occasions White headed national relief organizations: it was mainly for this work that he received a host of Chinese decorations.

White also imported new varieties of cattle and poultry, and pioneered new techniques of farming and irrigation. Always taking care to work closely with Chinese officials, he was often asked to arbitrate between rival war lords who were threatening the capital. Once his penchant for "good square talks" probably saved Kaifeng from an orgy of murder, rape and looting as he crossed and recrossed the dangerous no-man's-land between two armies to negotiate a settlement.

This was no desk-bound administrator. Still filled with restless energy, White was often on the move around his province. For years he bounced along the rough country roads on a motorcycle, much to the amazement of the peasants and (one suspects) to the gratification of his own sense of showmanship. The motorcycle was an indication of how White — a Victorian who had been born in an era which saw the invention of the telephone, the typewriter and the automobile — was always quick to adapt modern technology for his own purposes. Later, in his sixties, he would learn to fly an airplane.

Again we touch on White's complexity. For he was also a traditionalist and every inch a bishop: a Prince of the Church who delighted in both the dignity and the authority of his office. He demanded deference and rejoiced in ceremony. Thanks to Annie's careful attentions, he always looked the part: except when the motorcycle threw him into a ditch, his robes, his suits and his grooming were immaculate. With his good health and his straight, clear gaze, he radiated purpose and conviction: it was a rash man who dared to cross him. He had suffered too long in Fukien from the restrictions placed upon his work by hesitant superiors and uncooperative colleagues. Now he was in charge and no one was left in any doubt of his power.

Some of the missionaries who went to work under Bishop White found him much too dictatorial. Although he could sometimes talk them around — despite his autocratic ways, he had a certain charm and diplomatic skill — some had to leave his jurisdiction.

There was also conflict with missionaries from other churches, especially the Canadian Presbyterians, who had been established in Honan before the Anglicans, and who had given White a generous welcome. Soon White tried to involve them in his plans to establish schools for young Chinese. But the Presbyterians demurred when they came to realize that the Bishop would be making all the decisions. This was only one of several disputes; before long the Presbyterians became convinced that White was determined to control the work of all the churches in Honan. They felt he was too adamant in having his own way and too insistent that he — and he alone — should be their intermediary with the Chinese authorities. Although he was well aware of these criticisms, White never seemed to understand them. After all, he *was* the Bishop, wasn't he?

That was part of the trouble, since Presbyterians have a natural distrust of any bishop. By now, too, White had apparently outgrown those Calvinist and Low Church influences which might, had they persisted, have gained him a greater sympathy among the other missions. With his growing sense of hierarchy, he rejoiced in the full panoply and power of his princely office; moreover, his aesthetic sensibility, never totally suppressed, was re-emerging under the combined influence of Freemasonry and the Chinese culture which he found exemplified by the mandarins of Kaifeng, just as much as their counterparts in Foochow.

White had come a long way from the Glengarry world of Norwood: it is no exaggeration to state that he had been transformed by China. He had arrived as a priggish, intolerant youth, as fervent as any Methodist and as narrow as any Calvinist. Yet his early diaries show that the zealous young Christian who dreamed of Africa possessed a spiritual hunger which could never be satisfied by the conventional pieties of Victorian Ontario. From the start, he sensed he needed greater challenges.

China provided them. As a very old man, White would describe it as

> a nation which has absorbed all its conquerors and transformed everything that came into it — races, systems of thought, religions — and produced the most continuous and integrated tradition of civilization that the world has known . . . It is a world that has given more than it has received — the peach and the orange, silk and tea, porcelain and paper and printing, probably gunpowder and the mariner's compass, fine arts, learning and manners, and a moral philosophy second only to that of Christianity.

This is perceptive. It is also impersonal. Once he abandoned his diaries, White rarely tried to describe his feelings, so we can only speculate about the nature of his deepest responses. There could be a clue in some notes he wrote in Kaifeng on Christmas Day of 1917:

> China is as usual in a condition of uncertainty. Hardly a year passes but we feel the break-up of the nation is about to take place, and yet somehow or other the crisis passes and another arises, and China still remains intact! The Chinese are clumsy in their national and international dealings, and yet so diplomatic they can squirm out of any difficulty. They are persistent and conservative to a degree, and yet can accommodate themselves to any circumstances. *They are a remarkable people, and one cannot but feel they have been preserved nationally for some wise purpose among the nations of the earth.* [Emphasis added.]

By 1924, on his return from furlough in Canada, White was ready for a striking change of direction which would make him an apostle for that "wise purpose". This would involve a new career, first as a collector, then as a curator of those Chinese works of art in which he had sensed such a wealth of spiritual passion. It would also lead him to his most lasting achievement, and a personal fulfilment which the missionary of thirty years earlier could never have envisaged.

In Foochow, White had begun to appreciate the spiritual

power and psychological subtlety of a culture which had initially struck him as merely superstitious. In Kaifeng, he was even better placed for his renewed pursuit. For he was at the heart of the north China plain, the area from which civilization had radiated throughout the empire. The legendary founder of that empire, Fuh-hsi, was said to have been Honanese, while both Confucius and Lao Tzu, the reputed originator of Taoism, had taught there and served as provincial officials. All the great dynasties had established their capitals in the area, and Kaifeng was within easy distance of Loyang, Anyang and many other important archeological sites. White was also fortunate in his timing. This was a period of extensive construction and railroad building across north China; surveyors and work gangs were constantly unearthing royal tombs and other buried treasures. It was also a time of civil war and banditry; amid the turmoil antiquities and works of art became more readily available, and there were few effective controls on their export.

There was another fortunate coincidence of timing. Back in Toronto in 1924, White met C. T. Currelly, the curator of archeology at the new Royal Ontario Museum. For several years Currelly had been building an impressive Chinese collection, mainly with the help of George Crofts, a British fur merchant living in Tientsin. But Crofts became bankrupt in that same year, and could no longer help. With his growing interest in antiquities and his powerful position in Honan, White struck Currelly as an ideal replacement, especially since the Bishop was primarily interested in early bronzes, whereas Crofts had concentrated on objects from later dynasties.

White returned to China determined to fill the gaps in the ROM's collection. Few men could have been better suited to the task. Now in his early fifties, he had abundant energy, ingenuity and perseverence; he was well versed in the Chinese classics, and he had good connections with the leading mandarins and merchants. From Currelly he began to learn the intricate disciplines of scientific archeology; he was already in regular correspondence with two other Canadians who were authorities on Chinese art: Dr. John Ferguson, the first president of the University of Nanking, and Rev. James Menzies, a Presbyterian missionary at Anyang, who had made major discoveries of Chinese oracle bones. Both gave him scholarly guidance and practical help.

Over the next decade, White threw himself into the task with such determination that some of his colleagues in Kaifeng began to grumble that he was neglecting his mission work. But the Bishop felt that he had done as much as he could for the Chinese church. Now it was time to be a missionary-in-reverse: to give his own countrymen the chance to participate in the spiritual and artistic wealth of Chinese civilization. In view of his earlier prejudice, this was a remarkable change. Yet one factor may well have been constant. As a theology student, White had lectured his Wycliffe classmates on their lack of religious fervour. Never a man to tolerate complacency or any form of watered-down belief, he now seems to have concluded that the Western world was becoming increasingly secular and de-spirited, and increasingly in need of regeneration from the East. This would be the "wise purpose" for which he felt the Chinese had been preserved.

It was harrowing work which required not only the learning of a scholar and the sensitivity of a connoisseur but also the instincts of a detective, the tact of a diplomat and the wiles of a canny bargainer. There were forgeries to be detected, spies and informers to be hired, dealers to be haggled with, and officials and priests to be charmed and placated. Because he never entirely abandoned his mission work, White was seldom able to visit the graves and other sites. This was a major disappointment since it meant he rarely enjoyed the savage thrill of actual discovery. But he chose his intermediaries carefully, his own scholarship became impressive, and his instincts were usually acute. Aside from financial constraints, White had virtually a free hand in his purchasing, but when Currelly requested specific items, he would put his agents on the scent with formidable determination, even though the search might take a year or more. There was no restraining his enthusiasm. "The enclosed will take your breath away," he told Currelly in a note with one of his shipments, "for I have gone more than the limit, and overdrawn my bank account to do it . . . too good to let pass . . ."

Money was always a problem, but White was seldom hampered by the lack of it. When the museum board ordered restraint after the start of the Depression, he simply ignored the instruction, at one point building up an overdraft of more than $90,000. For he was seized with a vision — a vision that Toronto should have one of the world's great collections of Eastern art — and he refused to be deterred by the rumblings of cautious administrators. As he assured them in a barrrage of letters, an opportunity like this would never occur again, and the objects would soon be worth many times their purchase price.

During his decade of collecting for the ROM, White sent back several thousand items. If the quantity was impressive, the quality was even more remarkable. Thanks to White, Toronto has one of the world's foremost collections of early Chinese bronzes, and a trove of tomb figures which give an extremely detailed picture of Chinese life over thousands of years. Another major acquisition was the Mu Library, with about 50,000 rare volumes, some of them exceptionally important.

But White's most breathtaking purchases were the three gigantic wall paintings which have their own separate gallery in the ROM — a gallery which bears his name. The two side panels are Taoist processionals and the enormous fresco in the centre is a Buddhist paradise: all came from temples in Shansi province. The Buddhist painting is considered one of the world's major art treasures. It had been cut into eighty pieces by the priests of the temple and hidden from a rampaging war lord; when they were later facing starvation, the priests decided they had to sell their only security. Told by his informants that it was on the market, White quickly negotiated its purchase. Back in Toronto, it took years of cautious experimentation and careful workmanship to rejoin, restore and mount the pieces.

Seen together the frescoes have an overwhelming richness and subtlety, with the processions of Taoist deities complementing the more static formality of the Buddhist paradise. As White wrote of the latter: "Over the whole there broods a spirit of serenity and quiet dignity, an atmosphere which soothes the spirit of the beholder, and breeds contentment and rest." There is also a majestic sense of hierarchy which must have made a deep appeal to White's own feelings for ritual and ceremony — again, we sense the enormous distance he had come from Norwood.

White's great splurge of collecting lasted for less than a decade. He had begun to encounter stiff competition from wealthy connoisseurs and their agents; prices kept on climbing even during the Depression. Chinese officials had become increasingly concerned about the flood of their national treasures to the West; in 1930 the government in Nanking ruled that "all antiquities and relics shall belong to the state" — and banned their export. With civil war again breaking out — this time between the Nationalists and the Communists — and with the Japanese menacing from Manchuria, it became almost impossible to conduct business of any sort. Soon missionaries and other foreigners were advised to leave the interior for the relative safety of the treaty ports.

After more than thirty years in China, White was ready to welcome such advice. Despite his robust health, the pressures were beginning to tell. As he wrote in 1930:

> It requires a good deal of grace to live in China these days and I shall be glad when my work and my conscience allow me to leave. The constant strain and anxiety are very great, and sometimes one feels almost at the breaking point.

But when he finally returned to Canada in 1934, White was neither discouraged nor disillusioned. While he recognized that the political turmoil was bound to worsen, he felt that he had left his mission on a solid footing. For years he had struggled against Anglican leaders in Canada who were complacent about the ferment of nationalism in China, and determined that the Honan diocese should remain under their control. Instead, he had worked to keep the number of Western missionaries to a minimum, while insisting that they all had a thorough grounding in Chinese language, history and culture before they started their work. His main goal had always been to train Chinese converts to the point where they could take complete charge of the diocese: as he had written in 1924: "The missionary should have before him a picture of himself with his suitcase in his hand leaving China." On his return to Toronto, he won his final battle when the General

Synod agreed to appoint his Chinese assistant as the new bishop: by leaving his mission in the hands of the Chinese themselves, he felt he had done his best to ensure its survival. All this, of course, was a strong departure from White's earlier racial arrogance: it was another indication of how greatly he had changed.

Typically, White had new work to absorb his energies. Back in Toronto, Currelly had been avidly pursuing his dream of a vastly expanded museum. A new wing was opened in 1933: more than twice the size of the original building, it had eighteen galleries allocated to the Chinese collection. For years White had been bombarding Currelly with plans for the proper display and use of his treasures. His vision extended far beyond the ROM itself, for he argued that the Chinese collection should become the basis for a major program of Chinese studies — linked to the University of Toronto — which would make the city a leading centre for research and scholarship in Chinese art, archeology, history and other related fields. Both Currelly and the university authorities were receptive to the plan; they also recognized that White had the best chance to make it work. In 1934, he was named curator of the whole Far Eastern collection, as well as an associate professor of archeology at the university.

White was sixty when he left Honan: a time when most men are looking forward to their retirement. Instead he launched himself into his new career with unflagging enthusiasm. Plans and projects cascaded from his office. The Chinese collection was catalogued and exhibited with detailed descriptions of the geographical, historical and cultural background of the objects. Tours and lectures were arranged, as well as further research by graduate students. Scholars were hired and the library expanded. White maintained a heavy correspondence with authorities in other countries; he also began to produce a steady flow of articles, pamphlets and books, most of which were based on his own major acquisitions. Within a few years, the ROM's collection — and its curator — had a world-wide reputation. In 1943, the university sanctioned the importance of his work by establishing a School of Chinese Studies — the first of its kind in Canada — with White as its director.

On the face of it, White's character was still dominated by those practical, extraverted qualities which had made him such a forceful bishop in Honan. With his energy and administrative skill, he was almost an archetypal modern executive, swept up in a drive for achievement. Yet part of him — an even more essential part — remained resolutely non-modern, even non-Canadian. In his relations with his staff and colleagues, he was often arbitrary and impersonal, always demanding deference and obedience. As one of them remarked: "Bishop White could never adapt himself to this modern world. He remained at heart a medieval bishop, like Archbishop Baldwin of Canterbury who maintained the right to crown Richard Coeur de Lion." Other colleagues had a strong impression that he was not quite one of them, that his long years abroad had made him more Chinese than the Chinese, and that even his features had taken on an Oriental cast. Some said that *he* was the one who had undergone conversion. (In a formal portrait taken at this time, White appears in the full splendour of his bishop's robes, but the picture is dominated by a large Chinese decoration which he wears around his neck.) Certainly his experience in China had only reinforced his strong sense of hierarchy, and his instinctive feeling that a man in his position should never be challenged or corrected. It had also given him a remarkable talent for evading such challenges: his colleagues would often depart from meetings groaning in frustration over their inability to pin him down. Anyone who has ever lived in China will understand the technique of these evasions.

In his personal relations, White could be just as arbitrary and demanding. After all the long years of loyal work at his side, Annie had left China in a sick and weakened state; she died soon after their return. Many spinsters and widows in Toronto considered that a bishop would be a fine catch. Overwhelmed by their attentions, White told Canon H.J. Cody, chairman of the university's board of governors, that he would have to remarry or else leave town. So he wrote a letter of proposal to Daisy Masters, whom he had first met in 1915, and who had worked in the Honan diocese for many years. Then on furlough in England, Daisy was taken completely by surprise. Although she refused his proposal — and kept on refusing it — White was not to be deterred: he maintained a persistent stream of letters. As his biographer records: "She raised every obstacle she could conjure up, and White knocked them down as quickly as she erected them. Finally, when he proclaimed that the marriage was in accordance with the will of God, she could no longer refuse — coming as that argument did from a bishop." They were married in 1935, and Daisy was with him to the end.

If Bishop White could never entirely adapt himself to the modern world, he could also never accept the victory of modernity in his beloved China. While he had grown sympathetic to the rising force of nationalism, he was convinced that the new China which emerged from the Second World War would reject any political extreme, and follow the traditional "middle way" of Confucian doctrine, thus allowing ample opportunities for a thriving and indigenous Christianity. In this he demonstrated his conservative bias. Although his views on China had certainly changed, although his spiritual feelings and instincts had undergone a remarkable development, he was not a profound thinker, and he rarely showed much inclination to question the basic doctrines — whether religious or political — which he had absorbed in his youth. Unlike many Canadian Methodist and Presbyterian missionaries and their children, he was never a reformer and never attracted to radical ideas. He accepted the regime of Chiang Kai-shek just as readily as his parents had accepted the leadership of Sir John A. Macdonald. As early as 1936, he could confidently assert in *The Globe and Mail* that the Chinese peasants had already rejected Communism.

In late 1945, White was given a chance to test his convictions on the spot. His former diocese in Honan had been devastated through seven years of war, famine and flooding. On the appeal of his Chinese successors in Kaifeng, who remembered his endeavours amid earlier calamities, White was sent back to assist in the relief work. Typically, he was still working in his museum office late on the afternoon of his departure. At the last minute, he rushed out the door, flagged down a passing car, and announced loudly: "I'm Bishop

White. I am on my way to China and I haven't much time to catch my train. Please drive me quickly to the Union Station."

Once in Kaifeng, White tackled the relief work with much of his old energy. (He was now seventy-two.) But he was frustrated by rampaging inflation, official paralysis and sagging morale on the Nationalist side. The situation soon became hopeless. White left Kaifeng in May 1947; one month later the Communists launched their attack on the capital. By mid-summer, they controlled all of northern Honan. Two years later, Mao Tse-tung stood on the Gate of Heavenly Peace in Peking and proclaimed the victory of Communism over all the Chinese mainland.

Back in Toronto, White watched from afar as the new regime worked gradually but inexorably to constrain the Chinese Christians. Writing in 1952, he sadly described "a complete blackout" between the Canadian Church of England and its Chinese counterpart: "We dare not communicate with them, nor they with us."

There was another, more personal blow. Also in 1952, Bishop Francis Tseng launched a strong attack on White in a Shanghai Christian magazine. Tseng had studied under White in Toronto, returned to China in 1945, and was consecrated Bishop of Honan in 1949. He wrote that he had seen the Chinese collection in the ROM and had been filled with hatred to think that White had taken advantage of his position to steal these treasures under the cloak of religion, and had grown rich in the process.

White was deeply pained by this attack. He had not profited personally from his acquisitions: most had been purchased on the open market at current prices. More important, they had been acquired during a period when Chinese officials were indifferent to their fate: if White and other Western collectors had not removed them from the turmoil of the civil war, many would have been lost forever. White also knew that he and his competitors had literally only scratched the surface of China's buried heritage. In 1943, he predicted that "a great day for archeology in China" would dawn with the end of the war, and that what had been dug up so far "are but tokens of further treasures to be uncovered and deeper revelations to be unfolded."

This was highly perceptive, although White would never have predicted that Communists would be the ones to sponsor the remarkable renaissance of archeology which did in fact occur. Nevertheless, he would have been delighted with the extraordinary Chinese exhibition of new finds which Peking sent to the ROM in 1974. Yet it was just as well that he was no longer alive, for the Chinese were adamant that the museum should not advertise White's collection in connection with their own exhibits. One can sympathize with Chinese sensitivities. But many collections in the world's greatest museums are the result of invasion, looting, grave-robbing and smuggling; in contrast to these, White's purchasing practices are hardly reprehensible. It is only in recent years that "finders-keepers" has ceased to be the ethic of archeology, and that various nations including Canada have taken steps to prevent the export of their national heritage.

Despite the attacks and setbacks, White remained convinced that Chinese Christianity would eventually triumph over Chinese Communism. In 1954, he could anticipate a day when "we may once more be able to give help to our daughter church", adding that "we may be on the eve of a national conquest such as the Church has never seen in her long history — the conversion of a nation of five hundred million souls." He also wrote that China's future was of the highest importance to the whole world: "Whether this country is to be Christian is the greatest challenge — in the long view — that the Church is faced with today." If White ever became discouraged about the outcome of that challenge, he never let it show. In 1959, he told an interviewer he still felt the Chinese church was growing. Apparently he died in that conviction.

Yet the defeat of his cause had been obvious for many years. The assumptions upon which he had based his missionary career were regarded as totally irrelevant by the new Chinese leaders, who could only despise his sacramental vision. White's Christianity had been vanquished in China just as thoroughly and ruthlessly as Sutherland Brown's Anglo-Tory patriotism had been overwhelmed in Canada —

in both cases by that modern spirit of which Communism is just as much an exemplar as Western liberalism.

White's refusal to accept his defeat is staggering in its stubbornness. It seemed to be based upon more than wishful thinking; rather, it sprang from a rock-like will and a quite extraordinary faith. It may also have been rooted in profound necessity: a deep compulsion to assert that modern secularity could never triumph — at least, not ultimately — over spiritual forces which were a living reality for White, and which he had come to find as much in the Shansi frescoes as in the Christian communion.

We can imagine him in his later years standing before those magnificent Buddhist and Taoist paintings in the gallery which bears his name — a small, slight figure wrapped in contemplation. Not so much the powerful bishop now, but more like a monk in his cathedral. He was often seen like this, and on his tours of the other galleries he would pause for long minutes, absorbed in the simple splendour of a Tang vase.

Of course, the Chinese collection is White's greatest achievement, and it overshadows by far the failure of his missionary endeavours. That image of the monk in his cathedral wants to recur. For that is what White built for us — in the midst of the bustling and prosperous secular city, he founded a cathedral which glorifies a higher power and a universal order. In those great frescoes, he caught an intimation of eternity incarnate — as real and almost as immediate as in the Eucharist itself.

It was here that he came to contemplate and worship, almost to the end. In 1949, he had retired from his positions at both the museum and the university. At seventy-four, he was still vigorous, but he had finally recognized it was time to make way for younger men. He and Daisy withdrew to a cottage at Fonthill in the Niagara peninsula, but eventually this proved too remote, since he was still active in both church work and Chinese studies: in 1955 White moved back to Toronto. There he was in a better position to keep up his meetings and his correspondence with scholars in many countries, to serve on church committees, and to pursue his reading and writing on China and Freemasonry. (Rising at 7.30, he would often work until well past midnight.) There, too, he could be close to his real cathedral. For it was the Chinese treasures which still evoked his deepest responses. While he always delighted in his full dignity as a bishop, he also caused an Anglican colleague to complain that White talked incessantly about Chinese art, and that "I never once heard him mention theology or the Church."

Now he was like a pilgrim at the end of a long and arduous quest. For there was a wholeness to White — and a consistency of purpose — that had often escaped notice amid the many twists and turns of his various careers. On the face of it, the sensitive young introvert and fervent evangelist became an energetic man-of-affairs who all but lost his hunger for transcendence. At times — and especially during the early years in Honan — it seemed that his aesthetic and spiritual impulses had been permanently overcome by the demand for pragmatic achievement, that he had become nothing more than an ecclesiastical executive, a modern organization man in the service of a church which had largely lost its own spiritual bearings.

Yet White never abandoned his quest. It was a long way from the simplistic pieties of Victorian Ontario to the intense spirituality of the Shansi frescoes, but it was a route that White managed to travel because he retained a need to unite both sides of his nature — the practical and the reverent. Had he remained in Canada, this fusion might never have occurred: doubtless the bishop would have emerged, but hardly the curator. Instead, it was China which saved White from the banality of mere administrative achievement, and rekindled his religious and aesthetic fervour. It was China which showed him how a man can be active and contemplative, both Confucian and Taoist. Finally, it was China which made him a missionary-in-reverse, and which enabled him to put his practical gifts to work in building a cathedral as testament of his faith that man's spiritual passion must ultimately transcend our modern secularity.

Yet there is something ambiguous and covert about his triumph. The Royal Ontario Museum itself is an exact image of the man: a grey, gothic Victorian edifice which encases a passionate Oriental mystery. It is as though White always wore a mask — hiding his spirituality behind the dignity and authority of the bishop-curator — and never quite daring to reveal the intensity of his feelings. In his last years, some of his closest friends would compare him to a Taoist monk, resting on a mist-shrouded mountain peak, and serenely contemplating the flux of life in the valley far below. But Taoists also sing and dance and drink hot wine — it is part of their wholeness, and it is the lack of something similar in White, something more spontaneous and sentient, that flaws the wholeness which he finally achieved. It almost seems that he never entirely overcame the Victorian constraints of Norwood, and that a stubbornly residual Calvinism curbed him to the end.

Yet not to the very end. In a sense, his death seems more Taoist than Anglican. When White died on the 24th of January, 1960, at the age of eighty-six, it was after a gradual and peaceful preparation. For several days as he grew weaker, the Bishop was speaking in a Chinese dialect, possibly Fukienese, which nobody could understand. Also in his last days, and in a true Taoist spirit, he was laughing.

James Houston

When James Houston landed in the Arctic for the first time in 1948, he felt an instant shock of recognition. Those short, brown, exotic people, buzzing around him and talking a language he didn't understand — he couldn't explain it, not even to himself, but somehow he had always known them. And those extraordinary vistas — the icebergs shimmering in Hudson Bay, the great rivers, the endless tundra, the white mountains of Ungava — again it seemed that he had been there in the past, that this was a return. "You've been looking for this place all your life," he told himself. "And — this is the crazy thing — you're just up north of where you were born. It's not Tibet. This is Canada. *Your own country!*"

James Archibald Houston is a very modern man who has enacted — with apparent eccentricity but notable success — a very traditional Canadian impulse. This is the impulse which would have us seek our destiny — even our definition — in our northern wilderness. On that first trip to the Arctic, and through all the years he stayed there, Houston was acting out a role which has deep roots in the Canadian consciousness. As artist and author, as government administrator of a vast Arctic region, as prime mover in the renaissance of Eskimo art, he has had the temerity to make himself a living link between the modern world and that much older myth.

From the frozen Arctic tundra through the rocky lakes and stunted trees of the Precambrian Shield, the North is part of our historic experience, as are its native peoples. From the settler period to the present day, Canadians have used the North to feed our sense that we are different from other nationalities, whatever our specific origins. To Americans, the "frontier" was harsh, but also the source of opportunity and equality: it became one of their own most fecund myths. To Canadian pioneers, however, the northern wilderness was not so much a frontier as a presence: cold and brooding, inexorable and dangerous. To a notable extent, we have defined our national character in terms of its cruelty.

Essential to this conception is a physical and spiritual hardiness. Our "bracing northern winters," said the Toronto *Globe* in 1869, "will preserve us from the effeminacy which naturally steals over the most vigorous races when long under the relaxing influence of tropical or even generally mild and genial skies." During the decades which followed Confederation, the Canada First movement extolled the virtues of a northern location and a northern climate in moulding a "young giant nation" and a "race of men with bodies enduring as iron and minds as highly tempered as steel."

At the turn of the century, the immensely popular Glengarry novels of Ralph Connor portrayed a rugged and romantic pioneering world, with the landscape as an ever-present force which largely determined the destinies of his protagonists. Those who met the challenge best were those who displayed a muscular, red-blooded Christianity. Physical prowess, hard work and straight-dealing are the marks of Connor's heroes, while the virtues of his heroines are only slightly softer. In the same vein, there is no more archetypal Canadian hero than the manly, taciturn Mountie who imposes law and order on the peoples of the wilderness, making it safer for the settlers, the traders and the missionaries.

That vision has persisted: a vision of the harsh wilderness and its original inhabitants, with their challenge to our courage and ingenuity. It has persisted especially in our literature and public rhetoric. "I see a new Canada," John Diefenbaker proclaimed in 1958, on the eve of his sweeping election victory, ". . . A CANADA OF THE NORTH!" For our writers, it has often been a case of defining ourselves in relation to our native peoples. In terms of actual history, the Indians, Métis and Eskimos have been figures on the fringe of our concerns: exploited, patronized and rarely understood. Yet they have always loomed larger than their numbers, their practical impact or even our liberal guilt would seem to merit: witness the remarkable number of contemporary poems, plays and especially novels in which they have a leading part. Sometimes (as in George Ryga's *The Ecstasy of Rita Joe*) they function in that particular Canadian role of victim; more often (as in Leonard Cohen's *Beautiful Losers*) they play a variation on the noble savage theme: redemptive figures who are wiser, more honourable and more instinctive than ourselves. The Calibans of the Canadian consciousness, they proffer the lure of the exotic, the unrepressed, the natural.

Yet there is a crucial difference between what we feel, and how we act. Contemporary Canadians still use the North and its peoples to help define ourselves; in practice, however, we do as much as possible to insulate ourselves against them. In the rugged landscapes of the Group of Seven, and in Emily Carr's lush and mysterious rain forests, we still recognize an essential part of our heritage; but the way we live denies this recognition.

This is one of the stranger contradictions in the Canadian character. Huddled close to our southern border, most of us now reside in cities, and relatively few of us have seen the Shield, let alone the Arctic. For many, a weekend at the summer cottage passes muster for an outdoor life. Few of us know a single Indian or Eskimo; to the extent we think of them, they are a social problem, and a political embarrassment: a noisy obstacle to our further exploitation of their homelands. These days, manly virtues are hardly at a premium: we regard our Mounties with more suspicion than admiration, while our hockey players, those stalwart heroes of more recent decades, are now the high-priced pawns of cynical promoters, more inclined to slashing than to chivalry, and frequently humiliated by the Russians in a game we used to call our own. Even our racial composition has changed in a way which would have horrified the Canada Firsters, who held that only northerners — British, Germans, Scandinavians and Norman French — were hardy and masculine enough to be Canadian. Increasingly urbanized, hunched before our television sets or behind the wheels of our gigantic cars, protected by our double-glazing and our central heating, few of us pay more than lip-service to our wilderness heritage.

James Houston is a striking exception to this enervating trend: he has not only retained our traditional vision of the North, he has also *lived* it. Houston has been rash enough to enact our wilderness myth at the very time when most Canadians have been taking pains not to let it touch them — and this not only in terms of where he chose to live, and what he chose to do, but also in terms of the kind of person he has tried to be. For Houston has something of that compulsion which we have seen in White, and which we shall encounter even more strongly in Carr and Symons: an urge to transcend the blandness of our modern life, an urge to quest our deeper roots.

From the beginning, there was always a large measure of the outdoors in Jim Houston's life. Born in Toronto in June 1921, he grew up along the Don Valley, hunting for rabbits and pheasants in the nearby open country. As a boy, Ernest Thompson Seton had roamed the same terrain; young Houston was also reading Seton's books, and would later say they had helped to open his eyes to nature. Summers and holidays were spent at the family cottage on Lake Simcoe. These were common experiences for many middle-class boys of the time, but for Houston there was an added feature which foreshadowed much of his later life: early and intimate contact with Indians. His parents were of Scottish descent; from both sides of the family he inherited a fascination for native peoples and an ability to get on with them. His maternal grandfather, James Barbour, was a land agent with the Grand Trunk Railroad who often dealt with West Coast tribes. On his father's side, the family had run supply boats on Lake Simcoe before the days of the railroad, and counted many Ojibwa among their friends. Houston's father, a partner in an English clothing firm, also travelled widely and had an unusual affinity to Indians. He would always return from his trips to the Pacific coast with Indian gifts for Houston and his sister. One of Houston's earliest and most vivid memories is the alluring smell of moosehide from a pair of moccasins.

There were still Ojibwa around Lake Simcoe when Houston was a boy; most of the cottagers feared or despised them but Jim was soon spending time with them. He would meet old women searching through the bush or along the railroad track for medicine roots and healing herbs; one of them hugged him once and he never forgot how it felt: "She was soft, warm and brown as partridge feathers, and she smelled of wood smoke." His closest friend was Nels, an old Ojibwa who always wore Eaton's Catalogue rubbers over his moccasins, but who otherwise "lived beyond the commercial corruptions of this world, as self-sufficient and well-protected as a porcupine." Nels was the stuff of every young boy's fantasies: an older man who had nothing but disdain for the busy city world of schools and tight collars, and who lived in harmony with the wiser world of lakes and forests. Most mornings after breakfast Houston and his sister would rush to the gravel road and wait for Nels to return from fishing, "shambling like a light-footed bear, head down as though he searched for tracks in the dew." From Nels, Jim heard the old Indian legends of Nanibush and other gods, and learned Ojibwa tricks for catching fish and snaring game. These, too, he would never forget:

> It seemed to me then that the only education I wanted or would ever need I could gain right there in that old fish-smelling boat or stalking through the woods. From Nels I learned such invaluable things as the sound of the two little nervous clucks a ruffed grouse gives the instant before it thunders into the air, or how to whistle to a groundhog and have him whistle right back and stick his head out of his hole to see who you are.

To Houston the Indians were both exotic and familiar; their life was greatly different from his own, but still a part of it. His feelings for them were warm and sensuous, without a trace of condescension. This seems the clue to his later empathy for the Eskimos. An art historian would write of Houston's "empirical approach, his affection and respect for the Eskimo unclouded by sentimentality or paternalism". In the history of Eskimo art, it seems that old Nels the Ojibwa must have an honourary place.

Both of Houston's parents were Presbyterian, but there was

nothing dourly Calvinist about his upbringing. His mother was energetic and ingenious, enthusiastic about her children's projects and clever at making things, whether costumes or castles. His father had a certain flair for art; whenever he returned from one of his Western trips, his son and daughter would scramble on the bed beside him while he sketched pictures of the Indians, their masks and dances. Soon Jim was drawing for himself. When he was seven, an aunt asked him to illustrate a poem she'd written. Weeks later, he received a magazine with his drawing on the front page — and a cheque for three dollars. This was a revelation: watching the fathers of his friends, he had concluded that men were condemned to put on suits and ties, and spend their days at dreary toil in stuffy offices. Now it seemed that people might actually pay him money for doing something that he enjoyed almost as much as his fishing trips with Nels. At that moment, he decided he would be an artist.

Considering the time and the place, Houston was fortunate in having a family which gave him such encouragement. Toronto in the nineteen-twenties was a plain, sober and highly respectable city which laid great stress on all the Protestant virtues and had little use for anything as fanciful as art. But there were always exceptions: again Houston was lucky in having a teacher, Harold Hedley, at John Wanless Public School who encouraged his drawing and helped him to enrol in special classes at the Art Gallery of Toronto, where Arthur Lismer and other artists were trying to beat back the deadly grip of the Toronto philistines. Which is how it happened: a magical, ecstatic moment which set the course for everything that followed.

Houston was about eleven at the time. One morning at the Gallery, a teacher announced that Lismer, who was just back from a trip to West Africa, was coming to the children:

> All of a sudden we heard BOOM, BOOM, BOOM BOOM . . . tremendous African drumming . . . and this guy's about six-foot-four with this big tall dome of a head, and he's wearing this HUGE West African mask, and he comes in BANGING the drum and DANCING and I don't know what it did to the other kids but I nearly died. I thought WOW — I mean, that's IT! I

just thought — oh, my God, you could go out to far places . . . and he's come from AFRICA . . . think of it! . . . and these people are making just the right kind of masks . . . You see, until then I hadn't connected my art world with my other world, especially the Indians. But here was Lismer, tying it all together for me . . . the Indians, the Africans, the masks, the art . . . I just went wild!

From that moment there was never any chance that Houston would grow up to embrace the dreary proprieties and the narrow outlook of southern Ontario respectability. He was too open now, his senses too alert, his imagination too aroused . . . no, he was never going to subside into the mundane world that was already claiming so many of his schoolmates. Old Nels had opened one door, Lismer another: there would be no turning back.

When the Second World War interrupted his studies at the Ontario College of Art, Houston joined the Toronto Scottish Regiment and found himself serving first in Labrador, then in British Columbia. At Goose Bay he was fired up again when the pilots came back from their northern reconnaissances, talking with wonder about the Eskimos, their dogs, their snow houses and their cold, white landscape. This was another turning point: Houston sensed that the Eskimos and the North were part of that other world he had found among the Indians — and even more exotic, even more remote from the dreary cities to which most of his fellow soldiers were planning to return.

As hard as he tried, however, Houston was never able to join the pilots on their flights, never able to see the Eskimos for himself. For a while after the war it even seemed that he had lost the scent. His success as an artist for Victory Loan campaigns led to a cartoonist's job with a newspaper in Trois Rivières; with time out for further art studies in Paris, he went on to establish Valley Advertising, a small commercial art firm, in Grand'mère, and built a log cabin for himself beside the St. Maurice River. The firm was a success but it was hardly satisfying: Houston had solved the problem of making a living, but his life seemed dangerously routine and dull. Again he felt the lure of the wilderness, the call of the North.

Again he was looking for people without neckties and corsets, people who were different from those he saw slouching along the city streets. So, in 1948, he packed his sketch books and his sleeping bag, and went up as far away from them as he could get — up to the end of the railway at Moose Factory, where he began to draw the Swampy Cree Indians. This was better, but still he felt the Arctic up above him, attracting him like a magnet. Again there was the problem: how to get there? At that time, there were no regular flights to the Arctic; to hire a plane would cost several thousand dollars, money he could ill afford.

Then it happened: another lucky break that Houston turned to his advantage. On his last morning at Moose Factory — just as he was despondently preparing to go back south — a bush pilot had to make an emergency flight to Canso Bay, on the far northeast of Hudson Bay, taking a doctor to treat an Eskimo child who had been savaged by a dog. He was flying an old Norseman with pontoons and a single engine; they would have to come down every few hundred miles, roll out gas drums and fill the tiny tanks. Houston was young and strong; if he cared to help with the drums . . .

Many hours later there it was: the Arctic all around him. The Arctic and its people. It was indeed what he'd been questing all his life. It didn't matter that the doctor decided the child should be flown immediately to Moose Factory. There was no way Houston was going back with them. The doctor and the pilot pleaded with him, shouted at him, told him he was mad. Finally they left him in the settlement with his sleeping bag, his sketch pad and a can of peaches. The Eskimos were puzzled when he stayed behind, but they gave him food and shelter: a simple act of hospitality that would have enormous consequences.

Houston was there to make his own drawings; he had no idea that his strange, new, exotic friends might also be artists. At first it was a bit disconcerting when they clustered around him as he sketched, pointing to their likenesses and nodding their approval. Even worse, they began to take the pad away from him, and then his pens and pencils, and then they were at it themselves. Annoyance turned to admiration when Houston saw what they produced. For they were all natural artists. They had never been inhibited by a white man's education, had never suffered a blunting of their sensibilities, so they drew with the confidence of a child and yet with the skill of an adult.

That was the first revelation. An even greater one was soon to follow. An Eskimo called Naiomialook watched Houston sketch his wife, took away the drawing and returned some time later, holding out a closed fist. When Naiomialook slowly opened his fist, Houston saw the gift: a small caribou carved from soapstone. At first Houston thought it was something that Naiomialook's grandfather or even his great-grandfather might have made. He'd seen ancient Eskimo carvings in museums: charms and amulets as well as knives, harpoon heads and other tools. But he had no idea the Eskimos were *still* carving. When Naiomialook somehow made clear he'd done his caribou the day before

> I was overwhelmed. It looked so ancient. It could have been carved at any time. I became so excited. I thought, my God, that looks like something out of the caves at Lascaux! When Naiomialook opened his fist ... well, actually it came to me a day or two later, when I saw there was so much more of it around ... I swear I could somehow see the whole future ... not only to this day but far beyond my life. Children coming to museums in the year 2,000 ... I just *knew* it would be like that. I never doubted for an instant.

When the bush pilot made a return trip, Houston went back to Grand'mère with about a dozen more small carvings. By now he wanted desperately to live in the Arctic, and was only heading south to wind up his affairs. He wasn't quite sure how he would return, unless those carvings ...

Even Houston was surprised at the results when he placed his Eskimo sculptures on the mantelpiece at home. Small as they were, he didn't have to point them out when friends and fellow artists came to call. For the carvings commanded their attention; his friends praised them with an excitement that matched his own, and clamoured to buy them. There was similar enthusiasm for the carvings when Houston showed them to the Canadian Handicraft Guild in

Montreal. The Guild officials already knew about Eskimo art (Houston is the first to deny that he "discovered" it) and were quickly convinced that it should be developed for the benefit of the artists themselves. With $1,000 of Guild money, Houston was back in the Arctic the next summer; when he returned, the Guild sold all his purchases within three days. In 1950, Houston went back to the east coast of Hudson Bay for more than a year: this trip yielded over three thousand carvings. By now Montrealers were lining up for blocks and even camping overnight whenever the Guild announced an Eskimo exhibition; when the doors were opened, fights would sometimes break out in the rush to claim choice pieces. Prices climbed from tens to hundreds to thousands of dollars as government agencies, museums and business corporations joined private collectors in the hunt. By the mid-fifties, Eskimo art had become a national, even an international craze.

When people spoke with wonder about the extraordinary success of the Eskimo carvings, Houston would tell them not to be surprised — "just look at what they're up against." For he had a low view of most modern art, finding it bloodless and cerebral. Modern art seemed to reflect the city life that he had always turned his back on: a civilization which was increasingly estranged from its instinctive roots. Eskimo carvings, on the other hand, were the direct expression of a powerful inner world, and a belief in the unity of all living things. This, he felt, was their link to other forms of so-called primitive art. On an earlier trip to Mexico, Houston had become passionate about Aztec and Mayan art; in British Columbia during the war, he had his first contacts with Northwest Coast Indian carvers. In Quebec, and later in New England, he came to prize the wooden roosters and other birds which farmers had carved and painted and mounted on their barns. All these works seemed full of strength and confidence, the creation of genuine folk artists who were in intimate touch with the natural world, and totally conscious of their surroundings. In particular, Houston felt that the best Eskimo work was sacramental: a direct expression of the Eskimos' belief that life must be lived in harmony with nature, that their hunting was a religious act, that the seals and walruses they killed were part of the same spiritual universe as themselves. As he has written:

> The best Eskimo carvings of all ages seem to possess a powerful ability to reach across the great barriers of language and time and communicate directly with us. The more we look at these carvings, the more life we perceive hidden within them. We discover subtle living forms of the animal, human and mystical world. These Arctic carvings are not the cold sculptures of a frozen world. Instead, they reveal to us the passionate feelings of a vital people well aware of all the joys, terrors, tranquility and wildness of life around them.

By the time the passion for Eskimo art had begun to take hold, Houston was back in the Arctic, joyfully remote from the clamour of the cities. His trips to the North became longer and longer; finally he went back to stay. His work among the Eskimos had brought him to the attention of Ottawa; in 1953 he was named federal civil administrator for West Baffin Island — in effect he was governing 65,000 square miles of territory and 343 Eskimos living in thirteen widely separated camps.

These were golden days. Although Houston and his wife eventually built their own home in Cape Dorset, where they raised their two young sons, he was no desk-bound civil servant, trammelled by routine and bureaucracy. His work was with the Eskimos; since they were scattered and nomadic, Houston was almost always on the move. With his team of fourteen huskies, he ranged across the tundra on trips that often lasted for several months. He lived with the people and adapted himself to their ways, eating raw seal meat and learning to make his own snow house in little more than half an hour.

It was a dangerous life, especially at the start, when he was still a novice. A man could freeze or starve to death at any time, if he didn't take the proper precautions, if he didn't know how to use his eyes. Five times in that first year, Houston fell through the sea ice, narrowly escaping drowning. Once, when by himself, he was only saved because he had shot two seals, and was dragging them behind him. The seals stayed on solid ice, and Houston managed to pull himself out by clinging to their flippers. Another time he was persuaded only at the last moment not to build his snow house on a shelf which, by the next morning, had broken away and drifted out to sea. "Much later, the Eskimos told me: 'We sometimes thought we'd have to give you away. We didn't know what to do with you — you were so dumb!' "

As Houston learned the arts of survival from his patient tutors, he also shared their random joys:

> It was sheer pleasure. If the geese came, you went out with the geese. If the caribou moved, you moved with them. When the char were running, you went fishing. If you heard there was going to be dancing, singing and good times in one of the camps, that was where you went. It was like a dream. Few people can imagine the joy of such a life. You're so much your own man.

Even time was eliminated. In the early years a boat would bring mail and provisions once a year. Since the boat always had to set out again right away, letters from Ottawa in 1954 would be answered by Houston in 1955. Then those letters would receive their reply in 1956. . . . In the unchanging light of summer, or the endless dusk of winter, one day followed the next without division. There were no mornings and no evenings; Houston simply slept when he was tired, for as long as his body needed. He hardly ever knew the date. Soon he had abandoned his watch.

Freed from the tyranny of time — and the dreary pressure of routine — Houston also lost the burden of possessions. All that he needed, all that he wanted, he could carry on his dog sled, or else nature and his Eskimo friends would provide. To the boy who had tramped with old Nels through the forests of Lake Simcoe and always dreaded the return to Toronto, to the artist who sought the freedom of open spaces and the excitement of exotic peoples, it must indeed have been a dream come true.

It is a dream which has great resonance in our mythology and our literature. We think of Seton, who wanted to become an Indian, or Archie Belaney, who *did* become Grey Owl . . . and others who have gone native, turning their backs on the dreary cities, seeking an existence which is more natural and fulfilling.

It is also a dream which we can share, with Houston as our proxy. For most of us have felt a similar urge — as childhood fantasy, perhaps, or else amid the disillusionments of middle-age — an urge to live with nature while depending for survival on our strengths and skills. Racing with his huskies through the endless twilight of an Arctic winter, Houston is a modern Glengarry hero, stripped of sanctimony, with a touch of the Mountie and a dash of the *coureur de bois:* a man who lives out our fantasies and so becomes a proxy hero for us all.

The Eskimos called him Saomik — "Left-handed". From the start he felt at home with them, just as he had been at ease with the Ojibwa. As he came to know them better — and especially when he learned their language — his respect for them grew steadily. He noticed how well the Eskimos cared for their old people, honoured them, and relied upon their wisdom. He also saw how natural they were, how unafraid of their emotions. One day a man walked six miles across the ice, his eyes still red from a day of carving, his trousers covered with fine stone dust, to show Houston the walrus he'd just finished, to share his joy and passion. There were many times like that.

Houston had a friend, a successful hunter in his midforties, with a wife and five children, as well as an ancient father who was half-blind and infirm. Whenever Houston suggested a hunting trip, his friend would answer: "I don't know. I haven't asked my father." So they would go to the old man's tent, lift him to the door, and ask him where the hunting would be good. The old man would squint at the ice, sniff the wind, and give them his advice.

Early one morning, the friend came to Houston's tent, gave a polite cough, and scratched at the flap. "My father died this morning," he announced. "I came to cry with you." And so they sat down, and cried together.

As Houston learned to respect the Eskimo way, he also came to question the wisdom of the white man's paternalistic policies. On an inland trip in the central Arctic, his Eskimo guide showed him where a whole community had died in their snow houses. It happened because one of them caught tuberculosis, and was flown out for treatment. The Eskimos said he mustn't go, because he was very important to them. "But they took him anyway, and the people in his camp starved to death," Houston's guide recounted. "You see, he was the only one who knew where the caribou meat was cached."

Experiences like this began to temper Houston's enthusiasm for his job. In time they would lead him to write his best-known book, *The White Dawn*. Much earlier however, he was showing signs of being a most unconventional civil servant. Back in Ottawa, whenever one of his rare reports arrived, some of his superiors began to think Houston was going swampy. Nothing he did ever seemed to fit their preconceived notions of how the natives should be guided to a better life. They told him he was the only government administrator in the whole Arctic who wasn't requisitioning new buildings for his region — they couldn't understand how a man could be doing his job if he wasn't putting something up. Once they actually sent him some buildings, but he left them unopened in their crates. For Houston had come to feel that Ottawa was pushing ahead too fast, building communities and launching projects which had little meaning for the Eskimos themselves, and would often offend against their traditions. Like Herbert Norman, whom we shall see listening to the Japanese during the Occupation period, and resisting policies ordained from far away, so Houston was treating Ottawa's directives with growing scepticism. Instead he was turning to the Eskimos, asking their advice, relying on their wisdom.

Houston spent much of his time encouraging the Eskimos to create the carvings which were finding such a ready market in the south. He insisted that they should follow their own instincts and stick to their traditional themes. They must carve to please themselves, he told them: that was what the white man valued most. Especially in the early days, Houston was determined that only the best carvings should go south, so that the overall quality would not be diluted, or the reputation of the carvers compromised. But he also came to understand that the Eskimos had a sense of "face" which was almost Oriental. Too often, a promising beginner would be discouraged forever if his early efforts were rejected. So Houston would buy everything they brought to him. The beginner would not receive lavish praise for his work, but he would always get a Hudson Bay Company chit which he could use to buy tea, flour, cartridges, canvas or whatever else he needed: a chit which he could also show his friends and family as proof of his success. When the time came for a shipment to the south, Houston would separate the good pieces from the bad, and add the prices of the latter to the former. In the middle of the night he would pack the inferior carvings on a small hand sled, slip out of his dwelling, go half way across the frozen bay, and dump them down a tide crack into the sea. If anyone saw him, he would think Houston was emptying his toilet. So everyone received encouragement and a fair return for their work, but only the better carvings used to reach the south.

As the passion for Eskimo art mounted in the south, the carvers on Baffin Island were soon earning increased payments for their best work, and artists of equal stature were being discovered and encouraged at other communities across the Arctic. Yet life was still hard for most of the Eskimos. Not everyone could be a first-rate carver, but Houston was convinced there were many others, including women, whose natural skills had yet to be tapped. Again he was right. As he tells the story, this is how it happened:

> Oshaweetok, a famous Eskimo carver and good friend, sat near me one evening casually studying the sailor head trademarks on two identical packages of cigarettes. He noted carefully every subtle detail of colour and form, and he suggested to me that it must be very tiresome for some person to sit and paint every one of the little heads with exact sameness on an endless number of packages. I started to explain in Eskimo, as best I could, about 'civilized' man's technical progress in the field of printing little sailor heads, and the entire offset printing process. My explanation was not altogether successful, partly because of my inability to find the Eskimo words to describe such terms as intaglio and colour register, and partly because I was wondering whether this could have any practical application for the Eskimos.

Looking around in order to find some way to demonstrate printing, I saw an ivory walrus tusk that Oshaweetok had recently carved. The white tusk was about fifteen inches long. Oshaweetok had carefully smoothed and polished it and had incised bold engravings on both sides. Into the lines of these engravings he had rubbed black soot gathered from a seal oil lamp.

Taking an old tin of writing ink that had frozen and thawed many times, I poured off the separated grey matter. With my finger I dipped up the heavy black residue and smoothed it over the tusk. Taking a thin piece of toilet tissue, I laid it carefully on the inked surface and rubbed it lightly and quickly. Stripping the paper from the tusk, I saw that by good fortune we had a clear negative image of Oshaweetok's incised design.

"We could do that," he said, with the instant decision of a hunter. And so we did.

So printmaking was born among the Eskimos. With Houston's help, they were soon experimenting to find the best techniques. When proper ink and paper finally arrived from the south, Cape Dorset was engulfed with enthusiasm for the project. In the summer of 1958 the first series of prints were shown at the Stratford Shakespearean Festival. It was like Montreal, a decade earlier, when Houston brought down the first carvings. The prints were soon sold out; galleries and dealers began clamouring for more. With assistance from Ottawa, Houston spent his accumulated leave in Japan where he studied under leading printmakers. Returning to the Arctic in the spring of 1959, he gathered the best Eskimo printmakers and started to develop techniques which blended centuries of Japanese ingenuity with their own uninhibited talents. If the concept was new to the Eskimos, the images and ideas were based on their traditions, depicting birds, animals and humans as well as ancient legends of the spirit world. As this improved work began to reach the south, prices for the best prints began to rise from tens to hundreds of dollars and would eventually reach the thousands.

For the Eskimos it was an ideal occupation during poor weather, when hunting was impossible. Not only the men were involved: many of the women already had an art form of their own, based on skin appliqué, the ancient practice of cutting silhouette designs from animal hides to be sewn onto clothing as decoration. By making stencilled prints, the women were soon taking part in the project. Again with Houston's help, the Cape Dorset artists — carvers and printmakers alike — formed a cooperative to run their own affairs. This became a model for similar co-ops across the Arctic. To market the prints and carvings they still needed a contact with the south. This would be a white man — initially Houston. But when Houston left Cape Dorset in 1962, he advised the Eskimos not to take a civil servant imposed on them from Ottawa, but to hire their own employee whom they could always fire if he displeased them.

Once again Houston had helped the Eskimos to help themselves. When he arrived in the Arctic in 1948, there were no family allowances for the Eskimos and hardly any sort of government aid. The market for white fox and seal skins was at an all-time low that year, and the Eskimos on the east coast of Hudson Bay received only a pittance for their skins. It was only a matter of time before the federal government would start to intervene more frequently in their affairs, and before defence contractors and mineral companies would open up the North to thousands of white intruders. As the old way of life began to crumble before the onslaught from the south, Houston saw it would be a great boon for the Eskimos if they could develop an earning power based on their ancient skill as carvers — and in a way that left them with their dignity. As the art critic Charles Gimpel has written:

> The right man was in the right place at the right time. An artist with the knowledge of the technical problems involved, he perceived the merit and the spontaneity of the Eskimo art, yet had the wisdom and restraint not to interfere, but merely to guide and foster; an administrator he had to help the economy of this semi-nomadic people, living so near starvation level in their inclement country. Finally he brought to his work an astute twentieth century mind, for he knew that the markets of the world could and would absorb on different levels, not only the work of the top artists, but the work of the skilled artisan-craftsman.

"An astute twentieth century mind" — this is true, and crucial to any understanding of Houston's work and character. For he has used the techniques of modernity — especially a decided flair for publicity and promotion, as well as a fascination with technology — to revive a traditional art form, to make it an extraordinary commercial success, and to carve out a role for himself as a link between the ancient culture of the Eskimos and the modern world of the Western city dweller.

There are those who scoff at his achievements. Some art critics and social scientists argue that both the cultural importance and the aesthetic value of Eskimo art have been grossly exaggerated — largely due to Houston's energetic efforts. They maintain that the carvings are not based on any great artistic tradition, or even on the Eskimos' present experience, while the prints are simplistic drawings which have been converted into over-praised artifacts through a bastard mixture of white techniques and Japanese materials and style. According to the scholar and Eskimo enthusiast Edmund Carpenter: "Eskimo stone art was made for, used by and believed in, solely by Westerners . . . Having deprived him of his heritage, and even the memory of this heritage, we offer him a substitute which he eagerly accepts, for no other is permitted." While the art critic Sol Littman has written that Houston merely succeeded in romanticising primitive work to make it acceptable to sophisticated buyers, and that his descriptions of the spiritual and legendary qualities of Eskimo art are nothing more than "pure bafflegab".

But the best of the Eskimo art has a power and a formal beauty which have earned it a rightful place in the museums and galleries. It commands our attention and respect as much as a Henry Moore sculpture or a Picasso print; to quibble about the authenticity of its origins is nothing more than pedantry. Nor is it fair to blame Houston, the pioneer who sought to maintain the quality of the early shipments, for all the inferior work and plaster reproductions which have since been dumped upon a gullible public. In his definitive work, *Sculpture of the Eskimo*, George Swinton concedes that Houston's promotional enthusiasm endangered his credibility. But he adds:

It is often said that white men and white values have changed and corrupted Eskimo art. Changed — I agree, but corrupted — definitely not. Changed, because white influences stimulated the production of art at a time when it was necessary, at a time when art was almost dead. And it is here where lies the greatest achievement of the much maligned James Houston. It was his insight, his enthusiasm, and his promotional talent that sparked the entire development. There were others, too; many in fact. But Houston was the prime mover.

As for the Eskimos themselves, let us hear from Pitseolak, an elderly woman printmaker:

> Before Jim Houston came to Cape Dorset we had the people at the Bay who were here for the furs, and we were grateful to have them and very pleased to get tea, sugar and flour. But I think Saomik was the first man to help the Eskimos. Ever since he came, the Eskimo people have been able to find work. Here in Cape Dorset they call him 'The Man'.

So far we have encountered no traumas or desperate complications in Houston's life. So far we have a picture of unusual achievement and fulfilment. There is a clear line from the youth who fished with old Nels on Lake Simcoe, who despised a mundane city life, who was confirmed by Arthur Lismer in his passion for the exotic . . . a clear line to the resourceful optimist of the Arctic tundra, the enthusiast of the Eskimos and their art. So far we have seen 'The Man' as an almost mythic figure, a Ralph Connor hero strangely and stubbornly resurrected in our modern era. Yet there is a darker side to Houston: an aspect which makes him even more interesting, and which must qualify our judgment of him. It all came out in *The White Dawn.*

There was no doubt about his intention: Houston meant his novel to be a microcosm of the clash between the white and the Eskimo ways, a decisive statement of the white man's impact on the North. Set in the last decade of the nineteenth century, it is based upon a true story which Houston

heard on Baffin Island. (He still has a small carving which is a
likeness of one of the white protagonists.) Three American
whalers, lost and stranded on the island, are rescued and
adopted by a band of Eskimos. Under their leader Sarkak, a
masterful and mighty hunter, these Eskimos feel themselves to
be unusually fortunate. As the narrator of the story, Sarkak's
crippled son Avinga, explains:

> We were proud of our camp. It was the biggest on the
> whole coast. We had seven snow houses. Other families
> visiting from far camps gasped at the size of our igloos,
> with their long tunnels and big outer snow porches. They
> wondered at our rich abundance; so many children,
> meat caches, kayaks, sleds and dogs. There was nothing
> like our village anywhere. You would need to count all
> the fingers and toes of two men if you wished to number
> the hunters, their wives, the old people and the children
> who lived in our camp.

Ignorant of the Arctic and its ways, the strangers are
entirely dependent on the protection and generosity of Sarkak, who treats them at first with amused condescension, as
little more than awkward children. Here, of course, there is a
strong echo of Houston's own initial flounderings. When one
of the strangers falls through the ice, it recreates one of the
author's near-disasters. Regarded as inferior by their rescuers,
the intruders are called "the people with the heavy eyebrows",
or "the dog children" — a reference to an Eskimo myth which
accounts for the white race as the degenerate offspring of an
Eskimo girl and a huskie. At first, they seem to adapt themselves without undue difficulty to a way of life which, for all
its hardships and dangers, is described with lyrical enthusiasm:

> From the coming of the geese until the darkness returned
> in autumn, people lost all track of time. The strangers, at
> first, tried to keep the order of the days and nights, but
> soon it was lost to them, and they did not care, and we
> did not care. The sun wheeled endlessly above our heads,
> and we hunted and ate and laughed and lay with our
> women. Only the rise and fall of the tide had any mean-

ing for us during the short softness of summer.

But the aliens carry within them all the aggressive individualism and moral corruption of the white man's world; before long they have begun to undermine the social cohesion and traditional values of the camp. Some of the first manifestations are relatively trivial, but they stir the apprehensions of the Eskimos. When the strongest of the strangers engages a visiting giant, Nukinga, in a wrestling match, he refuses to play by the established rules; cleanly beaten, he launches a treacherous counter-attack, and has to be pulled away. The Eskimos are dumbfounded:

> 'Someone should open him up with a knife,' said Nukinga, 'and look inside him to see what kind of a soul he has that makes him play a game like that. I think that man has lost his soul.'

> But Sarkak and Atkak and Poota crowded up to him and said, 'No, no. Do not say that. These strangers do not know how to play our games. They do everything wrong. They surprise us every day by their differences . . . After all, you must remember that these foreigners know very little about life. They are violent, savage people.'

It becomes clear to the Eskimos that the intruders have little of their own reverence for the natural world, that they are predators rather than communicants. After a daring and successful walrus hunt — during which the strangers make their share of kills — Avinga describes how they sing loudly and boastfully on their way back to shore:

> I wished I could have understood the words of their song, even though it was wrong of them to sing out there on the sea right after such a great killing. We knew that the waters must have been swarming with the souls of the dead walrus, and at this time it was important that we show them respect, not triumph. For had they not come to us from some distant place and given their flesh to us so that we might live? Still, even with the foreigners rudely singing, we managed to reach the shore without another mishap, which made me think again that these round-eyed people lived by other rules and perhaps

would not be hurt by disobeying our taboos.

But Avinga is wrong. Soon the strangers are sleeping with the young girls, gambling with the hunters, and challenging the authority of Sarkak and the other elders. When they distil a potent brew from frozen berries, they launch a drunken orgy which completes the band's physical and moral disintegration. Eventually the Eskimos retaliate by executing the foreigners. But it is already too late: Sarkak has banished himself to the wilderness, the band is broken up, and only Avinga survives to tell their story.

The White Dawn is full of ironies which Houston employs to underline his moral: a bleak, tragic view which indicts the white man for his destructive impact on so-called primitive cultures. As he portrays them (without false sentimentality), the Eskimos are a warm, generous and cohesive people, living on the brink of starvation, but also in close harmony with nature and themselves. It is the intruders who are awkward, aggressive and selfish — in conflict with each other and themselves. Two of the whalers are little more than selfish oafs, but the third, whom the Eskimos name Kakuktak, is much more sensitive. This is the greatest irony of all, since it is Kakuktak, the well-meaning liberal, who is ultimately the most culpable.

Like Houston himself, Kakuktak struggles to learn the language and to understand the customs of his rescuers. In a grim self-parody by the author, he also makes drawings with a pad and pencil. To Sarkak and the others, Kakuktak is the intruder whom they find the most sympathetic, the one most likely to understand and accept their ways. Yet it is Kakuktak who eventually challenges Sarkak, destroys his pride, and precipitates the final calamity. When the whalers are executed, there is no suggestion that the Eskimos can redeem themselves and regain their traditions; just the opposite, since the book ends with the prophetic return of the whalers' vessel. Significantly it is Kangiak, Sarkak's favourite son and a likely future leader of the band, who decides to foresake his roots and seek his future with the white men.

Since its publication in 1971, *The White Dawn* has appeared in more than twenty-five editions and many languages around the world; Hollywood has also made a movie of it. Much of its appeal is based on the sheer drama of the tale, and Houston's skill in telling it. Yet there may be a deeper reason for the novel's enormous success. It appeared at a time of declining confidence in Western civilization, when our sustaining liberal doctrine of progress-through-technology had been revealed as spiritually hollow, and when the virtues of other traditions — Eskimo, East Indian or whatever — had come to seem increasingly attractive. No longer could we feel that aggressive optimism which sent generations of missionaries, merchants and soldiers into distant lands as proponents of a way of life which, they were sure, the natives would regard as more enlightened than their own. For we understood too well the fatal impact of such an arrogant interference: while *The White Dawn* is a microcosm of our own Arctic experience, it has disturbing parallels with Vietnam.

Yet it is strange that Houston should be the author of such a bleak and pessimistic parable. For a start, he is such an obvious optimist. In middle-age, the man is humorous, vivacious and spontaneous, with a strong, square face, deep-set eyes, thick black hair and bushy eyebrows. It is almost the face of some rugged movie star, except that it is usually too animated and too comical for that sort of role, and Houston is too often springing to his feet, moving restlessly around the room, acting out his stories, and laughing like a cheerful clown.

Then there is his own career among the Eskimos: this also seems out of kilter with his novel's perceptions. True, Houston has always had a deep sympathy for other, more exotic cultures. He can hardly be accused of that arrogance and racialism which our missionaries and administrators have often betrayed among the Eskimos and Indians, and which the best and the brightest of the American technocrats lavished so lethally on the Vietnamese. Instead he has functioned like Bishop White as a missionary-in-reverse, showing us how foolish we are when we despise our native peoples, how much we have to learn from them. But Houston's career in the Arctic *does* manifest a basic liberal optimism, a belief that different cultures can meet and mingle to the benefit of all, a UNESCO-view of progress through togetherness. While he

always urged the administrators in Ottawa to be more cautious and sensitive in their incursions, he worked even harder
to open up the cultural channels between the Eskimos and the
white man's world. On the face of it, his career is in conflict
with his novel's central thesis.

To Houston himself this conflict seems more apparent
than actual. When he wrote *The White Dawn* he *was* pessimistic about the Eskimos' future. Since his first encounter with
the Arctic it had suffered a painful transformation through
the building on the DEW line, the invasion of the oil companies and the influx of bureaucrats with all their flow charts
and blueprints, all their schemes to "modernize" the natives.
All around him he saw the new buildings springing up, with
the Eskimo children herded into schools to learn disciplines
they might never need, and whole communities induced to
give up their nomadic, hunting lives and so become dependent on the white man's bounty. As the Eskimos lost their ties
to the land, as they began to abandon their accustomed ways,
he saw confusion, despondency and savage drinking, even
among many of the carvers and printmakers. He called it "the
tender trap"; he had no doubt that the bureaucrats were well-
intentioned, but he was equally certain they were trying to do
too much, too quickly. He came to feel that the 20,000 Eskimos in Canada were bound to succumb to the overwhelming
impact of the white man's culture, that even their art could
hardly survive for long. He also had second thoughts about
the movement he himself had launched, deploring the flood of
inferior carvings and plaster imitations, as well as the way in
which some of the artists squandered their earnings on gambling and drink (although he never expected them to follow
our own materialistic standards, which place high value on
mere possessions such as cars and houses).

The White Dawn was written out of these perceptions.
Since 1971, however, Houston has become less pessimistic. On
more recent trips back to the Arctic he noticed a resilience
among the Eskimos. They were still being drawn inevitably
into the white man's world, but it seemed that many of their
younger leaders were using the white man's language, the
white man's education and the white man's political techniques to fight for their rights, their land and their traditions.

It seemed they might, after all, avoid the tender trap; they might, after all, defeat the threat of cultural extinction. As for the art movement, even the most modest carvings have value if they enable an Eskimo to earn his living with some dignity, doing work that he knows and enjoys, rather than surviving on government handouts. Above all, everything is made worthwhile by the best of the prints and carvings:

> I wouldn't change any of that . . . just to uncover that talent and have it burst into flame . . . to have those people show you what has been hidden there in the tundra, hidden within themselves . . . it's worth it. It's worth it for the good people and the best of their art. Akeeaktashuk, Oshaweetok, Parr, Kenojuak, Oonark, Tiktak, Pudlo, Pitseolak and others . . . those great folk artists will go down in the history of Canadian art.

Only time will justify Houston's renewed optimism, or else confirm his novel's starker vision. But there is another issue here which does not concern the Eskimos; it does concern the man himself. When he talks about the Eskimos, Houston emerges as a cheerful pragmatist, a man who abhors the evil that is often done to them, but who remains convinced that they can come to terms with the modern world, and benefit from its blessings . . . just as *he* has come to terms with it, and prospered from it, despite his initial compulsion to escape it. Unlike the other subjects of this book, Houston has apparently been successful in living with modernity, especially in recent years.

Houston left Cape Dorset in 1962 to join the Steuben glass company in New York City as associate director of design. This was a startling switch: from the lonely tundra to the nervous clamour of Manhattan; from a world without watches to the high-pressured demands of a business career. It was, in fact, an abrupt reversal of the pattern which had, until then, dominated his life.

Houston explains it this way. By 1962, the Eskimo co-op was well established, and the art was at an all-time high in quality and earnings: by leaving, Houston could prove the

Eskimos had reached the point where they could look after themselves. He might easily have gone somewhere else in the Arctic, but this would have only meant that he was repeating himself. For most of fourteen years he had lived and worked in the North; he knew little of the outside world, and he wondered whether a business career would cripple him. Yet at forty-one, he wanted a new challenge.

Sometimes he thought he had made a mistake. Twice he almost pulled out abruptly. Once, when he was walking in the heart of Manhattan, he passed a garbage can with a Christmas tree inside . . . someone had tossed in a match and the smell of burning pine was wafting out . . . "Goddamn it," he thought, "I'm going back to Canada *today!*" Another time he was lying in bed early one morning in his brownstone on East 69th Street when he heard the unmistakable sound of Canada geese flying overhead . . . they, too, seemed to be calling him back. But he stuck it out, rising early every morning for two hours of writing and drawing before he went to work, turning out a series of children's books on Eskimo and Indian life, and then *The White Dawn.* Yet he had never felt at ease in any city. While retaining his job with Steuben, Houston bought a 160-acre property in the woodland of Rhode Island, where he lives with his second wife, Alice, in a colonial farm house that was built in 1751 by one of the early English settlers. Although comfortable and modernized, this was closer to the wilderness, with its stands of maple, oak and pine, and the constant birdsong in the tangy air. It was also an appropriate setting for working on a novel he had long been planning.

With *Ghost Fox,* Houston remains consistent in his vision. If this later work lacks the stark tragedy of *The White Dawn,* it is an equally engrossing narrative which explores a similar confrontation — in this case, the clash between New England settlers and hostile Indians during the middle decades of the eighteenth century. Again based on a true story, it concerns Sarah Wells, a young girl who is kidnapped by Abnaki Indians, who are allied with the French, and taken back to their village in Canada. After much ill-treatment and a perilous attempt to escape her captors, Sarah is eventually married to an Abnaki brave; in time she comes to value the natural Indian life much more highly than the narrow world of her own family. Once again, the white men are portrayed as ignorant and treacherous intruders. Once again, there is no attempt to glorify the natives, but they are shown in much closer harmony with their surroundings and themselves. As one of the Abnaki says, in a passionate oration:

> The whites talk endlessly of trading or buying the land from us. What right have they to buy the land? What right have the humans (i.e. the Indians) to sell it? From whom did they buy it? How little these whites know about life. Even we humans may not own the land — or the rivers that come rushing down the gorges or the rain that falls or thunder or lightning — or rainbows or the moon or sun and stars. These are sacred objects beyond possessing. Both we and all the sacred animals that live here may rest for a little while, beside these magic lakes — observing their reflected images. Seeds flow from our loins and new humans and animals and trees and grasses come forth as we ourselves grow old. When winter comes, we all of us will fall like needles from the pine.

"How little these whites know about life." That was what Sarkak said, in almost identical words. It is the core of Houston's vision in his novels: an indictment of our narrow, thrusting selfishness, a reminder that other peoples, for all their own faults, often retain an outlook that is more humane and more sacramental, with a touch of that reverence for life which we have largely lost. (This is what Carr found among the Indians, and Symons among the Moroccans.) Sarah comes to share that vision — more fully and successfully than Kakuktak, the well-meaning liberal of the earlier novel. In the end, she is recaptured by English soldiers and restored to her family. But she is appalled by their hypocrisy and sanctimony (they now regard her as irredeemably tainted): when the Indians come for her again, she joins them willingly, and goes back to find her husband in the forest.

Unlike his heroine, Houston is now too much a part of the modern world ever to think of going back to the wilderness for good. With his New York job — and a New York lawyer to negotiate his lucrative contracts with publishers, book clubs and movie producers — he has achieved an international success that is rare among Canadian artists and authors. Yet when Sarah rejects the white man's life, one suspects a certain wish-fulfilment in the writing, even a hint of something unresolved in Houston. For if he lives so successfully in the modern world, much of his work — more important, much of his compulsion — is still centred on that exotic other world which he first encountered in 1948. He keeps his contacts with the Arctic, serving as chairman of the Canadian Eskimo Arts Council. He has also worked as technical adviser on award-winning National Film Board documentaries on Eskimo life; when *The White Dawn* was made into a movie, Houston was associate producer and wrote the screen play. Characteristically, he also stood guard with a rifle on location, in case a trained, 700-pound polar bear took exception to any of the other actors. More recently, he has been promoting West Coast Indian art, another part of our northern heritage which, like Carr, he has also come to value for its instinctive power. Above all, he tries to return to the Arctic at least twice each year.

This is a fundamental pattern. As William Morton has written, the "alternative penetration of the wilderness and return to civilization is the basic rhythm of Canadian life, and forms the basic elements of the Canadian character." While few of us enact this rhythm any longer, this is still part of how we view ourselves. Here, again, we can see Houston as our modern Glengarry man: a proxy hero for us all.

We can, but we don't. For Houston has not become an archetypal figure to his contemporaries. If he were an American, he might have long since achieved the romantic aura of a Hemingway. Yet he has not gained any popular image among Canadians, any status as a cultural icon. In 1974, an article by John Ayre in *Saturday Night* was appropriately entitled: James Houston: The Neglected Hero. As Ayre maintained:

> Perhaps the image of Houston offends something deeply embedded in the darker layers of the Canadian psyche — something that rejects the idea of happy earnest heroes who disappear into the white vacancies of the north and come out years later suspiciously unscathed,

still happy and full of accomplishments to show for their time. The example of Houston violates cherished Robert Service myths that depict the Arctic as a monstrous death-dealer. By all rights, Houston should have gone mad and left a gangerous leg or a frost-bitten ear on a snowbank somewhere in Baffin Island.

In other words, Houston does not fill that distinctive Canadian role of victim which Margaret Atwood has identified as a central preoccupation of our literature, and our conception of ourselves. He seems too happy, too unscathed. Perhaps the greatest irony of Houston's life is that he has succeeded in becoming a modern Ralph Connor hero, succeeded in living the stalwart-man-of-the-wilderness myth, at a time when his countrymen were demanding a much more brooding, guilty and crippled version of that hero.

Put another way, Houston as author and cultural promoter has not struck the popular Canadian imagination as a spokesman for the North. Despite the enormous success of the Eskimo art movement, and the widespread appeal of *The White Dawn*, he has not attracted nearly as much attention as Farley Mowat, that other great enthusiast of the Arctic and its peoples. Partly this is a matter of masks: on the one hand, the modern Glengarry man; on the other, the bearded, kilted, crotchety Scot with his fondness for the bottle and his outrageous sallies against any and all establishments. With our propensity for victims, we cherish Mowat as an angry, roaring lamenter for various doomed species. Houston, on the other hand, remains too cheerful, too optimistic, to engage our deepest responses.

Again this indicates an important difference between Houston and the other subjects of this book. Like the others, Houston felt stifled by the oppressive limitations of the modern spirit. Like the others, he turned to other cultures for a more sustaining vision. Like the others, he has sought to share that vision with us. But unlike Sutherland Brown, Carr and Symons, he never rejected the modern world; much more than White or even Norman, he returned to work within it — adapting many of its techniques for his own purposes — with considerable success, notable panache and few apparent qualms.

Yet in his novels — and with his ardent promotion of Eskimo art — Houston champions a sacramental vision and a reverence for life which modernity has always sought to denigrate. There is a world of difference between the warm soapstone of an Eskimo carving, which is meant to be passed from hand to hand, and rubbed and fondled until it gleams with the oils of the flesh . . . and the cold crystal of a Steuben bowl, which is designed to be admired, but seldom touched. This is the paradox that remains in Houston's life . . . and the hint of something still to be resolved.

Lt-Col. James Sutherland Brown, 1917.

Brig. James Sutherland Brown in retirement, Victoria, B.C., 1947.

William White, the young man, Ottawa, 1893.

Bishop White wearing the Decoration of the Excellent Crop, presented to him by the Chinese Government.

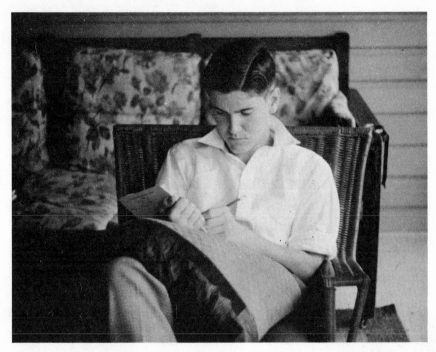

James Houston sketching at the family cottage on Lake Simcoe, c. 1933.

below: James Houston at Cape Dorset, Baffin Island, 1958. Photo credit: Charles Gimpel.

James Houston at his
Rhode Island home.
Photo credit: Watson.

Herbert Norman (with his dog) and family in Nagano, Japan, c. 1912.

above: Herbert Norman, c. 1955. Photo credit: Garnet Hollington, National Film Board.

left: Herbert Norman, graduation, Victoria College, University of Toronto, 1933.

left: Emily Carr as a young girl.

right: Emily Carr with her dog.

below: Emily Carr as an older woman.

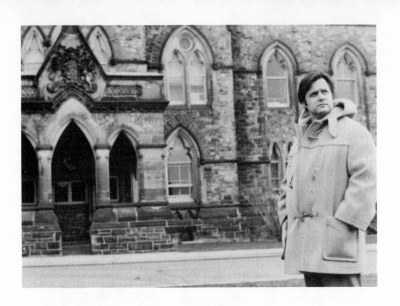

above: Scott Symons on his return from Morocco, 1975. Photo credit: Peterborough *Examiner*.

top left: Scott Symons outside the Houses of Parliament, Ottawa, 1969.

left: Scott Symons as curator of the Canadiana Gallery at the Royal Ontario Museum, c. 1962.

Herbert Norman

Early on the morning of 4 April 1957, passersby on a busy street in central Cairo noticed a tall, grey-haired man walking back and forth on the flat roof of a nine storey apartment building. For a few minutes, the man sat down on the parapet, with his back to the street and his head between his hands. Then he stood up, removed his jacket, carefully folded it and placed it on the parapet with his watch and glasses. On the street below, a woman screamed and men shouted at him to go back. Instead he turned away from them and stepped off the edge, falling to his death in a parking lot.

Within hours, the suicide was a *cause célèbre* in Washington, London, Paris, Tokyo and other major cities. For the man was Herbert Norman, the Canadian Ambassador to Egypt, and his name was already widely known: only three weeks earlier, a subcommittee of the United States Senate had revived allegations that the ambassador, who was playing a key role in the resolution of the Suez crisis, had been for many years a Communist.

Norman was forty-seven. Aside from the notoriety evoked by the Senate investigation, he was eminent in two respects: as a renowned scholar of Japanese history, and as a diplomat who had just achieved his greatest personal triumph. After the British, French and Israeli invasion of Suez, it was Lester Pearson, then Canadian External Affairs Minister, who proposed the first United Nations peacekeeping force, who negotiated its acceptance by the major powers, and who later received a Nobel Peace Prize for his efforts. But it was Herbert Norman in Cairo who had gained the confidence of President Nasser, and who finally persuaded him to permit the landing of the UN troops.

Norman's suicide aroused indignation throughout the Western world: he was widely seen as an innocent victim of that fanatical cabal of witch-hunters which had flourished under the leadership of Sen. Joseph McCarthy. (An editorial in *The Times* of London was headlined "Reckless Persecution".) Across Canada the initial anger was heightened and prolonged when President Eisenhower and Secretary of State Dulles responded to the tragedy in a perfunctory and patronizing manner. "As usual I shall not criticize anybody," Eisenhower blandly told reporters. "Indeed, it is my hope that the thing can now be dropped. . ." For weeks on end, the ensuing crisis dominated the front pages of Canadian newspapers and question time in the House of Commons. As politicians and editorial writers launched diatribes against Washington, Canada's relations with the US reached their lowest point in decades. To add to the furor, Canada was heading into a federal election: the Conservative opposition under John Diefenbaker began attacking Pearson and the Liberal Government for being evasive, weak and inconsistent in their responses. Like most political crises, however, the Norman affair was soon overtaken by more immediate events. It dwindled out amid the clamour of the campaign, and was almost totally forgotten in the excitement of Diefenbaker's upset victory. Since then it has become little more than a footnote to accounts of the McCarthy era, an occasion for pious asides by Canadian historians or a few paragraphs in the memoirs of former statesmen.

It is ironic that Norman should be remembered — if at all — as a victim of that messianic thrust which characterizes American politics at their worst and which, when thwarted, demands the sacrifice of scapegoats. For Norman was a fervent internationalist without a trace of enmity toward the United States: he never shared Sutherland Brown's obsession with the threat from the south. Moreover, as an historian he had often cited the American Founding Fathers as members of his pantheon of democratic heroes — together with the English Levellers, the French Encyclopaedists and a host of others, whether famous or obscure, whom he revered as "apostles of freedom".

Norman's importance — his real claim to remembrance — is based on his struggle to enact this Enlightenment tradition amid a century which so often swamps humanist values in orgies of irrationality and violence. His fate was to fail in that attempt, and to be crushed in the conflict between the two dominant modern ideologies — Communism and liberal-capitalism. His opponents — the men who brought him down — were particular Americans acting at a particular time for their own particular motives. But they were also surrogates for all the dehumanizing forces of our era, whether they act in the name of American liberalism, Soviet Communism, or any other aggressive creed.

All these modern forces are the bastard offspring of that humanist tradition in which Norman found his own sustaining vision — this is the real irony of his struggle. At the end, he seemed to recognize this irony, and to affirm an even higher allegiance. By then, however, it was much too late.

Egerton Herbert Norman was born on 1 September 1909 in Karuizawa, a Japanese summer resort. He was the last of three children: his sister Grace and brother Howard were then six and four years old. Their father, Daniel Norman, was a Methodist minister who had been born on a farm just north of Toronto; their mother, Catherine Heal Norman, was a farmer's daughter from the Goderich area. It was all English blood: Daniel's father came from Somerset, while his mother was a Quaker of United Empire Loyalist descent; Catherine's parents were both from Devonshire. Daniel Norman had come to Japan as a young missionary in 1897 and was to remain there with his wife even in retirement, not returning to Canada until 1940.

His religious background was crucial for Herbert Norman. Although he would later question the relevance of Christianity to the modern world, his outlook was always pervasively marked by the Canadian Methodist tradition. Unlike the tougher-minded doctrines of the Calvinists, Methodism is a compassionate creed which concerns itself with social tasks; among its components are often to be found utopianism and a sense of brotherhood which extends far beyond national boundaries. Methodists provided much of the impetus in the growth of Canada's socialist parties; as they battled with Calvinist individualism, they enacted the Christian ethic of supporting the weak against the strong. This is the moral base from which Herbert Norman's own radical politics were to spring; although he would be strongly shaped by other traditions, there is a sense in which he would always remain a secular Methodist missionary who advocated social reform as the only rational path toward justice and freedom.

This impulse came to him at an early age, for there was often political talk in the Norman home, which was in the provincial Japanese city of Nagano. As a student in Toronto in the eighteen-nineties, Daniel had attended early Marxist meetings; while he never thought much of Communism (and was notably unimpressed with the Soviet Union when he crossed it by train in 1930), he was always concerned with social responsibility as much as individual salvation. The same could be said of his eldest son, Howard, who also became a minister, developed moderate leftwing views, and had a strong influence on his younger brother.

Although the talk around the Norman table often reflected Daniel's broad international interests, large portraits of Jacques Cartier and Sir Isaac Brock above that table were a constant reminder to the Norman children of the homeland they had never seen; their parents also took pains to tell them stories of the pioneering days. Yet nothing in Herbert Norman's writings indicates that he was ever deeply excited by his Canadian heritage. In all his books and essays (which have enormous scope), there are few if any references to events and personages from Canadian history. This was partly because his Methodist background gave him an instinctive international outlook; it was also due to the stronger and more immediate impact of Japan.

There was no attempt to shield the Norman children from their surroundings. Daniel Norman was a tolerant missionary whose living room was often filled with Japanese seeking help with their problems. His children played with Japanese friends, and became so fluent in the language that in later years, when speaking on the telephone, Herbert was often mistaken for a native. From an early age, his imagination was aroused by reading tales of Japanese heroes, includ-

ing the classical story of *The Forty-Seven Ronin*. These were feudal retainers who beheaded a rival lord after he had caused
the death of their master, and who then gave themselves up to
the authorities and were condemned to hara-kiri. This enormously popular tale exemplified the virtues of Bushido — the
feudal code which stressed unquestioning loyalty and obedience, and which regarded hara-kiri as an act of honour and
courage, and a final proof of integrity. According to Howard
Norman, both he and his brother were deeply impressed when
they read this story as teenagers.

Children of missionaries often have trouble assimilat-
ing their dual heritage. The missionaries themselves sometimes evolve a romantic identification with their adopted
country — like Bishop White in China. Born in that country,
their children tend to be more critical. Sensing that they can
never fully belong to any nation, they are influenced by both
their ancestral and adopted countries, often to their confusion
and dismay. "Poor Japan!" Herbert was to write to his parents from Toronto in 1932, during the Japanese aggression
against Manchuria. "I feel all the fierce unreasoning loyalty
one does to one's native land, but I cannot stomach that
Bushido rot." By that time, Bushido had been revived by the
Japanese militarists to rally the people behind their
expansionist policies. One can see how it would offend against
Norman's libertarian instincts, but one can also suspect, with
hindsight, that he had been more deeply influenced than he
then realized by some of its concepts — especially the concept
that valued honour above life.

Yet there was no automatic conflict in Norman
between his Methodist and Japanese heritages. In Japan,
unlike in China, Christianity was little tainted by imperialism, and the missionaries seldom gained a dominant position
within the churches. Although it was never widespread among
the people, Christianity was taken up by a large number of
intellectuals and politicians as an alternative to the Confu-
cian-Shinto-Imperial tradition. Japanese Christianity tended
to be progressive and anti-establishment: the founders of the
Socialist and Communist parties were both Christians. There
was little here to trouble a sturdy Methodist conscience.

Despite his early exposure to Japanese friends and

Japanese customs, there was one sense in which Norman had a sheltered childhood. Like his sister and brother, he remained at home, and was tutored by his mother, instead of starting school at a normal age. Only when he was eleven did he leave Nagano to attend the Canadian Academy at Kobe, which had been founded by Canadian Methodists. By then, Herbert was growing into a tall, blond, athletic youth. He drove himself hard, playing baseball, basketball and tennis, serving on the student council, and helping to put out the student magazine. In all these endeavours, he showed an aspect of his character upon which his friends would always remark: a sunny, extraverted disposition and a strong sense of humour which usually made him the most entertaining of companions. But there was another side to Norman which became evident at this time to his family and closest friends: an inward-looking and melancholic streak which would sometimes overcome his usual cheerfulness. Norman could never entirely suppress or sublimate this darker side of his nature; in later years, under the pressure of his persecution, it would develop into a chronic anxiety. At Kobe it began to emerge when, at age sixteen, he developed tuberculosis.

After a year at a Japanese sanitorium Norman was sent to Canada to spend another year at a hospital near Calgary. During his confinement he began to show a new seriousness and gravity which might have occurred under any circumstances, but which was certainly precipitated by his illness and the gloomy surrounding of the Calgary san. "I don't know what has caused the change," he wrote to his parents, "but except with my most intimate friends, I have become too taciturn and reticent . . . I take no pains to carry on conversations with many people, causing often painful gaps of silence." His fellow patients were part of the problem: coming from such a sheltered and religious background he was troubled to find himself thrust among so many iconoclasts, cynics and agnostics — "distorted minds as well as bodies."

As another result of his confinement Norman became a prodigious reader. Poring through books of history, philosophy and political theory, he became increasingly concerned with the plight of his fellow man, especially in Asia and Africa. This was a logical outcome of his Methodist upbringing; his initial response was far from radical. Within a few years he would be calling himself a Marxist, but at seventeen he was assailing that "irascible old Teuton philosopher". Rejecting both Communism and capitalism — and still calling himself a Christian — he could only wistfully conclude that "less extreme and stubbornly dangerous arrangements can surely be devised."

While his reading had given him a formidable intellectual arsenal, Norman had nevertheless lost two years of formal schooling. Cured of his tuberculosis he took his Grade Thirteen at Albert College in Belleville, where his brother Howard was among the teachers. Then, in 1929, and at the age of twenty, he entered Victoria College in Toronto: the chosen university for children of Methodist ministers. Mature for his age, and bursting with intellectual curiosity, he was hardly a typical freshman. While his field was classics his reading ranged extensively through literature, philosophy, politics and economics. His professors were delighted by his sophistication; his fellow students were often intimidated by his erudition. But he did strike up a friendship with an attractive girl from Hamilton, Irene Clark, who would later become his wife. Typically, he courted her with Greek and Latin poetry.

It was at Victoria that Norman encountered another dominant influence on his thought and sensibility: the Greek philosopher Epicurus. Perhaps because of that chronic anxiety which he could seldom appease for long, he was drawn to the philosopher's calm approach to such weighty questions as religion, death and suicide. To Epicurus the object of living is to obtain all possible pleasure. But real pleasure is nothing gross and sensual: rather it means a body free from pain and a mind free from trouble. Nor is this a purely selfish doctrine, for Epicurus also held that giving pleasure to others is one of the highest goods and that friendship is one of man's most precious possessions.

Norman found affinities between Epicurus and the Japanese part of his heritage: not the "Bushido rot" but the enlightened hedonism and intellectual serenity which so many Japanese and Chinese philosophers have advocated as components of a balanced life. Epicureanism and Oriental thought also share another characteristic: both suggest that if everyone followed his true instincts, everyone would be good. Norman always retained this optimistic bias: he never seemed to comprehend man's propensity to evil.

Another Epicurean dictum — "Live unknown" — also became part of Norman's personal philosophy. For Epicurus political activity is to be avoided since it can only lead to notoriety, controversy, partisanship, the distortion of truth and the disruption of tranquility. As both scholar and diplomat, Norman would shun personal publicity; despite great persecution, he would resist all attempts to portray him as a martyr. Even as a student in Toronto he showed no desire for fame, nor any attraction to a public life. During his student years, however, the Great Depression engulfed the Western world. Given that his social conscience was already aroused, it was inevitable that he should be drawn into the political turmoil of his time.

Except for his year in the Calgary san, Norman had so far led a sheltered life. His childhood had been comfortable and now he was sailing ahead on scholarships; absorbed by his studies he had little direct knowledge of how most men around him were struggling to survive. When a United Church minister asked Norman to help him deliver baskets of food to some of the unemployed, Norman was horrified to discover that these men were living in caves on the banks of the Don River. As he told his friends, there must be something drastically wrong with a society which compelled some of its members to live in holes in the ground — and nearly starve to death.

About the same time, Norman's libertarian instincts were aroused when the federal government began to imprison Communists and other radicals in the Kingston penitentiary; to Norman the cruelest part of their confinement was the fact that they were not allowed to read — a "diabolical prohibition" which he felt placed Canada below even Bulgaria. "No more carping at Russia," he told his parents in a letter. "Whatever they do to the bourgeoisie we politely reciprocate."

Back in Nagano the family was troubled by such outbursts, and Daniel responded with descriptions of the tyranny in the Soviet Union. In reply Herbert did not deny the tyranny; like the other apologists of the day he pleaded that the Russian Revolution was only fifteen years old and that "such a tremendous social upheaval needs time for readjustment. It need not hang its head before the world or speak the language of cringing apology before capitalism with its stupid wars and soul-crushing system."

He was still not a total convert to Communism. Although he considered Marxism to be "a remarkably acute touchstone" for understanding historical events, he conceded that it lent itself easily to distortions. He also thought that Stalin was narrow, without an international outlook, and he feared that a growing bureaucracy might yet betray the goals of Lenin and the other original Bolsheviks. He was much more strongly drawn to the banished Trotsky whose theory of permanent revolution was more in tune with his own internationalism. This, too, did not go down very well in Nagano. "You call Trotsky a fanatic, father," Norman replied. "Then if any man is true to his ideals, however wrong they may seem to another, he is a fanatic, every saint of the church is a fanatic and every man loyal to his conscience is a fanatic. The gentle sceptics and cynics like Anatole France who write beautiful epicureanism and accomplish absolutely nothing are the only people free from fanaticism."

For the time being Epicurus had lost his sway. Norman was now twenty-four and engulfed by the passions and polemics of the nineteen-thirties. He was also on his way to England and further studies at Cambridge, where leftwing attitudes were even more prevalent than at Toronto, and where his own thinking would become even more radical. At Cambridge, too, he would sow the seeds of his ultimate destruction.

Norman graduated from Victoria College in the spring of 1933. With the scholarship to Cambridge, where he would study medieval history at Trinity College, he seemed destined for an academic career. In his first letters to Nagano, Norman wrote that he was impressed with the cosmopolitan atmosphere of Trinity and the sophistication of his tutors and fellow students; in retrospect, Victoria seemed decidedly parochial.

He also found that Cambridge was seething with radical politics. With the Depression worsening and with Fascism on the rise in Germany, Italy and Japan, it was taken for granted that any intelligent student would be somewhere on the left. As one of Norman's friends at Trinity recalled: "The only people who didn't lean left were the dull ones — the muscle boys, the drunks and the hunters." Many of the most brilliant scholars at Cambridge were already Communists — either openly or secretly — and a high proportion of these were at Trinity. The first Communist Party cell at the university had been formed in 1931; Norman was surprised to find that even his landlord, a Mr. Bell (who was also the college electrician) called himself a Communist — "although a quieter, less complaining labourer I never saw," he told his parents.

Early in his first term Norman began attending tumultuous meetings of the Cambridge University Socialist Society, the focus of most leftwing activities and often a battleground between Communists and social democrats. In this heated atmosphere his political views became honed in arguments such as he had seldom enjoyed in Toronto. Norman's room at Mr. Bell's was often filled with friends — many of them Chinese, Japanese and Indian — everyone talking at once but with Norman's somewhat nasal Canadian voice always heard above the others. At other times he would be seen striding down the college paths: a tall, blond figure surrounded by smaller, darker Asians. But his closest friend — and the strongest influence upon him at that time — was an Englishman. This was John Cornford, the son of the classicist F. M. Cornford and the poet Frances Cornford, and the great-grandson of Charles Darwin. Himself a poet of considerable promise, Cornford had plunged into politics with a furious dedication, joining the Young Communist League in the spring of 1933. He came up to Trinity that autumn — the same time Norman arrived — and was soon organizing meetings and demonstrations as well as scouting prospects for the Party. Although he was only seventeen when he arrived at Cambridge (nearly six years younger than Norman), Cornford was already a commanding personality. With dark, curly hair, high cheekbones and deep-set eyes he was a romantic, gypsy-like figure with enormous magnetism and an overpowering ability to convince others of the rightness of his beliefs. Cornford also enjoyed flouting the bourgeois conventions of the time — dressing indifferently, often going without a shave, cleaning his fingernails with a breadknife and living openly with a woman comrade.

One vignette describes Cornford at the end of his examinations: "He and a Canadian friend had been priming themselves with brandy during lunch, and were marching along singing ribald snatches, clearly fancying themselves as a pair of Wild West tough men." Although he was far from the only Canadian at Cambridge this may well have been Norman, for the two men were close. Most of Cornford's friends shared his political views or were soon converted to them. In March 1935, Cornford left the Young Communist League to become a full-fledged Communist. Soon after, by his own account, Norman followed him into the Party.

To this day, there is no available record of how long Norman remained a member of the Communist Party, or whether his membership ever involved anything more than attending meetings and study sessions. As we shall see, it can be surmised with considerable certainty that he was never active in the Party after he became a Canadian External Affairs officer in 1939. During and after the Second World War, moreover, his basic political instincts were those of a social democrat — this, at any rate, is the clear evidence of all his writings.

There is no need to wonder that he became a Communist in the nineteen-thirties. This was one of those periods when a certain climate of conviction settles on a whole generation, particularly its best members. To most, it was obvious that urgent action was needed to prevent war, halt Fascism and cure unemployment. It was not yet clear that these goals would prove difficult to reconcile; rather it seemed that a mixture of pacificism and Marxism might attain all three. To many, Marxism was simply another branch of the Western humanist tradition. As André Malraux told a New York audience in 1937: "Democracy and Communism differ on the question of the dictatorship of the proletariat, not on fundamental values."

Not everyone who held such beliefs became a Communist; those who did were convinced that the Western democracies had lost all purpose and conviction and that only the Soviet Union had the will and the strength to resist the menace of Hitler. Few had any direct experience of life under Communism; like Norman many had doubts about the nature of Stalin's regime. But they suppressed those doubts for the sake of what seemed the most pressing objective of the time: the halt of Fascism.

This objective became even more urgent when civil war broke out in Spain in July 1936. By then Norman had graduated from Cambridge with another BA and was studying Japanese history at Harvard on a three-year Rockefeller Foundation Fellowship. He had married Irene Clark on his return from England; as the young couple settled into the academic world at Harvard it still appeared that Norman would devote the rest of his life to scholarship. But many of his Cambridge friends were serving with the International Brigades in Spain; Norman was tormented by the thought that they were in the front line against Fascism while he was safely sequestered many thousand miles away. True, he was sending part of his stipend to the Loyalists, and Irene was collecting food and clothing. But this hardly seemed enough, especially when one of his friends, a New Zealander called MacLaurin, was killed in the fighting near Madrid in late 1936.

Norman thought seriously of going to Spain himself, but concluded that his total aversion to pain and violence as well as his complete helplessness in military matters would make him of little use to the Loyalists. Yet the emotional pull was strong and he couldn't help wondering how MacLaurin had died and whether he himself could have stood such hardship and danger. Then came even worse news: in late December 1936, John Cornford was killed on the Cordoba Front. He had just turned twenty-one. "For the past three weeks," Norman wrote in a letter, "I've been trying to shake the gloom that has settled on me after receiving the news of the death of the best friend I had in Cambridge, John Cornford, killed by Fascists in Spain . . . I was influenced by him more than any of my friends there and under his tutelage I entered the party. I not only respected him and his gifts, both intellectual and political, but loved him."

His grief strengthened Norman's conviction that Spain offered decisive proof of his political views. These views had grown in part out of his Methodist humanitarianism, but Norman now regarded Christianity as incapable of meeting the challenges of the era. As he wrote to his brother Howard in early 1937: "I can't accept the view that preaching Christ is the highest endeavour of human life . . . the real standard-bearer for humanity, for liberty and man's right to develop freely — is communism."

Like so many of his generation, Norman was impressed by the fact that only the Soviet Union was offering material help to the beleaguered Spanish Loyalists. By failing to resist the spread of Fascism in Europe, the Western democracies were demonstrating their impotence and futility. More than ever it seemed imperative to support the Russian Communists, especially when it became evident that Hitler, with his aid to Franco, was using Spain as a testing ground for his own ambitions. So Norman accepted without question Stalin's purge of his rivals in the great Moscow Trials which began in 1936. In letters written at the time he made clear that he regarded the "confessions" of Zinoviev, Kamenev and the other old Bolsheviks as the literal truth, as well as conclusive proof of a widespread plot by Trotskyites and Fascists. Rejecting all allegations that the Trials were rigged, he saw them as a vindication of Soviet justice.

We now know that the Trials were frame-ups and that the confessions were obtained through a mixture of torture, drugs and psychological pressure. Even at the time, evidence to this effect was widely available in the West. Like Norman, however, many Western sympathizers of the Soviet Union — including liberals and socialists as well as Communists — refused to accept this evidence. It was simply impossible for them to believe that the Soviet Union, the hope of all progressive forces and the only apparent bulwark against the Fascists, could be guilty of such duplicity. This was outright naivete; in Norman it seems linked to his lack of any strong sense of evil.

Norman was working even harder at Harvard than he had at Cambridge; apart from his studies in Japanese history

— which were to earn him both an MA and a PhD — he was also learning to read Chinese, a task which demanded enormous application. But as the Fascists continued to triumph in Spain, and as they came to the fore in his own Japan (especially after the attack on China), it still seemed wrong to hide among the academic cloisters, doing nothing. So Norman helped to establish the Canadian affiliate of the American Friends of the Chinese People; he also attended an informal discussion group at Harvard devoted to "the study of American capitalism from the Marxist point of view". He was an early contributor to the radical journal *Amerasia* and in 1938 he became associated with the Institute of Pacific Relations in New York: both the journal and the institute were later attacked by the witch-hunters of the McCarthy period as being heavily infiltrated by Communists.

There was some truth in these charges. We do not know whether Norman himself was an active member of the Party at this time, but there is no evidence that he had begun to temper his enthusiasm for the Soviet Union as the sole opponent of Fascism. Yet although he was very much involved in the immediate issues of the day — and although his responses were sometimes naive — his philosophical point of view was the direct antithesis of narrow partisanship or dogmatic advocacy. This is clear from the first of his books, *Japan's Emergence as a Modern State,* which he began writing at this time and which affirms his basic stance as a traditional humanist.

When *Japan's Emergence* was published in 1940 it established Norman, who was then only thirty-one, as one of the leading Western scholars on modern Japan. For more than a decade — until his political persecution was followed by his academic denigration — it was considered the most important study of Japan's emergence from feudalism in the latter half of the nineteenth century. It was also seen as a pioneering work, since Norman was the first Western historian to draw on the research of Japanese Marxist scholars and to adopt, in part, an economic analysis of Japan's evolution to a modern state. At the time — and even more during the nineteen-fifties — this led other historians to describe the work as Marxist.

Despite its methodology, however, *Japan's Emergence* was no more Marxist in its basic vision of history than Herbert Norman was Communist in his fundamental outlook. Throughout the book Norman refused to accept Japan's transformation as preordained by any abstract principle, Marxist or otherwise. Moreover, he had consulted virtually all the primary sources (Japanese scholars commented on his extraordinary diligence), and he drew more upon non-Marxist historians than their Marxist counterparts. While he was clearly attracted to the social conscience of the Marxists, he emphatically dismissed — in his own words — "all preconceptions based on a 'class-struggle' interpretation."

To open *Japan's Emergence* at any page is to grasp the nature of Norman's sensibility. The style is lucid, graceful and often eloquent — the direct opposite of the cumbersome jargon which modern social scientists usually inflict upon their readers. There is a deep concern with people — not as abstract units but as suffering and aspiring individuals. Above all, Norman disdains all cultural arrogance and ethnocentricity. Discussing Japan's development from the Meiji Restoration of 1868 to the Russo-Japanese War of 1905 he remarks:

> Much has been written to express the delighted amazement of the Western traveller, journalist or diplomat as he warms to the spectacle of a nation so quick in learning the industrial arts of the Occident, so precocious in mastering the diplomacy of the Christian powers. This often condescending admiration whose object is worthy of a more understanding if less effusive appreciation, becomes at times quite fatuous in its talk about the "miracle" of Japan as if, somehow, Japanese development had transcended all the laws of history and nature.

This could have been written with equal force about Western and especially American reactions to Japan's recovery in the aftermath of the Second World War. In fact we have here — in 1940 — the roots of Norman's later opposition to Washington's policy of "modernizing" the Japanese. For the moment let it stand as an indication of an historical approach which is free from dogmatism.

By his own admission, Norman was "addicted to history". He wrote of the "magical pleasure" of reading about turbulent events in the calm of his study, adding that "to cast one's mind into the past and to have described vividly for one the passions and ambitions, the hopes and disappointments not only of great men, but of people like ourselves, is to feel an intimation of man's immortal spirit."

While his exemplars were the great masters from every era, Norman was mainly a legatee of the Enlightenment. He believed that man was essentially good and could achieve true freedom through the exercise of his reason, as applied to the study of his history and his institutions. As he wrote in another essay:

> I venture even to go so far as to say that the world is out of joint, not so much because people are basically wicked, but because of lack of cultivation, in the broad sense of the word, lack of intelligence, tolerance and reason. If enough people had these qualities, it would be virtually impossible for dictators to deceive their people so completely as to what was desirable and secondly as to what was possible.

This passage defines Norman as an archetypal liberal. Again we note the strong belief in human goodness, and the lack of any sense of evil. We may also start to wonder whether Norman was not, in many ways, a most remarkable anachronism: an avatar of the great humanists and rationalists of the Enlightenment, somehow preserved in amber for two centuries and then let loose amid all the disasters of our modern era, to try to make sense of the Enlightenment's legacy. For the drama of his life is his attempt to enact that Enlightenment vision in the face of overwhelming evidence to the contrary. At this time he had already lived through the Depression, the rise of Fascism and the start of the Second World War. The greatest horrors of that conflict still lay ahead, as did the paranoiac furies of the Cold War, including his own persecution. It now remains to be seen whether he could sustain that noble vision through all this further turmoil, or whether he ever came to question it.

Despite his devotion to scholarship it is not so strange that

Norman became a diplomat. In the winter of 1938-39, as he worked on the final draft of his PhD thesis (which became *Japan's Emergence*), he must have given hard thought to his future. His formal education was coming to an end, he had a wife to support and he would soon be thirty. The Depression had forced universities to restrict the size of their staffs; despite his outstanding record there was no guarantee that he would find a worthwhile teaching post. When he heard that the Department of External Affairs was looking for Far East experts it must have seemed too good an opportunity to let slip, since it offered both security and the chance of returning to Japan.

This last was important because Norman had no intention of abandoning his studies and his writing, nor did he see any automatic conflict between history and public service. Instead he would be following that Victorian tradition of European scholar-diplomats who had written so extensively on China and Japan. These were mainly gifted amateurs such as Sir George Sansom who regarded the writing of history as a proper pastime for a man in public life.

Norman was quickly accepted when he applied to External Affairs in 1939. At this point he underwent his first security check. These checks were routine for all new foreign service officers, and it has never been established whether Norman then disclosed that he had joined the Communist Party while at Cambridge. He arrived in Tokyo in early 1940 to serve as language officer and third secretary at the Canadian Legation. Aside from his normal duties he was soon busy looking up old friends, attending the Kabuki theatre (sometimes three or four times a week) and pursuing his studies. Yet he was depressed by the totalitarian atmosphere of Tokyo, especially when he discovered that many scholars whose work he had been using were imprisoned or otherwise intimidated by the military regime.

He had no doubt that war was coming. With the wives of other Canadian diplomats, Irene returned to Canada in May 1941. On Pearl Harbour Sunday, Norman and the rest of the Legation Staff were placed under house arrest. Their confinement lasted for seven months; Norman spent most of this time in the Legation library, reading and brushing up on his Japanese. To the Canadian *chargé d'affaires,* D'Arcy McGreer, Norman was an ideal fellow prisoner, since his flow of amusing conversation was inexhaustible. In the course of a single evening he might discuss Persian poetry, the wines used in Italy at the time of Catullus, the pungent writings of John Aubrey (the seventeenth-century London diarist) or the personal idiosyncrasies of such writers as Cervantes and Voltaire. On other occasions he would explore such subjects as how the unicorn got his horn, the mating habits of African tribes or the sewage system of ancient Rome.

Norman bore his knowledge lightly, and shared it wittily. It was the result of his hungry curiosity and his prodigious reading in several languages — aside from English and Japanese, he read Greek, Latin, French and German, and could find his way in Italian and Chinese. His memory was also remarkable. Some years later, during a party in Ottawa for visiting scholars from France, there was a long discussion on Baudelaire. To illustrate a point, Norman recited a verse, pausing in the middle of a line. One of the French scholars challenged him: "Why do you stop there?" "Because there's a comma," Norman answered. After some argument, a volume of Baudelaire was consulted, and Norman was proven right.

The Canadian diplomats were repatriated in June 1942. On the way home they exchanged ships at Lorenzo Marques, in Mozambique, with a group of Japanese who had been interned in the United States. On the gangplank, Norman met Tsuru Shigeto, a Japanese scholar who had been part of the same Marxist study group at Harvard. It was a fateful encounter, for Tsuru asked his friend to retrieve some papers he had left behind in his apartment in Cambridge, Mass. Later in the year, Norman went to Tsuru's apartment where, with unfortunate timing, he encountered agents of the FBI. This was an indication that even in 1942, American authorities were already on the track of Communists and other radicals. Whether or not he was aware of the danger, Norman apparently reacted with a nervous bluster which betrayed his political innocence. He identified himself as a Canadian foreign service officer and intimated that he was on government business. Already sceptical, the agents became even more suspicious when Norman had to admit under close questioning that his visit was unofficial. Finally they let him go, but the damage was done. If there wasn't already an FBI file on Norman, this was when they opened one.

Norman spent the next three years in Ottawa. In his spare time he completed his second book, *Soldier and Peasant in Japan: The Origins of Conscription.* Published in 1943, it traced the roots of Japanese militarism and aggression to the introduction of conscription during the Meiji period (1868-1912). Like all Norman's work it had strong contemporary significance. Writing in the midst of the Pacific War, Norman maintained that the road to democracy in Japan — which the Meiji Restoration had opened and then blocked — could be regained only with Japan's defeat in the war, at which time the victors could "help the Japanese people themselves to secure that liberty and freedom which they have so far been too misguided and weak to accomplish unaided."

Taken out of context, that passage has a patronizing tone: it suggests a cultural arrogance which was notably absent from *Japan's Emergence.* In fact, Norman was always the least arrogant or ethnocentric of men: in Japan — and, later, in New Zealand and Egypt — he took pains to immerse himself in the peoples' customs and to understand their particular impulses. In the full context, Norman's criticism of the Japanese as "misguided and weak" clearly applied to their leaders. Like all his books, *Soldier and Peasant* was marked by a strong feeling for the common people, whose democratic instincts Norman described as being sounder than those of their rulers. Far from lapsing into cultural arrogance, he was searching for some *indigenous* tradition of democracy on which the Japanese could build their postwar politics.

Yet there remains a deeper sense in which Norman can be accused, if not of racial arrogance, then of a rationalist innocence which was to manifest itself throughout his career, and play a major part in his destruction. His Enlightenment vision, his passion for freedom, his faith in man's essential goodness, even his residual Methodist evangelism . . . all these produced a conviction that men of all nations could order their affairs in a sane, civilized and democratic manner, if only they could be educated out of their fears and prejudices.

As he wrote in that essay already cited, the world was out of joint because men lacked "cultivation", not because they were basically wicked.

With hindsight we can see how Norman's vision of an indigenous Japanese democracy was bound to conflict with the demands of American foreign policy in the immediate postwar period. As a diplomat in Tokyo his views of Japan's past and future were often at variance with those of Gen. MacArthur and his aides. Moreover, while Norman became a Communist at Cambridge, and while his accusers would base their charges mainly on his activities and associations at Harvard and New York, there are grounds for suspecting that the enemies he made in Tokyo were the instigators of his persecution.

These conflicts would not take long to emerge, despite Norman's warm reception by the Occupation authorities. He had returned to Asia immediately after the Japanese surrender — first to the Philippines and then to Japan — to arrange the repatriation of Canadian prisoners. Once in Tokyo he was recruited — with Ottawa's blessing — by the US military authorities at the headquarters of SCAP (Supreme Commander for the Allied Powers for the Occupation and Control of Japan). Under Gen. MacArthur's authoritarian direction, SCAP was running everything that mattered in the defeated and devastated nation. Because of his background Norman was thrust into the massive task of interrogating and classifying thousands of Japanese politicians, military leaders, businessmen and intellectuals — both those who had supported the military regime during the war and those who had been imprisoned for opposing it. In the last few months of 1945 we have the extraordinary spectacle of Norman, a Canadian diplomat of decidedly radical tendencies, serving as effective head of the US Army's Counter-Intelligence Corps in Japan, working in a huge office on the ground floor of the Dai-Ichi Building, opposite the Imperial Palace, and supervising a major, a captain, five lieutenants and twenty-five enlisted men, as well as a larger number of Americans in closely related sections.

It was hectic and exhilarating. Ravaged by bombing and traumatized by defeat, Tokyo was struggling to regain some semblance of normal life. In his letters Norman wrote of scrounging food and lodging from the Americans, of visiting the Imperial University and the Meiji Library, and of trying to trace old friends among the Japanese intellectual community. After years of repression — and in some cases imprisonment — liberal and radical scholars were starting to re-emerge; Norman found that he gained more from an hour's conversation with the leading historian of the anti-imperialist school than he could have learned from days of plodding research. In October he drove with an American officer to a prison outside Tokyo where he was able to tell sixteen important political prisoners, including two Communist leaders who had been locked up for nearly twenty years, that MacArthur had ordered their release. It was, he wrote, "the most exciting experience of my life."

Before long Irene had joined him, the couple had moved into the Canadian Legation, and Norman had given up intelligence work to assume full-time duties as chief of the Canadian Mission to SCAP. At thirty-six he was effectively an ambassador. While this was an indication of Ottawa's high regard, it by no means guaranteed that Norman would have much sway in SCAP where MacArthur, who was running Japan as an American fiefdom, had little interest in the views of any of his wartime allies.

Yet Norman's influence was substantial at this time, even though it had little to do with his official role. Rather it derived from the enormous esteem in which he was held by Japanese intellectuals. His command of their language and his deep knowledge of their traditions were apparent from the start; by 1948, when both *Japan's Emergence* and *Soldier and Peasant* had been translated, Norman was widely seen as the foreigner who had the most sensitive appreciation of both their past history and their present problems. Amid the humiliation of military defeat, his books offered Japanese intellectuals a means of understanding their historical experience and of charting a future course which would be based on their own customs, rather than merely imposed upon them by their conquerors. Japanese read these books with pride and hope, drawing encouragement from Norman's concentration on their traditions, and especially the struggle of ordinary men against the tyranny of their rulers.

Norman returned to these themes in his public speeches, some of which were also published. At a memorial service for his father in Nagano in 1947 — after apologizing for being rash enough to speak to Japanese in their own language and about their own history — Norman noted that authoritarianism and intellectual repression were the dominant pattern of feudal Japan but added that "in spite of centuries of isolation and regimentation, I believe it is a remarkable tribute to the inherent humanity and decency of the common people in general that there is considerable evidence that the feudal authorities did not succeed in brutalizing the people or in converting them into fanatical chauvinists."

Norman's influence was also enhanced by his personal friendships with leading intellectuals. At this time the Japanese were already overwhelmed by a host of Western scholars and linguists, mainly American, who had been pressed into service by the Occupation. The Japanese found most of them narrow in outlook and unrewarding in conversation. But a leading Japanese scholar, Masao Maruyama, would later write: ". . . no one would ever think of classifying Herbert Norman with that steady post-war stream of scholars 'specializing' in Japan and the Far East who are generally ignorant of anything of the history and culture of Europe. He was a historian of the world before he was a historian of Japan. If one could lead the conversation skilfully enough, there was almost no limit to what one could learn from his inexhaustible fund of scholarship."

It was Norman's charm and consideration as much as his scholarship which delighted his Japanese friends. On one occasion the distinguished scholar Kazuo Watanabe drank too much at a Legation party and fell asleep. When Watanabe woke up several hours later, feeling thoroughly ashamed of himself, Norman offered him another drink and a lift home in his official car. The following midnight Watanabe's phone rang. It was Norman, asking if he could come over and bother Watanabe for a minute. Soon Norman appeared with a bottle of whiskey. After the two friends drank and talked, Norman professed to be tired, whereupon Watanabe invited him to take a nap. Norman did so. "I couldn't forget this incident," Watanabe later said. "To save my face, Dr. Norman tried to lose his."

Such sensitivity to Japanese feelings was lost on the brusquer officials at SCAP, but MacArthur himself had a shrewd appreciation of Norman's stature. It was upon MacArthur's urging that he agreed to tutor Prince Mikasa, the Emperor's brother. The Supreme Commander realised that this request from the Palace was an extraordinary honour for any foreigner, especially since Norman would be instructing the Prince in *Japanese* history. Among the diplomatic community it was noted that MacArthur granted more time to the Canadian envoy than he did to many ambassadors from more important nations. More crucially, much of the initial Occupation policy was based in part upon Norman's work as an historian. His concept of the dictatorial and feudal nature of the Tokugawa and Meiji periods had made a deep impression on American experts; it clearly influenced SCAP's early directives, especially those relating to land reform, the new constitution and the proposed dissolution of the zaibatsu business complexes.

Norman viewed MacArthur with a mixture of admiration and exasperation. His reports to Ottawa are filled with wry comments on the Supreme Commander's grandiloquent manner, both in his public pronouncements and in his private conversation. "The General's words steam along like warships with no great cargo of meaning," Norman wrote on one occasion, while on another he refered to "the evangelical style with which we are becoming familiar in Japan." It was always difficult for Norman to determine where MacArthur really stood on any matter, especially the key issues of political and economic reform, despite their frequent meetings. MacArthur was given to lengthy monologues which were almost impossible to interrupt; with his remarkable memory Norman would listen patiently, return to his office and then dictate a detailed account without the help of notes. At times he heard the General castigate the die-hard Japanese conservatives for the Occupation's difficulties, while on other occasions he listened to similar diatribes against the Communists and their allies in the trade unions.

But it soon became obvious to Norman that his hopes for the Occupation were not being fulfilled. In its early directives SCAP had professed to be embarked upon a "democratic revolution" — to Norman this implied a continuation of the aborted revolution of the Meiji through sweeping reforms which would shatter the ultra-conservative oligarchy which had led Japan to war. Nor was this merely Norman's personal view: official documents make clear that the Canadian Government was also convinced that the Japanese militaristic traditions could be overcome only through basic reforms in the constitution, labour laws, land tenure and education. By 1948, however, both Norman and his superiors in Ottawa were expressing concern that these reforms were being steadily abandoned. This basic change of direction — which soon became known as the "reverse course" — had been ordered from Washington as part of its emerging Cold War strategy of containing Communism on a global basis. The Americans were distressed when their initial reforms — including Mac-Arthur's release of thousands of political prisoners — unleashed a leftwing movement of surprising strength. This was seen as a direct threat to Washington's new policy of establishing Japan as an industrial and political bulwark against Communism in Asia. As a result of the "reverse course" thousands of leftwing labour leaders, government officials and journalists were fired from their jobs in response to SCAP directives, a 150,000-man national "police" force was recommended as a first step toward remilitarization, and economic reforms were halted to permit increased production and investment, even if this meant failing to break up the zaibatsu. In his dispatches to Ottawa, Norman began to question MacArthur's optimistic pronouncements about the progress of the Occupation and warned that reactionary forces were far from vanquished.

Nor were he and Ottawa alone in their views. When the "reverse course" began to unfold, a clear conflict emerged in SCAP between proponents of the new policy and many civilian officials who were strong advocates of reform. These reformers directed their ire at Maj-Gen. Charles Willoughby, MacArthur's chief intelligence officer, who spent most of his time hounding Communists, socialists and trade union activ-

ists. A Prussian who had come to the United States as a teen-
ager, Willoughby kept a picture of Franco in his office. (He
was later to retire to Spain.) This was hardly a man to inspire
confidence in any friend of John Cornford; it seems that Norman's suspicions were fully reciprocated, since Willoughby
was later to testify in closed session at the Senate hearings in
which Norman's name first emerged. While he refused to discuss Norman at a subsequent public hearing, it is doubtful
that his private testimony in any way contradicted the accusations of the Senate investigators.

Although Norman could hardly hope to change the
views of Willoughby and the other hard-liners in SCAP, he
could still try to influence his real constituency: Japanese
opinion. In the summer of 1949 he seized every possible spare
hour at the Legation to write one of his most important studies: *Ando Shoeki and the Anatomy of Japanese Feudalism.* This is a
remarkable book for many reasons, not least of all because
Norman chose an obscure eighteenth-century iconoclast, who
was unknown even to most Japanese intellectuals, in order to
remind contemporary Japan of its own radical and democratic traditions. At the outset Norman made his intention
clear: he had been trying for some years to discover any
impressive evidence from the centuries of Japanese feudalism
of a philosophy vindicating resistance to unbridled authority
and repression. He had all but abandoned his search when he
discovered Shoeki, whom he praises for his "sweeping and
unqualified condemnation of feudal rule".

Again we may note Norman's pervasive bias. By his
own admission, he had encountered extreme difficulty in finding a Japanese figure who exemplified Enlightenment values;
that few Japanese had even heard of Shoeki might have led
another historian to question whether classical Western concepts of freedom were, in fact, relevant to Japanese experience, and whether Japan *had* radical and democratic
traditions. Many Japanese intellectuals were delighted to
make the acquaintance of such an intriguing forerunner; we
may still suspect, however, that both Norman and his readers
failed to confront the deeper question which was clearly raised
by the selection of the obscure Shoeki as a liberal exemplar.

In other ways, too, *Ando Shoeki* tells us a great deal

about its author. Except for some of his shorter essays this is the most personal, eloquent and moving of Norman's works. It is clear that he felt a deep identification with Shoeki, whom he describes as passionate in his convictions, his pursuit of knowledge and his hatred of man's inhumanity to man. For all his passion, however, Shoeki is seen as akin to Epicurus, since his sense of humanity and his intense curiosity were devoted to developing a philosophy which could give peace and calm to the mind:

> Finally I like to see Shoeki as a simple country doctor . . . reserved yet not cold, neither haughty nor fawning, humane but not condescending, valuing friends but socially not ambitious; stoical in manner but sanguine in outlook; studious of books but more of the living world around him; a man who could look with keen but friendly eyes on Nature and his fellow men, learning from them and so able to teach them. Above all else he was a lover of peace and the pursuit of peace; hence in the proper sense, a *civilized* man.

This comes close to describing Norman himself. As Norman placed Shoeki in a classical tradition of libertarian thinkers he also defines his own intellectual and political credo:

> Men reach the same goal through different experiences and by different paths. Shoeki's social and intellectual milieu was completely foreign to that of the ancient Epicureans, the Levellers of seventeenth-century England, the *encyclopedists* of eighteenth-century France and the fathers of the great North American Republic. Yet spiritually he was akin to them all. Nourished on classical Chinese philosophy particularly as interpreted by Japanese thinkers, he comes to conclusions phrased in words essentially similar in content to those used by apostles of freedom and equality throughout the world.

While *Ando Shoeki* is revealing of Norman's own sensibility, its author's main purpose was to provide Japanese intellectuals with the example of a notable forerunner who had defied authoritarian rule. He had always believed that

true progress toward freedom could only spring from indigenous roots. Now — as he confided privately — he hoped that
his book might help to turn the Japanese away from their fixa-
tion upon American-style democracy, as imported by SCAP,
by reminding them of their own populist exemplars. This is
where we see Norman in clearest focus as an opponent of that
modern spirit which, through the pursuit of absolutist goals,
was swamping the Enlightenment values from which it
derived. Specifically he was opposing the "modernizers": an
apt title which was given to all those American politicians,
diplomats and historians who sought to impose upon the
Japanese a vision of their history and their future which had
little to do with their own traditions but which instead would
create a liberal-capitalist nation akin to, and allied with, the
United States. This was Norman's real heresy — much more
so than his youthful adherence to Communism. For he was
challenging not just specific American policies in a specific
part of the world, nor even just the main thrust of all American foreign policy. Rather he was defending human individu-
ality and human particularity against that basic modern
doctrine of progress-through-technology which threatened to
entrap mankind in a bland, homogenized and conformist destiny. In resisting the "modernizers" Norman was reaffirming
his commitment to an older tradition of freedom and social
justice in which his own sensibility found its deepest roots.

Here is one of those painful ironies which resound
through Norman's life. For Norman applied his advocacy of
indigenous traditions to Japan, rather than to his own country. By ignoring his Canadian heritage he could become, without any apparent qualms, a member of the civil service elite
which denigrated that heritage, fostered a creeping conti-
nentalism, and so became a willing collaborator in American
imperial schemes. In turn, this collaboration would play its
part in Norman's own destruction.

Ando Shoeki was published in 1949; a Japanese translation appeared in the following year. Unlike *Japan's Emergence* it
was largely ignored by Western scholars, to whom Shoeki
himself seemed too obscure to matter. But Japanese intellectuals praised the book as original and important; some called it
Norman's major contribution. Norman's hope that the book

might have some practical effect now seems decidedly quixotic, however, and a further indication that he never comprehended the power of the forces against which he contended. By the time the translation appeared, the "loss" of China to the Communists had bolstered Washington's determination to contain the Red Menace. In Japan itself the "reverse course" had ensured that conservative forces grouped in the Liberal-Democratic Party and the giant business complexes were firmly in control, and that the "modernization" of Japan would proceed along lines acceptable to Washington. With the outbreak of the Korean War in June 1950, Japan's emergence as an American satellite was made inevitable. Not only was MacArthur using the Japanese islands as home bases for the United Nations forces but the war gave an enormous boost to the Japanese economy, to the direct benefit of the politicians and industrialists who were the prime advocates of the American connection.

For Norman the war meant further differences with the hard-liners in SCAP. There is no indication that he ever questioned Ottawa's support for initial UN action against the North Koreans, but he argued strongly against the UN advance on the Yalu River on the ground that it would lead to Chinese intervention. This was the direct opposite of the advice that MacArthur was receiving from Willoughby and his other experts: their intelligence was responsible for the disastrous failure of MacArthur's "Home by Christmas" offensive; their mistrust and resentment of Norman could hardly have been lessened when he was proven right.

Norman seems to have retained good relations with MacArthur himself. When Pearson visited Tokyo in early 1950 the Supreme Commander thanked him for Norman's services, adding: "He's the most valuable man we have." Since the two men were still meeting regularly this was probably more than courtesy, even if MacArthur was still addicted to monologues and rarely sought the Canadian's advice. At their final meeting, in October 1950, with UN forces pressing their advance toward the Yalu, MacArthur was adamant that the Chinese would never intervene. Even if they did, he added, his air force would cut their troops to pieces and would reduce Mukden, Shanghai and Peking to ashes, even without atomic bombs. MacArthur was clearly in an expansive mood, especially since he was still relishing his triumph at Inchon, where his amphibious assault had turned the tide of the North Korean advance, as well as providing the Supreme Commander with a notable opportunity for gilding his own legend. As Norman informed Ottawa:

> General MacArthur described his feelings in taking the gamble in the Inchon landing as recalling to his mind the early study of Wolfe's campaign in Quebec, when the latter had decided upon storming the Plains of Abraham against the advice of all his staff. The General, who is very sensitive not only to his place in history but also to the minute details attending it, mentioned that he also, on the evening before the landing in Inchon, had read Gray's "Elegy" and fully appreciated Wolfe's sentiments.

This is vintage Norman. It shows that quality which gives so much vivacity to his books: a fascination with the quirks and foibles of the great, an awareness that much of history is to be explained in terms of individual passions rather than impersonal forces. However much he may have been horrified by the threat to level Peking and Shanghai, Norman could still be entertained by the General's eccentric grandeur.

Despite the pressures and the disputes, Norman was apparently still enjoying his role as diplomat. That he was working in Japan certainly added to the pleasures of the job: he loved visiting Japanese bath-houses and restaurants, scouting the best locations for viewing cherry blossoms in the spring, visiting antique shops with Irene to add to their collection of screens, prints and vases and — above all — spending long evenings in relaxed and rambling conversation with his Japanese friends. But Norman was now committed to the diplomatic life, wherever it might take him. In a letter to Pearson just after the latter's Tokyo visit, Norman discussed his next posting. Pearson had mentioned Moscow as a possibility but Norman argued against this, pointing out that it would be a difficult place in which to pursue his Far Eastern interests. Instead he mentioned London, or a period back in Ottawa, as more desirable; he also raised the longer-range possibility of a posting to Peking. But he concluded that he would do his best wherever the Department decided to send him.

Despite this apparent equanimity Norman was actually a very worried man. It is always dangerous to take his reports and letters at face value: even during the last weeks of his life in Cairo, his dispatches to Ottawa were as painstaking as ever while his letters gave little indication of his inner turmoil. Like most men of abnormal sensitivity Norman wore a mask. To colleagues and acquaintances he was the brilliant scholar-diplomat whose sparkling conversation seemed to indicate a sane and balanced nature, enlivened by a strong sense of humour and instinctive courtesy and dignity. Only to his family and closest friends did he reveal that chronic anxiety which lay behind the mask. During those last months in Tokyo he appeared to some of his friends as deeply worried and almost neurotic in his fears. As he told one friend, he had recently discovered that he was under investigation by US Counter-Intelligence, one of whose agents had even started dating his secretary.

Rather than paranoid fantasy, this was almost certainly the truth. It would be another year before Norman was publicly denounced by the Senate investigators. By Pearson's own account, however, the accusations had already surfaced in 1950, while Norman was still in Tokyo, in the form of a private communication from the State Department to External Affairs. For the time being there would be no question of Moscow or any other posting. In late autumn Pearson summoned Norman home to Ottawa on "special duty" — a euphemism for investigation.

It was the worst of times to be accused of Communist associations. When the first Cold War shocks in Europe were followed by Mao Tse-tung's conquest of China and the sweeping Chinese victories in Korea, Americans saw themselves as the intended victims of a monolithic Communist movement bent on world domination. Rightwingers who had fervently espoused Chiang Kai-shek as a frontline fighter for the "free world" were incapable of understanding Mao's appeal to his own people and sought to explain Chiang's defeat in terms of a conspiracy which had been hatched in Moscow, and aided and abetted by traitors within the State Department and their allies in the diplomatic service of other Western nations. With elections looming in 1952, Republican Congressmen were especially anxious to unmask such Communist agents — at home and abroad — since their "treachery" could then be linked to the policies and practices of successive Democratic administrations.

There is still no precise account of how Norman had come to the attention of the witch-hunters. Many of the Americans under investigation had worked with the Institute of Pacific Relations and had written for *Amerasia*; this would have brought Norman's name at least to the fringe of the inquiries. His 1942 encounter with FBI agents in Tsuru's apartment was certainly a key incident, but several of Norman's colleagues were convinced that American Counter-Intelligence agents in Tokyo had taken the first crucial steps. The agents' suspicions would have been aroused by the Canadian diplomat's opposition to the Occupation's "reverse course", and his contacts with leftwing Japanese. These suspicions were presumably conveyed to Washington; it later emerged that in late 1950 the FBI had asked the RCMP for any relevant information on Norman. As it turned out the Mounties had a letter sent to them in 1940 by one of their secret agents which stated that a "Professor Herbert Norman" was a member of the Communist Party of Canada. The Mounties had never taken this letter seriously, since the supporting evidence was clearly inaccurate, but they had kept it in their files, and had no qualms about passing it on to the FBI in October 1950.

This was a frightening example of how the routine exchange of raw security information had made the Canadian Government the accomplice of the most ruthless elements in Washington. In October — and again in December — the Mounties assured the FBI that their own investigations (ten years earlier) had led them to dismiss the charge. Despite this assurance, the FBI relayed the accusation against Norman to the Senate's subcommittee on Internal Security, which was in the throes of a massive hunt for Communists.

Alerted by the State Department that Norman was under suspicion, Pearson brought him back to Ottawa in November and told him he would have to submit to the most exhaustive investigation that any Canadian civil servant had ever undergone. According to Pearson's later account the interrogation lasted six or seven weeks; according to Norman's friends it was a traumatic experience which left him shaken and deeply disturbed. The details have never been made public but when Pearson reviewed the evidence he found nothing that would challenge Norman's loyalty. Much later — after Norman's death — Pearson said Norman had at one point acknowledged that "he had had mistaken beliefs and had been following a false ideology." This was the closest he ever came to stating that Norman had admitted to his Communist connections. But Pearson also stated emphatically that while Norman had been an officer of External Affairs — in other words, from July 1939 — none of his contacts or his actions "could in any way be questioned from a security point of view."

After reviewing the evidence in early 1951, Pearson told the State Department that Norman had been cleared of all suspicion. To demonstrate his confidence to the Americans, he appointed him to be Canada's acting permanent representative at the UN in New York. This was a temporary posting: Norman was back in Ottawa when the storm finally broke.

On 7 August 1951, in public testimony before Sen Pat McCarran's subcommittee on Internal Security, an avowed ex-Communist professor called Karl Wittfogel said Norman had been a Communist in the late nineteen-thirties. As usual in such witch-hunts the evidence was ambiguous, inconclusive and largely inaccurate in terms of dates and places. Subsequent testimony which linked Norman to the IPR — and to the release of the Communist leaders in Tokyo — was even more tenuous. In a series of statements Pearson revealed that Norman had already been fully investigated in Ottawa, reaffirmed his complete confidence in the diplomat and castigated the subcommittee for releasing such "unimpressive and unsubstantiated allegations." As proof of Pearson's confidence, Norman remained at the head of External's Far Eastern Division; in a further gesture of support, Pearson took him as his chief adviser to the Japanese peace treaty conference in San Francisco. After signing the treaty for Canada, Pearson handed the gold pen to Norman, saying: "I'm giving this to the person who really did the work."

At this time — and again in 1957 — many Canadians praised Pearson for his courage in supporting Norman; other Canadians attacked him for weakness and vacillation. Given that Pearson almost certainly knew what most Canadians strongly disbelieved — that Norman *had* been a Communist — the occasional confusion and ambiguities in his public statements now seem understandable. But the real point is that Norman had already been betrayed by his own government's close links with Washington — as seen in the RCMP's unhesitating compliance with the FBI's request for information. Such security exchanges were the logical result of Ottawa's continentalist policies. By 1951, Ottawa had so mortgaged our independence that Canadian officials provided the spurious evidence which would further the destruction of a Canadian citizen by American politicians — and the Canadian Government could then do nothing but engage in ineffectual protests.

Years later, a Canadian newspaperman would recall how he had met Pearson and Norman on their arrival in San Francisco, and found that by then they were treating the allegations as a complete joke, even to the point of laughing at the coincidence which had brought Sen McCarran to the conference on the same train. There is something pathetic about this vignette: it suggests an almost wilful innocence. (Pearson, of course, was also the son of a Methodist minister.) But it also reminds us of Norman's strange duality, for on the evidence of closer friends he was still a deeply worried man, and far from reassured by Pearson's jovial support.

In fact, Norman had never fully recovered from the trauma of being investigated by his own government; then there had been the even greater shock of seeing his name screaming at him from the headlines. Never had the Epicurean dictum — "Live unknown" — seemed more apposite. Trying to cheer him up, a friend told him he was not a villain but a hero, especially to his colleagues. Very quietly, Norman replied: "I don't want to be a hero."

Refusing all interviews, Norman declined to answer the charges except to refute one specific, minor allegation that was demonstrably false. To add to his torment, the crucial charge — that he had been a Communist — was true and he knew it might at any time be repeated with stronger and more accurate evidence. With some formality he solemnly assured his brother and sister that he had never broken his oath of secrecy to the Canadian Government. But he could not escape a feeling of deep remorse and shame — a feeling which seems Japanese in its nature and intensity — for having let down Pearson and the other colleagues with whom he had worked so happily for the past decade. His deep anxiety now came to the fore; for the rest of his life it would seldom be appeased. Brooding by himself, or engaging in lengthy, tortured conversation with close friends, he wondered if his torment would ever end.

Despite Pearson's public support Norman soon had cause to suspect that his career had, in fact, been permanently damaged. In mid-1952 he became head of External's Information Division: this suggested he was being shunted aside. In early 1953 he was named High Commissioner to New Zealand. This was a small mission with only two senior officers: many observers felt that Norman was being banished, or at least put a long way out of sight. There was probably some truth in this, although a senior official later maintained that Norman's superiors had chosen New Zealand because they recognized his nerves were shattered and he needed time to recuperate.

For all the tranquillity of life in Wellington, Norman was never to recover fully from the initial shock of his persecution. To friends and colleagues he showed an obsessive interest in reports of Washington's continuing witch-hunt. Nor was his own involvement allowed to be forgotten: New Zealand publications often carried reminders from the local Social Credit League that the Canadian envoy had been accused of being a Communist and was being "tucked away" among them.

To most New Zealanders, however, Norman was far from a pariah. His distinction as a scholar was widely recognized; on several occasions he attended meetings of the cabinet to advise on Far Eastern matters. This was an extraordinary tribute: it again demonstrates Norman's ability to inspire the confidence of foreigners, whether they were the Japanese Imperial Family, the New Zealand cabinet or, later, the Egyptian President. While his academic achievements were appreciated, while he had the advantage of the high reputation which Canada's foreign service then enjoyed, this unusual acceptance can only be explained by more personal qualities. Despite his intellectual sophistication Norman was totally guileless. His appearance and his manner were frank and open. Although he was now in his mid-forties he was still youthful in his enthusiasms; even though his lanky frame had taken on extra weight he still looked in some way like a school-boy. People trusted him instinctively.

Like Shoeki, Norman was "studious of books but more of the living world around him". He was fascinated by the Maori people and often visited their villages. Before long he could talk knowledgably to groups of farmers about the problems of sheep-grazing. As a close observer of the natural world he delighted in finding parallels and congruencies in the vast lore of history and literature which his remarkable memory could always bring to bear. He became intrigued by a famous local dolphin who was free but thoroughly tame, bouncing rubber balls and frolicking with children in the ocean. Describing these exploits in a letter he recalled — with considerable detail — references to similar tame dolphins in both Pliny the Elder and Pliny the Younger, as well as the Greek poets Anyte, Anchias and Antipater. This led him into a lengthy digression on the dolphin's place in Western mythology and made him wonder whether there were any Japanese dolphin legends.

Such a sensibility could never be entirely satisfied by the diplomatic life. In other letters Norman complained of not having enough time for his studies. While in Wellington, however, he managed to write several essays on the general problems of history and the historian's craft which were later published in Japan; he was also working on "some lesser-known figures of the late Tokugawa and early Meiji periods". This was very much in character; as the Japanese scholar Masao Maruyama later wrote, Norman had "an affection for the lesser names". According to Maruyama, it was no coincidence that Ando Shoeki and John Aubrey were among his favourite characters because "he was less interested in the politicians and the generals and the orthodox scholars who stride boldly through the main streets of history than in the heretics, the slightly cynical withdrawn satirists, the wing-players who tend to be pushed aside in the over-hasty business of teaching history." Norman suspected any doctrine which held that one man, or one group of men, could change the course of history through a single, decisive act, including revolutionary violence. He held that Clio, the Muse of History, was left unmoved by brave deeds, the marching of armies or the declamations of statesmen. Rather she was impressed by the laborious efforts of many different people who slowly and determinedly advance their civilization by safeguarding and extending its basic liberties.

This was the main theme to all his writing. During his time in New Zealand, however, Norman's books were suffering a subtle denigration in the one nation which, above all others, has constantly proclaimed its devotion to the cause of liberty. While there was nothing crude about this denigration — Norman was never placed on any formal black-list — its effects were decisive: for the best part of two decades Norman and his pioneering work were almost totally ignored by his academic peers in the United States. To the extent that they were occasionally considered, his books were dismissed as Marxist; much more often they were not only removed from curricula but also banished from bibliographies.

There was no conscious conspiracy, but by the early nineteen-fifties the great majority of American Far Eastern scholars had begun to hew the State Department line on Japan. Many served as government advisers and one even became Ambassador to Tokyo. These experts developed a view of Japanese history which conformed to the "reverse course" of Occupation policy by presenting Japan as an attractive model of triumphant progress toward the glories of an American-style society. In the midst of the Cold War, the Americans were concerned to present Japan as an alternative model to Communist China for other developing countries. This led most American scholars to concentrate on the positive aspects of Japan's emergence as a modern power, and to ignore or depreciate the enormous costs of this process, including the political oppression, the widespread poverty, the unequal economic growth, and the fact that social cohesion was maintained through preserving feudal and militaristic traditions. Since Norman had stressed these factors in his books, they also had to be ignored.

The Japanese themselves always thought differently. When Norman was about to return to Ottawa in 1950, two hundred of Japan's most distinguished scholars gave him a banquet and presented him with a book of their brush signatures. Throughout the period of his political persecution and academic neglect in the United States, Norman's books were kept in print and used as basic texts in Japanese universities. To the Japanese, Norman's books are now classics: in the late nineteen-seventies his Japanese publisher launched a complete edition of his work, including many essays and studies which have never appeared in English.

Norman's reputation as a scholar is secure — and not only in Japan. By the late nineteen-sixties younger American historians, moved by the debacle of Vietnam to question the basic tenets of American foreign policy, had begun to reconsider Norman's work. The first formal step came in 1968 at a special meeting of the Association for Asian Studies which was devoted to Norman. By 1975 his scholarly rehabilitation seemed complete with the publication of a selected edition of his writings with a lengthy and appreciative introduction by the historian John W. Dower.

Norman never lived to see this revival of his reputation, or to continue his scholarly work. The essays that he wrote in Wellington were his final contribution. This, of course, was never his intention. In his letters he spoke of his increasing concern that diplomacy was keeping him too far off his main interest: "I have felt that if a suitable opportunity were available I would decide to take the plunge into the academic sea." Since 1950 he had been in touch with the University of British Columbia about establishing a Far Eastern department; despite his general neglect by American scholars he also received teaching offers from Yale and Princeton.

On several occasions Norman seemed about to take the plunge; instead, in early 1956, he accepted the posts of

Ambassador to Egypt and Minister to the Lebanon. Norman and Irene had no children: his life was his work. He still enjoyed diplomacy, and the posting must have seemed too good to refuse. It was a turbulent period in the region: Ottawa's offer of such an important assignment was a firm indication that his career had not been permanently damaged. Pride alone must have urged acceptance; his scholarly curiosity was also aroused by the opportunity to spend some years in the Middle East. As Norman prepared for the move with renewed optimism, he had no reason to anticipate the disastrous coincidence of the Suez War and his renewed persecution by the Senate subcommittee.

There was little time for study after Norman arrived in Cairo in late August 1956. He had prepared for the assignment by devouring scores of books on Middle Eastern history. A British diplomat would say: "He's been here less than a month and he seems to have done more reading about this area than I've done in ten years." Once on the spot, however, he was thrust into the diplomatic crisis provoked by Nasser's nationalization of the Suez Canal. At their first meeting, when Norman presented his credentials, the President was clearly impressed by the ambassador's understanding of Egyptian history and prolonged the ceremony to talk at length — and very openly — about his difficulties with the United States, Britain and the Soviet Union. In his report to Ottawa, Norman was sympathetic to Nasser's anti-colonialism and impressed by his "simple and frank manner". This latter opinion was not to survive further months of often tortuous negotiations (in the following March, Norman would tell Ottawa that Nasser's behaviour was morose and turbulent), but Norman never lost his sympathy for Egyptian aspirations. In private conversation in September, he acknowledged that Nasser threatened Western interests, but argued vehemently against the use of force by Britain and France; several months after the invasion he would still be castigating the aggressors in his letters. His instinct was always to side with the underdog, and to find virtue in the struggle of any people to regain control of their own destiny after generations of foreign domination. As he told a visiting correspondent in the midst of the crisis: "You cannot dismiss men's arguments just because they are shabbily dressed, eat with their fingers and think in a manner strange to you. The Suez dispute is like a quarrel between such men and suave fellows — club members who read the same papers, went to the same schools and never speak discourteously. You have to remember the fellow in beggar's robes might be right."

When the invasion took place, Norman was stranded with Irene in Beirut, where he had gone to present his credentials as Minister to the Lebanon. With the cessation of hostilities he hastened back to Cairo, resuming work in an atmosphere of tremendous pressure which would never be entirely dissipated. Since the embassy stenographers had been evacuated to Rome, Norman and his senior colleagues had to do all their reporting by hand for several weeks. Often working from eight in the morning until after midnight he struggled to keep Ottawa informed of the subtleties of Egyptian moves. Colleagues on the receiving end of these dispatches noted how Norman always seemed able to penetrate the official rhetoric to disclose the underlying motives of the Egyptians, explaining their thoughts as well as their deeds.

Most crucially, Norman became a key figure in Pearson's plan to interpose a United Nations peacekeeping force between the belligerents. In further long interviews with Nasser, Norman had already gained the Egyptian leader's respect and trust. This was decisive since the President had long suspected Pearson of being pro-Zionist; in general he also distrusted Canada for its role in the formation of Israel and its membership in the Commonwealth. When Nasser balked at permitting UN troops to land in Egypt, Norman obtained an audience on his own initiative. Two hours later he returned to his residence in jubilation. It had taken enormous persuasion (including a digression on Canadian history to convince the President that the Queen's Own were in no way a British regiment), but Nasser had finally agreed to admit the UN contingents. A few days later the first of the blue berets set foot on Egyptian soil.

Despite this triumph, there was little easing of the pressures on the Canadian Embassy. The presence of Canadians in the UN Emergency Force raised a host of problems, both political and logistical; the Embassy was also looking after the interests of the departed Australians. Norman was still working long hours, with only an occasional game of tennis for relaxation. With its police state atmosphere, its endless dry heat and its suspicion of all foreigners, Cairo was a tense, depressing capital; among the diplomatic community everyone was on edge and tempers were often frayed. Even Norman, that most gentle and considerate of men, found himself unduly annoyed when he was pestered by beggars on the street.

For six months Norman had stretched himself to the limits of his endurance. In February 1957 he was complaining that he was "very tired and rather depressed" and that he lacked his usual pep and energy. By the end of the month he reported in another letter that his spirits and stamina had revived but those were among the last hopeful words he ever wrote. On March 12 the Senate's Internal Security subcommittee returned to the attack, again releasing testimony which named Norman as a Communist.

There was nothing new to the charges, and no apparent reason for Norman to be singled out again. While the power of the witch-hunters was now in decline, the subcommittee had been doggedly pursuing its investigations throughout the five intervening years. One of its main targets was still the State Department which the investigators persisted in regarding as a sanctuary for traitors. On this occasion their intended victim was John K. Emmerson, the counsellor at the US Embassy in Beirut. Emmerson had also worked for SCAP in Tokyo and had gone with Norman on that official visit to the prison where they had announced the release of the political detainees, including two Communist leaders. This episode had long excited the suspicions of Robert Morris, the subcommittee's counsel (in effect, its chief prosecutor), who had first raised it as part of his case against Norman in 1951. Now he returned to the subject in his interrogation of Emmerson: when Norman's name came into the testimony Morris seized the chance to tell the Senators that "we have quite a few security reports which have a great deal of information to the effect that he (Norman) is a Communist . . ." Emmerson maintained he had no reason to believe Norman had ever been a Communist but the Senators were more interested to learn that the two men were still friends and had met in Beirut during the previous October, when Norman had presented his credentials. Despite persistent questioning of Emmerson — both on March 12 and again on March 21 — Morris failed completely to establish any sinister motive for the Beirut meeting, but this did not deter him from repeatedly mentioning the security reports on Norman and recalling Karl Wittfogel's charges against him in 1951. For days on end Norman's name was back in the headlines.

Although Pearson again spoke out in his defence — and sent a strong protest to the State Department — Norman could not be consoled. While he tended to his duties — and was still sending penetrating political reports to Ottawa throughout the whole of March — he became distant and aloof, often taking long drives by himself into the countryside. To his colleagues he seemed distraught and absent-minded; to his closest friends he confided his fear that his persecution would never end. Again and again he recalled his harrowing interrogation by the Mounties in 1951; he was convinced he would now have to return to Ottawa to face a similar ordeal.

Everyone realized he was close to breaking. His doctor prescribed sedatives and an immediate vacation. At first Norman refused to leave his post; at Irene's urging he finally agreed to take a holiday in Spain, provided they stayed close to the Canadian Embassy so he could keep in touch with events. On April 3 a telegram was drafted asking Ottawa's permission for the leave: it was to be sent the next morning. That evening the Normans went with friends to see a movie. This was *Mask of Destiny* which was described at the time as a brooding Japanese classic which suggested that death holds the answer to many of life's problems. After the movie Norman seemed relaxed for the first time since the charges had been renewed; he made plans with his friends for a croquet game the following afternoon.

On the next morning Norman left his residence on foot, telling Irene and his chauffeur he was going for a walk. He went to a modern apartment building where a close friend lived, took the elevator to the top floor and stepped out on the roof. Then, after those preparations which seem very deliberate and even ritualistic, he fell backwards to his death. His ashes were flown by the RCAF to Rome, and buried in the Protestant cemetery.

When a man takes his own life, we can never be certain of his motives. In Norman's case we can cite his physical and mental exhaustion, his deep-rooted anxiety and — perhaps above all — his conviction that he would have to face yet another interrogation, that he might have to implicate old friends and colleagues, that there would be no end to his dreadful persecution. Only death could release him from his suffering.

Yet his suicide seems more than an act of weary and neurotic desperation. It was too carefully planned, too public and dramatic; it reminds us of his complex heritage. Very likely, Norman found some solace at the end in the teachings of his old master, Epicurus, with his calm approach to death and his conviction that suicide is often the only sensible way of escaping insupportable despair. Oriental philosophers also teach that the body is merely a dwelling place to be abandoned at the will of its owner. The Japanese especially have long regarded self-destruction as a release from shame, an act of honour and courage, and an ultimate proof of sincerity.

This was how Norman's suicide was regarded by many of his friends who shared a similar Japanese background. As one of his former teachers at Kobe wrote: "He had entered most fully into Japanese thinking and spirit. Bushido was as much a part of him as his Christian heritage. He chose the Japanese solution when he could not see the way ahead." These old friends saw Norman's suicide as neither cowardly nor as an admission of guilt, but as a brave gesture of defiance to his enemies. For all his life and in all his work he had been a fighter in the cause of freedom; when it appeared that he would finally be vanquished by the forces of fanaticism and tyranny, he took the ultimate step which would affirm his own integrity, while passing the burden of shame and guilt back to his adversaries.

It was too Oriental and too subtle to be appreciated in the corridors of Congress where Robert Morris posed for pho-

tographs, smirking as he held up a newspaper with the headline: Envoy Accused As Red Kills Self. But it was how Norman's death was interpreted in the country of his birth. At a
memorial service in Tokyo his Japanese friends spoke of his
profound knowledge, his embodiment of Western humanism,
his modesty and tolerance and his sympathy for the oppressed.
"He was one of the few bright stars of mankind," one of the
scholars said, while another added that "only such a person as
he could be worthy of the task of providing a bridge between
East and West." In Nagano, his boyhood friends expressed
their grief by gathering in the flooded rice fields and floating
small bamboo boats, as they had done with Norman in their
youth.

There is one more piece of evidence to be considered. In a letter to his brother Howard which was found in his desk, Norman wrote in full:

> I am overwhelmed by circumstances and have lived
> under illusions too long. I realize that Christianity is the
> only true way. Forgive me because things are not as bad
> as they appear. God knows they are terrible enough. But
> I have never betrayed my oath of secrecy. But guilt by
> association as now developed has crushed me. I have
> prayed for God's forgiveness if it is not too late.

In a second note — this time to Howard and his wife
Gwen — Norman again asserted his complete innocence. He
added: "My Christian faith, never strong enough, I fear, has
helped to sustain me in these last days."

As a student Norman had abandoned Christ for Marx;
throughout his adult life he had been a rational humanist
whose attitude toward any higher authority was, at the very
least, sceptical and agnostic. Yet on the eve of his death he
reaffirmed the earliest of his beliefs: "I realize that Christianity is the only true way."

One explanation springs to mind, although it is only
just barely possible. The two brothers were very close, and
Howard was a minister who had never lost his own Christian
faith. We have seen how Norman was always deeply consider-

ate of other people's feelings; even in his final turmoil he may
have sought to ease his brother's grief, and to give him some
consolation, by counterfeiting a last-minute reconversion.

But this is hard to accept. The words themselves —
even the urgency of the handwriting — have a painful sincerity which seems far beyond contrivance. Words and ideas
were crucial to Norman; it was never his way to simulate false
thoughts or feelings.

So we are left with the much greater — and enormously important — possibility that Norman was compelled
at the end to reassess all those beliefs on which he had based
his adult life. If so, this is not only reassessment: it amounts to
recantation.

"I . . . have lived under illusions too long." Specifically,
he had lived under the illusions which he derived from
Enlightenment humanism. There is a paradox here. As
George Grant has noted, it was the freedom-loving Enlightenment which gave birth, over two centuries, to its apparent
opposite: the homogenizing modern state with all its dreadful
tyrannies. Based on a belief in man's rationality and goodness
— and a very superficial sense of evil — these Enlightenment
illusions had created that modern spirit which sees man, not
as part of some natural order, but as the master of his own destiny. No longer subordinate to a divine law, man is free to
remake the world according to his own desires. For if man's
essence is his freedom, if there is no context of reverence and
obedience to something greater than man, then there are no
limits to the evil which men can inflict upon each other.

In his note to his brother, Norman suggests that he
came, at the end, to some such awareness. As an avatar of his
Enlightenment exemplars, he was apparently forced to acknowledge that his noble vision was incapable of countering
that modern evil of which his own persecution was a small but
significant part. He had been misguided in his invocation of
the great rationalists, since he had failed to see that their doctrines were the origin of all those modern tyrannies which he
had opposed in their name. When Norman was crushed in the
conflict between Communism and liberal-capitalism, it was as
though Thomas Jefferson or Benjamin Franklin had somehow
come to grief at the hands of Richard Nixon.

By reaffirming his Christianity, Norman was asserting that true freedom can reside only in a philosophy which contains some concept of human limitation, some adherence to a higher order, and which in turn implies the idea of God. In a quite different way, Norman reached, at the very end, a similar belief to that which had informed Bishop White's last decades. Both men started with a hearty evangelism, attuned to good works and social progress; both finished with a much more profound view of man's spiritual needs.

As an historian, Norman cherished the ambiguities in human nature. Certainly his own suicide remains ambiguous. We can regard it in terms of his Japanese heritage — as a release from shame, and an act of defiance to his enemies. Or we can see it, as I prefer, in terms of his note to his brother, as acknowledging a higher purpose which modern man so wilfully ignores. Both impulses probably played their part in the turmoil of his final, desperate resolution. Whichever one we choose to emphasize, Norman's suicide seems the noblest of all his affirmations.

Emily Carr

A street in Victoria in the early nineteen-thirties. Buster Brown and Emily Carr are walking toward each other. Buster is headed for Government House; he steps out briskly and proudly, as though on parade. With his gleaming shoes, his Savile Row suit and a freshly-cut camellia in his button-hole, he is every inch a Tory gent. Ten years older than Brown, Carr has already turned sixty; she is a large, squarely-built woman who makes few concessions to her femininity. She wears a baggy Mother Hubbard dress and an old felt hat, and pushes a rickety baby carriage which is filled with shopping bags and strange movements. Six or eight great shaggy sheep dogs are gambolling in her wake.

As Brown draws closer to this eccentric apparition, the sheep dogs bound around his legs, and a Javanese monkey in a bright red and yellow costume sits up and chatters at him from the carriage. At first nonplussed, and disturbed by the lack of decorum, Buster is quickly amused. He tips his bowler and proclaims a hearty "Good morning, Madam"; then he steers a path through the dogs and continues on his way. Chuckling to himself, he decides the poor old dear is bonkers.

Carr says nothing to him. For a moment she feels a stab of resentment, even anger. To her, this immaculate and stiff-backed personage is clearly one of those pompous Victorians who have always snubbed her, always scorned her work: the sort who belong to the Island Arts and Crafts Society and are smugly satisfied with genteel paintings of rose gardens, the more like photographs the better. "You're quite right, Woo," she tells the monkey. "He is a silly fool." Then she trundles on with gloomy resignation; back at her house, the lodgers will be clamouring for attention.

And yet . . . imagined encounters to the contrary . . . imagined reactions to the contrary . . . Brown and Carr have much in common at this time. Each is an outcast; each has a high romantic vision which their society rejects. To the modern pragmatists and technocrats, to the businessmen and bureaucrats, Brown's Tory patriotism is just as irrelevant as Carr's passionate and God-filled paintings.

Alienated from the dominant Canadian culture, both Brown and Carr are exiles. Brown is an exile *in* Victoria: the one Canadian city above all others where he can act out, with dignity and pathos, his role as patriot and Anglophile. Because she makes greater demands and has a greater goal, Carr is an exile *from* Victoria: she lives in the city but finds it hostile to her vision; this drives her every spring to that caravan in the woods which is her real home and from where she plunges ever deeper into the trees, ever deeper into her art.

Since childhood, Carr has been a rebel. She rejects the narrow conventions of a decorous society, and scorns Victoria for its ersatz English stuffiness. This is her immediate heritage, yet her quarrel is not only with Victoria but with all those aspects of contemporary Canada which stifle her sensibility. About this time she gives a talk in which she deplores "modern ways" because they break man's links to the inner world of his spirit, because they deny the possibility of a life which is rooted in faith.

So Carr turned away from the modern city, toward the ancient forests. Initially she drew inspiration from the Indians who taught her how to *see*, deeply and directly, without the "formal tightness" she had learned at art school, and without the picture-postcard prettiness which her society demanded. The Indian carvers showed her the unity of all nature, and how to catch the inner intensity of her subjects. At first she hesitated on the verge of the lush rain forests, as though fearful of their brooding power. By this time, however, she was thrusting into the trees, seeking her God among the firs and pines and cedars, striving to express her own transcendent feelings. Finally, in her last great paintings, she would dare to fuse those two qualities which modern Canada so greatly fears: spirituality and true sensuality.

Emily Carr was a Victorian. This has more to it than the place of her birth, or even the date of her birth. Just as the young Will White and the young James Brown were stirred by the imperialistic traditions of their day, so Carr was marked by many other influences with which we also associate the adjective Victorian.

It was a very Victorian home in which she was born, on 13 December 1871, in the midst of a driving blizzard. She had four older sisters; a younger brother was to follow. As she described them in her books, her parents were archetypes of their era. Her father, Richard, was stern and domineering; her mother, also Emily, was delicate and uncomplaining. Her father's religion was Presbyterian and grim; her mother's was Anglican and gentle: it was Calvinist rigidity which ruled inside the home. Great store was set on appearances, on scrubbed faces and picking up your toys, on parading to church each Sunday morning and reading the Bible each Sunday evening. Dolls were banished on the Sabbath, and never undressed in the parlour. Throughout the week there were cold baths every morning, while childish pleasures — anything joyful and spontaneous — took second place to Richard's sense of decorum, and to his own comfort and convenience. Everything had to be straight and right for Richard Carr; he liked to follow a routine of mechanical precision, and he was meticulous in the tiniest details, even in the folding of his table napkin. A full-bearded patriarch, he ruled by inspiring fear and reverence; according to Emily: "He ignored new babies until they were old enough to admire him, old enough to have wills to break."

Richard Carr embodied everything that his youngest daughter was to reject. Born in England, he had ventured widely as a young man in Europe, Central America and Mexico, before making a small fortune in California as a purveyor to the Gold Rush prospectors. After his marriage, he moved to Victoria (where he established a successful wholesale grocery business), because he wanted to live under the British flag.

Yet he was often vexed by his surroundings. When he arrived in Victoria in 1863, it was only just emerging from its origins as a Hudson Bay post. Although the blockades to keep out Indians and wild animals had been torn down, the small town still had a raffish, frontier exuberance. Even during

Emily's childhood, there were only a few streets with shops and plank sidewalks. Cows roamed freely along the muddy lanes, and the livery stables gave off warm smells of horse manure. The ramshackle saloons were boisterous with sailors and prospectors; there were always Indians camping on the beaches. At the other end of the social scale, the more dignified English settlers felt a very Victorian compulsion to impose order on this chaos; if they were going to live in an outpost, it must at least be civilized. So it became imperative to push back the frontier and deny the wilderness, to build churches and inculcate a stern religious atmosphere, to drive English carriages and read English magazines.

This compulsion was especially marked in Richard Carr. According to Emily, he always thought everything English was better than anything Canadian. When he built his home on a choice lot opposite Beacon Hill Park, he surrounded it with acres of cowslips, primroses and hawthorn hedges, turning Canadian wilderness into a neat and tidy English garden. Richard made sure that his own cows were kept within their pasture; he enclosed his property with tall, strong fences. On their walks, he forbade Emily even to look at the saloons.

In short, Richard Carr was a notable example of what Northrop Frye has called our garrison mentality. Initially this mentality erected physical barriers against all those hostile forces which lay beyond the precarious homestead. It survived in an age of towns and cities because it included not only a fear of wolves and frozen forests, of Indians and Americans, but also a terror of the soul, a terror of what is savage and passionate in ourselves. So the barriers became cultural and psychic: values were imported from the mother country, and natural impulses were rigorously controlled. To some extent, Sutherland Brown shared this outlook, but Buster hardly strikes one as repressed. With Richard Carr, on the other hand, the garrison mentality was carried to its psychological extreme: a fearful denial of all that was sentient and spontaneous.

Richard's youngest daughter refused to be constrained. The signs were there from the beginning. "This one should have been a boy," her father said, appalled by her stubbornness. She had no use for crisp frocks and clean hands; resenting the polite formality of garden parties, she preferred to play in the yard, singing to the cows and mothering the chickens. She was bored when people talked about their trips back to the Old Country, but she was excited by tales of Indian villages up the coast and of the days, still fresh in many memories, when Victoria had been a fort. Although the town was becoming tamed and stuffy, it was surrounded by an overwhelming abundance of natural beauty: open fields and rocky beaches, the mountains and the straits, and especially the deep virgin forests. Soon Emily was escaping the nagging of her older sisters and the stilted conversation of their ultra-English friends by riding her pony beyond the town and into the forests: the "deep lovely places" which would be the basis of her art.

Yet she had to escape even farther, in order to find herself. Before she could appreciate and reclaim the source of her inspiration, she had to break loose from a family and a town which were stifling her.

Her mother died in 1886; at the age of fourteen Emily was deprived of the one person who had brought love and warmth into her childhood. When her father died two years later, she was left in the care of her eldest sister. Edith Carr was in her early thirties when she took charge of the household; she treated Emily as a child and whipped her with a riding crop. By threatening to strike back, Emily finally put an end to the beatings, but she was still tormented by Edith's tongue. Her other sisters were prim and pious, and gave her little support. As Emily was to write in her old age: "Outsiders saw our life all smoothed on top by a good deal of mid-Victorian kissing and a palavar of family devotion; the hypocrisy galled me."

She also conceded that she had been the "disturbing element" in the family, and had often provoked her sisters. She may well have exaggerated Edith's tyranny, since her spirit would always demand a large amount of opposition, and since she was often inclined, in her autobiographical writings, to special pleading. Yet there is no doubt she had to break away, if only to avoid being smothered by her sisters' Victorian constraints.

Art was the chosen path. She had long been drawing pictures, including an accomplished portrait of her father. Although there was no artistic tradition in the Carr family, her parents encouraged her interest; indeed, all the daughters had special drawing lessons. This was an accepted part of a Victorian education; art was regarded as a genteel pastime for young ladies, though nothing more. With Emily, however, the pastime became a passion; it was also a means of deliverance. At the age of eighteen she told her legal guardian of her ambition. "Is this Art idea just naughtiness, a passing whim?" he asked her. "No," Emily replied, "it is very real — it has been growing for a long time."

Her guardian, a crusty Scot, was startled but sympathetic. Since there were no proper facilities in Victoria, he agreed that Emily should study at the School of Design in San Francisco. Yet her deliverance was still not complete, since Edith turned her over to English friends who had moved to San Francisco, and who had equally strict notions of propriety. Emily chafed under their nagging, and resented the necessity of paying calls on other family friends, but she found all the freedom she needed in the school. Learning to draw and paint was her only concern; she took little interest in her clothes or in any sort of social life. She remained so innocent that she could tell her landlady — with lyrical enthusiasm — about how she had strolled past romantic little houses with red lanterns over their doors, and pretty women looking out their windows. Her landlady promptly and bluntly instructed her in the facts of life: "Half an hour later I crept up to my own room at the top of the house afraid of every shadowed corner, afraid of my own tread smugged into the carpet's soft pile. Horrors hid in corners, terrors were behind doors . . . Mrs Piddington spared me nothing. Opium dens in Chinatown, drug addicts, kidnappings, murder, prostitution she poured into my burning, frightened ears, determined to terrify the greenness out of me."

Emily's prudishness was just as formidable as her innocence, and equally Victorian. Her parents had taught her that the human body was indecent, something to be hidden. She was shocked at the art school to discover that some of the classes used live models, and primly declined to participate.

Only later, in London, could she bring herself to sketch from life, finding that the model's beauty "swallowed every bit of my shyness . . . Here was nothing but loveliness."

Her closest friends were other girls, fellow students at the school. Then, as later, most of her passion went into her art. "Make her mad and she can paint," one of her teachers said, conceding that she had some promise. But no one spotted any unusual talent. During her three years in San Francisco, Carr was limited to the normal student exercises: still-life studies, portraits and working from plaster casts. Best of all, she liked outdoor sketching. This was a sign of where her genius lay; by her own account, however, all this early work was humdrum and unemotional: "As yet I had not considered what was underneath surfaces, nor had I considered the inside of myself."

By 1894, when she was twenty-two, Carr was back in Victoria. Her guardian had decided it was time for her to settle down; there was also some suggestion that her studies were a burden on the family estate. It was the first of her many home-comings; she found that nothing much had changed. Edith still treated her as a child, and the atmosphere was still sanctimonious. One of her sisters wanted to be a missionary, and they were all involved in the newly-founded YMCA; to Emily it seemed the house was always full of people praying.

Over the objections of Edith, Emily had the cow barn converted into a studio where she began giving drawing lessons to children. The income from these lessons was important, since she was now determined to go even farther afield to pursue her own studies. There were still no teachers or artists of any stature in Victoria; she had found that even San Francisco had nothing to offer in the way of galleries or exhibitions. A visiting French artist had told her that Paris or London were the only places to learn to paint; she began to save for the trip, storing her money in an old shoe which she hung from the rafters.

Although she still had much to learn in terms of technique — although she still had not looked very deeply inside herself — Carr had already found the subjects of her greatest art before she left for Europe, even if she didn't know this at the time. In 1898, a family friend took her to Ucluelet, an isolated mission on the west coast of Vancouver Island. She stayed for several weeks; it was her first prolonged experience of Indians, and she was drawn to them as Houston would be drawn to the Ojibwa and the Eskimos, and for the same reasons. Shy at first, she was soon attracted by their openness and natural dignity. They were so different from the pious Victorians; she felt she could understand them, despite the language barrier. When she met the village patriarch, "the stare of his eyes searched me right through." The verdict was favourable: as the chief told the missionaries, Carr had no fear, was not stuck up, and knew how to laugh. Soon the Indians were calling her Klee Wyck — The Laughing One.

Then there was the forest. It seemed to her immense and unfathomable, tangled and untamed, even menacing. It attracted her and repelled her at the same time. Nothing in her training had equipped her to tackle such an enormous subject; at this stage, she wasn't even sure it *could* be tackled. Hadn't the French artist told her the Canadian West was too crude and vast to paint? So she hovered at the edges of the trees, sketching Indians and boats and houses. At twenty-six, she was still not ready for the deeper quest.

In another year, Carr had saved enough money; she arrived in London in the summer of 1899. Although she was to stay in England for more than five years, she rarely felt at ease there. In particular, she was depressed by London with its dirt and noise, its fogs and foul odours, its crowds and frenzied pace. ("The clamorous racing of hot human blood confused, perhaps revolted me a little sometimes.") She was bored in museums and disappointed in art galleries; even the parks were much too crammed. Only in Kew Gardens did she find any relief, discovering a grove of British Columbian pines and cedars, rubbing the needles between her hands, and breathing in the fond, familiar scent. Acutely homesick for her western landscape, she was just as disappointed when she travelled outside the capital. Her parents had always praised the English countryside, but she found it much too small and pinched and gentle. There were grand trees in the forests, but they, too, had been tamed; she missed the turmoil of undergrowth, the throbbing colours, the sense of space.

Scornful of the snobbery of her middle-class landladies, she delighted in playing the role of rough colonial. Again saddled with introductions to family friends, she resisted their attempts to polish her. After only a few months, she knew that she would never be a London lady: "I swore to myself I would go home to Canada as Canadian as I left her."

As always she found solace in her work. At first she studied at the Westminster School of Art; later she was happier in artists' colonies at St Ives, in Cornwall, and Bushey, in Hertfordshire, where she could sketch outdoors. From her teachers, she learned to look more deeply into nature, to see the sunshine in the shadows, the movement in the foliage. But she was as stubborn as ever in following her own instincts; in St Ives she refused to paint the white boats in the glaring sunlight on the beach; she preferred the wood behind the town. It wasn't vast or deep or dark enough, but the ivy-draped trees were solemn and majestic.

By now she was a striking woman, even something of a beauty, with soft brown curls, smoky grey eyes and thick arched eyebrows which gave her an almost Oriental look. Despite her squarish build, her hands were delicate and her feet were small and graceful. Since she was nearing thirty, the older ladies who tried to keep a watch on her became determined she should marry before it was too late. If they could only smoothe her rough edges, and tame her vivacity and independence, she might even do for one of their sons. But Carr made clear she had come to study, not to find a husband; she resisted all attempts to pair her off with eligible Englishmen, and rebuffed a love-struck suitor who had pursued her all the way from Victoria. Some years earlier she had fallen in love with another man in Victoria, but he had shown little interest. Now she simply refused to be distracted from her purpose; when one of her suitors told her he could support her and her love might grow, she answered scornfully: "It is not support; it is not money or love; it's the work itself."

She was pushing herself hard, taking every class she could, often working late into the evenings, almost always feeling tired. When friends cautioned her about the hectic pace, she told them that her funds were limited, that she had to make the most of her opportunity. But the strain was too much: after returning from Bushey to London, she fainted and fell down the stairs of her rooming house. The doctors diagnosed acute anemia, and prescribed a complete rest and freedom from all worry and exertion.

For the next eighteen months, Carr was confined to a Suffolk sanitorium. This was a desperate time for her; like Herbert Norman she discovered that sans were filled with sad and hopeless people, coughing their lives away. She hated her confinement and the rigid regulations: more than anything, she missed the space and freedom of her western wilderness; more than ever, she realized how much it meant to her. She became so depressed that her doctors despaired of saving her; by her own account, all that kept her alive were the song-birds she caught in the garden, tamed, and brought inside to share her room.

Eventually the doctors prescribed a new treatment of strenuous massage and exercise: this made her well enough to leave. But she was still exhausted, and it seemed that her eagerness and ambition had been killed. At the start of her illness, she had pestered her doctors to let her get back to work; now she had lost all desire to paint. Her instinct told her that she would recover her spirit only by returning to her native roots, that to stay in England was to suffocate. Too proud to face her friends, she slipped through London straight to Liverpool, convinced that her achievement in the last five years amounted to nothing but struggle — "just struggle which doesn't show." At the age of thirty-two, she thought she was a failure.

On her way back to Victoria, Carr spent eight weeks with friends on their ranch in the British Columbia hinterland. Riding through the fields, growing stronger in the fresh, clean air, she knew her instinct had been right, that she needed "the breath and westerness that was born in me, the thing I could not find in the Old World." Then Vancouver, and the ferry to the Island: "Never had her forests looked so solemn, never her mountains so high, never her drift-laden beaches so vast. Oh, the gladness of my West again!"

Her sisters hoped that England and illness had tamed her; they were soon disillusioned. One of her sisters owned a mare; nearly everyone was shocked when Carr rode out *astride* her. No woman had ever done that before, not in Victoria. Even worse, she was smoking — although not in public, and not even in the house: Edith made her go out to the barn.

Although she was now considered a spinster, Carr disdained to join her sisters in the religious and charitable work which was deemed suitable for a woman in that condition. As her health returned, she made clear that she was still determined to be an artist. To support herself, she moved to Vancouver, attracted by an invitation to teach the Ladies' Art Club. But she found that Vancouver was as snobbish and colonial as Victoria: "The Art Club, knowing I was just back from several years of study in London, expected I would be smart and swagger a bit. When they saw an unimportant, rather shy girl they were angry and snubbed me viciously, humiliating me in every possible way." When Carr actually dared to criticize the ladies' work, they fired her.

Thus began the most durable of all the myths surrounding Emily Carr. It is a myth that Carr herself assiduously fostered in her later writings: the myth of a solitary artist oppressed by philistines who ignored or ridiculed her work. As we shall see, the legend became even more pervasive when Carr reached middle-age; for the moment it should be noted that she was never as neglected as she liked to maintain. Even before her departure for London, there were some who appreciated her skills, although they failed to predict her greatness. In 1894 her pen and ink sketches won first prize in a competition over the work of professional artists, and also gained an approving mention in *The Daily Colonist.* When she returned to Victoria in 1904, the editor of *The Week* gave her steady work as a cartoonist. After her dismissal by the Vancouver ladies in the following year, she had no trouble setting up her own studio and attracting a host of young pupils. From 1906 to 1910 she showed her paintings at most of the regular Vancouver exhibitions, again winning reviews in the newspapers which were generally favourable, if not notably enthusiastic or sophisticated.

Carr seldom acknowledged this acceptance. In her

books — as well as in talks, articles and letters — she would accuse the critics, galleries and general public of neglecting and dishonouring her work. "My pictures were hung either on the ceiling or on the floor and were jeered at, insulted," she wrote in her autobiography. "Press notices were humiliating." Since this was never more than very partial truth — since she always had at least a few fervent supporters and many more admirers — it seems she had a need to feel rejected, to be an outcast and a rebel. This went back to childhood, when she first set herself against family authority. She would always remain abnormally sensitive to the reactions of her two closest sisters — Alice and Lizzie — and any sign of resistance to her work on their part aroused all her old resentments. Both sisters were obviously out of their depth when they looked at her paintings, and usually kept silent. But Carr invariably interpreted their silence as condemnation. On a two-month visit to Emily in London, Alice had never even asked about her work — "It was then that I made myself into an envelope into which I could thrust my work deep, lick the flap, seal it from everybody." To the end of her life, Carr would be hurt by her sisters' lack of understanding. This touched her more deeply than anything the critics would ever write; it seems to have nurtured her stubborn belief that nearly everyone was set against her.

    If Carr's sense of rejection was largely self-imposed, it was also necessary for her growth as an artist. On this level, the myth becomes convincing. Although her work always gained some acceptance, the praise was often patronizing and unperceptive: in her journal, Carr complained about "those beastly empty write-ups, varnishing the 'you' and ignoring (or worse) the thing you've been struggling for." On one occasion she was visited in her studio by three artists who had been hostile to her work, and to all modern art, but who now seemed genuinely appreciative of her paintings. Instinctively, Carr was suspicious. "Oh, Emily, Emily," she wrote, "be very careful. Strive earnestly toward the real. Let nothing these or any say satisfy you or puff you. It is a trust. Seek earnestly, reverently." In short, Carr sensed that bland acceptance would be more deadly than vigorous hostility, since it could make her satisfied with her second-best, and turn her away from the deeper quest. So she resisted the praise of the half-informed, the friendship of the dimly sentient, knowing their embrace could prove fatal to her growth. If she needed to feel rejected, that at least guaranteed she would not be suffocated.

And so she turned increasingly to the wilderness. Her stay at Ucluelet in 1898 had stirred her interest in the Indians and the forests; soon she was travelling every summer to Indian villages in the remote northwest of the province, to the Queen Charlotte Islands, the Skeena River and beyond. These trips were hard and dangerous. With her sheep dog as companion, Carr travelled by canoe, gas-boat and stage wagon; she carried her own food and bedding; she slept in missions, schools, lighthouses, Indian cabins and tents; she braved treacherous tides and sudden storms.

Carr was always explicit about her debt to the Indians. "Indian Art broadened my seeing, loosened the formal tightness I had learned in England's schools. Its bigness and stark reality baffled my white man's understanding." Like Bishop White, she found in an alien art a vision which drew out her own deepest feelings. Sketching the giant Indian totems, she came to see how their carvers had caught the inner intensity of their subjects, "the hidden thing which is felt rather than seen." When white Canadians portrayed the beaver as their national emblem, they belittled him, giving him only his surface representation. When the Indians carved him, they emphasized his huge front teeth, his strong hands and cross-hatched tail; they showed his energy and courage, the part of him that would still be beaver even if he were skinned.

It was a hard lesson to learn. Carr's Indian sketches from this period — her drawings and watercolours of native villages and totem poles — were freshly observed and technically competent. As she noted, she had learned more in England than she realized at the time. But they lacked any semblance of her later power and emotion. For she was still on the surface of things: "The new West called me, but my Old World heredity, the flavour of my upbringing, pulled me back. I had been schooled to see outsides only, not struggle to pierce."

Yet she decided, once more, to turn to the Old World for help. By now she knew that her western landscape — the totems and the forests — were the only subject for her art. She also knew that the Indian vision — direct and powerful — was what she had to emulate. But *how* to do it, that was the real problem. Somehow she had to find a broader, stronger technique. There was no one in Victoria or San Francisco who could help her; even in London, artists were still too narrow and conservative. But she had heard about a "new art" in Paris. It claimed bigger, broader seeing; her instinct told her this might be the way.

Travelling with her sister Alice, Carr arrived in Paris in the summer of 1910. At the age of thirty-eight, she again became a student, enrolling at the Académie Colarossi. This was the leading school for the new, post-Impressionist art: it was what Carr had wanted, but she found it hard going. She was the only woman in her class, and she understood little French; when the teachers stopped in front of her easel, chattering and waving their arms, she had little idea whether they were praising her work or condemning it. The classrooms were hot, stuffy and crowded; much of the time she felt faint and weak. Then a serious attack of measles kept her in hospital for three months; as in London, doctors told her she must keep out of big cities or die.

With Alice in tow, Carr went to Sweden, where she took the hot salt-baths. At this point, it might seem that her experience in England was repeating itself, that she would have to return to Canada with nothing to show for her time abroad but illness and frustration. But she was much less dispirited than she had been in the English san, for she was now much more certain of the direction her art should take. Impressionists such as Monet, Degas and Renoir were still alive and working in Paris. Carr had seen their paintings and those of their disciples. With its bold use of light and colour, and its clean, simplified forms, this new art spoke to her directly. She sensed there were techniques here that she could use, and a way of seeing that could open up her western wilderness.

After recovering her strength in the clean Swedish air, Carr returned to France in the spring of 1911. Leaving Alice in Paris, she went to Britanny to study under the English painter Henry Gibb, a post-Impressionist whose landscapes appealed to her as "luscious, brilliant and clean". Now she was in her outdoor element, tramping the countryside, making friends among the farmers, and sketching in the towns and fishing villages. Impressed with her progress, Gibb told her she would be among the foremost painters — women painters, he quickly added — of her day. But he was troubled by her intense determination: "You work too hard! Always at it. Easy! Easy!"

But she was happier and healthier now, and there was no danger of a relapse. Her instinct had been right: the new way of seeing was what she needed. Her watercolours from Brittany — both landscapes and interior scenes — were more vigorous and sensuous than anything she had done before; she was now less concerned with documentary representation, and more involved with strong patterns of form and colour. At last she was getting below the surface of her subjects.

Gibb was not alone in admiring her work. Two of her paintings were hung in the 1911 Salon d'Automne in Paris — the most important annual *avant-garde* exhibition — along with the work of such modernists as Bonnard, Léger, Gris, Vlaminck and Duchamp. This was clear recognition of her potential, an indication she could aspire to be an artist of international stature. In her autobiography, Carr mentions it only in passing. It seems she gave scant thought to remaining in Europe, among critics and fellow artists who were her peers, and who could have helped her to make even greater progress. Money may have been a problem, since her share of her father's estate was dwindling, but there are few signs that she was even tempted to remain. When she told Gibb that her far West had no artists, no exhibitions and no art talk, he said impatiently that her silent Indians could teach her more than all the chatter in cafés. This was also her own instinct. Solitary by temperament, more than somewhat puritanical, and in no way an intellectual, she felt little attraction to the expatriate life, especially in such tumultuous cities as Paris or London. Europe could teach her technique, but it could never satisfy her hunger for the wilderness. Years later, in Victoria, a friend would tell her it was a shame that she was stuck, unnoticed and unknown, in such a remote corner of the world. "It's exactly where I want to be," she told him. "This is my country. What I want to express is *here* and I love it."

Returning to Vancouver in late 1911, Carr opened a studio and gave exhibitions of her latest paintings. It was the first time that British Columbia had seen such modern work; by Carr's own account, all it received was "insult and scorn". Some people laughed openly at the paintings, she later complained, while even her friends talked idly and kept their eyes averted from the walls.

Again this was only partial truth. There may well have been people who scoffed at her work, but the press notices were in no way scornful. While one critic was taken aback by Carr's new techniques, and complained of her "blinding" colours, most of the reviews were favourable. But even the best notices were somewhat patronizing: to Carr, this must have been more disturbing than outright attack. By converting such half-hearted appreciation into humiliating rejection, she again showed her reluctance to be accepted on any terms other than the most demanding.

There was another reason for Carr's hostility to the local arbiters of taste. She found them ultra-conservative, and more English than the English themselves. While they might acknowledge her work with faint praise, they much preferred the genteel tradition of English landscape painting. They were afraid of art that was passionate, that probed beneath the surface, that made large statements. In short, they exemplified the garrison mentality — her father's mentality. They stood for everything that had tried to cramp and stifle her, from childhood on. When Alice and Lizzie told her she must abandon her "new way of seeing" if she wanted to survive as an artist, it only increased her feeling of rejection, and bolstered her determination to persist.

So she soon turned her back on Vancouver. In the summer of 1912 she made more harrowing journeys up the coast, to the Queen Charlotte Islands and remote Indian villages on the Skeena and Naas Rivers. Again she was rejecting a decorous city life for the dangers and hardships of the wilderness; again she was drawn by the power and mystery of the forests. Since many of the Indian villages and totem poles were soon to disappear, her paintings from this summer were important anthropological records. More crucially, they employed the techniques she had learned in France, especially bold colours and simple, rhythmic forms, to achieve a new strength and authority. But there was still something lacking in these paintings, as though she was seeing her country through the eyes of the Impressionists, without a distinctive vision of her own. To achieve the intensity of her later work, she would finally have to explore "the inside of myself."

There now began the strangest and most perplexing period of Emily Carr's life. The main facts are well-known: in 1913 the Carr sisters were forced by rising taxes to subdivide their father's property, and to sell off most of it. Returning to Victoria, Carr borrowed money to build a two-storey house on one of the lots. The house had four apartments: Carr turned one of them into a studio where she could live and paint, and planned to support herself by renting the other three suites. She had been told it would be a comfortable living, but with the outbreak of the First World War, rents slumped and prices rose. Unable to afford help, and always pressed to meet her mortgage payments, she gave up her studio, moved into the basement, and spent most of her time working as landlady, repairman, gardener and janitor. To augment her income, she hooked rugs and fired pottery in a home-made kiln, and also began breeding and selling English bobtailed sheep dogs.

    This arduous regimen began in 1913 when Carr was forty-one; it was to continue without change until she was fifty-six, and she would not finally cease to be a landlady until she was sixty-four. During these middle years of her life, Carr could have been expected to reach the peak of her artistic powers; instead, she wrote: "I never painted now — had neither time nor wanting. For about fifteen years I did not paint." In her book *The House of All Sorts* — a collection of stories about her life as a landlady — she portrayed herself as the constant victim of boorish and selfish tenants, adding that she was always being snubbed and cheated, insulted and even physically attacked. She felt she had struck bottom when she had to turn the upper floor of her home into a Ladies' Boarding House, filling it with demanding and quarrelsome women. "Tenants tore me to shreds," she wrote, while bemoaning the lack of privacy and solitude, the lack of any time to paint. Her only solace was her dogs, on whom she lavished most of her affection.

Other accounts make clear that Carr, as usual, brought much of her trouble on herself. No longer "The Laughing One", she was now lonely, embattled and increasingly vindictive. She had the worst possible temperament for a landlady, being much too impatient and intolerant. Suspicious and quick-tempered, she reciprocated every slight, whether real or imagined. Once she turned a pail over the head of a woman who refused to pay her rent; she drenched another lodger with a garden hose. By her own admission, "I know I hurt my tenants sometimes — I wanted to; they hurt me!" As a child, she had been a formidable adversary within the family; now she turned her wrath on anyone who aroused her displeasure, and not only her tenants. When her water supply broke down one day, she phoned the Mayor. "This is Miss Emily Carr speaking. You are a great fool. The Town Council are all fools. The City Hall is packed with fools!" Then she hung up, without even mentioning the water, in the middle of the Mayor's spluttering reply.

This was a temperament that needed to create its own opposition. As Carr embellished the myth in later years, it was public scorn, as much as economic necessity, which forced her to abandon her painting and become a landlady. "The people of Victoria strongly disapproved of my painting because I had gone from the old conventional way," she claimed. Nobody bought her pictures, she added, and nobody sent her any pupils. In 1916, she was visited by Marius Barbeau, a federal government anthropologist who had also travelled among the Indians of northern British Columbia, hearing stories of the strange woman artist who had come to their villages. Obsessed by her local rejection, Carr told Barbeau she had given up any hope of gaining success.

Again, however, this rejection was far from absolute. There were always a few people who bought her work, and tried to encourage her to keep on painting. Even the Island Arts and Crafts Society — the object of her deepest scorn —

exhibited some of her pictures in the early nineteen-twenties. Nor is it true that she abandoned her art entirely for fifteen years: there are at least two dated canvases from this time.

This is not to deny the hard reality of Carr's position. There is no doubt she had been unlucky in setting up her apartment house on the eve of the war, and that her circumstances then made it difficult for her to find the time and energy to paint. But Carr seems to have abandoned her art for psychological as well as economic reasons. As she wrote in her autobiography, it wasn't only that she lacked the time: she didn't *want* to paint. With their bland indifference, Vancouver and Victoria had sapped her confidence; it seemed better not to paint at all than to keep on floundering to earn the lukewarm praise of the half-informed. She needed a community which understood and honoured her compulsions: a community of fellow artists who could give her practical help and sensitive encouragement. At the outset of middle age, she despaired of ever gaining such support.

Isolated in Victoria, Carr had no idea that there were artists in eastern Canada who were doing comparable work and fighting similar battles. Nor had she any reason to suppose that easterners might be interested in her vision of the West. So she was surprised — and initially unimpressed — when she received a phone call in 1927 from Eric Brown, director of the National Art Gallery in Ottawa: Carr was so out of touch with the art world, she didn't even know that Canada *had* a National Gallery. When Brown, who was visiting Victoria, asked to see her work, she told him tartly she was no longer an artist, and most of her paintings were in storage. Somewhat grudgingly, she allowed that he could come to see the few canvases that were hanging on her walls.

Brown had been hearing about Carr for several years from Marius Barbeau and H. Mortimer Lamb, a Vancouver mining engineer and a connoisseur of modern art. At first Brown had shown little interest; finally he decided to see Carr, and her work, for himself. While Carr looked on — "indifferently apart" — Brown studied the paintings on her walls. To Carr's surprise, he asked her to send several of her canvases, as well as pottery and rugs, for an exhibition of West Coast art, native and modern, to be held at the National Gallery in

November. The Gallery would pay the shipping costs; there would also be a railway pass so Carr could travel East herself. Her sisters were even more astonished, but also impressed: they offered to keep an eye on the lodgers in her absence.

On the morning of 10 November 1927, Carr boarded the train in Vancouver: nothing would ever be the same for her again. Twenty-six of her paintings were shown in the Ottawa exhibition, which then moved to Montreal and Toronto. The show was only a partial success, but Carr's own work was highly praised. This was a lot different from the polite tolerance of the Island Arts and Crafts Society; for the first time, Carr had national — and enthusiastic — recognition.

She had also found what she needed most of all: a community of fellow artists whose aspirations matched her own. Until Brown's visit, she had never even heard of the Group of Seven, although one of its members, F. H. Varley, was teaching in Vancouver. Now, in Toronto, she found their work a revelation. After visiting Arthur Lismer, A. Y. Jackson and Lawren Harris in their studios, Carr wrote in her journal: "Oh, God, what have I seen? Where have I been? Something has spoken to the very soul of me, wonderful, mighty, not of this world . . . Oh, these men, this Group of Seven, what have they created? — a world stripped of earthiness, shorn of fretting details, purged, purified; a naked soul, pure and unashamed; lovely spaces filled with wonderful serenity."

Soon she realized that the Group of Seven had been fighting *her* battle: contending against critics and collectors who held that pine trees were unpaintable, that the whole Canadian wilderness was too raw and ugly to be rendered into art, and that Canadian painters should express themselves through the softer, mistier tradition of English landscape painting. Instead they were painting the Canadian lakes and forests with majesty and power, finding an austere beauty in the vast spaces of the North. Exploding out of the garrison mentality, they were daring to celebrate a God-filled wilderness.

This was what Carr had tried to do herself, but without the same success, without the same intensity. She had wanted to see beneath the surface, to express the essential spirit of her subjects. That was the way of the Indian carvers; it was also part of the new art in Paris. Carr had come to see her artistic ambition in religious terms: as she acknowledged in her journal, it was God whom she had longed for, and quested in the forests, and failed to find. Now she saw God in the paintings of the Group. It was the work of Harris that excited her the most, especially his tranquil spaces filled with light and serenity. They had a holiness about them; they drew her spirit into them.

To Carr, the Group of Seven were giants — "people who really count and are shaping a nation." She accepted invitations to their homes and studios with diffidence, even trepidation; but some of them had already seen the exhibition in Ottawa — to her great excitement, she found she was treated as an equal. They said she had caught the spirit of the West and its people more than any other artist who had been there. Harris even asked her to criticize his paintings: "You are one of us," he told her.

Yet she felt rebuked by their achievements, and their dedication. These men were big and courageous, and not deterred by scornful criticism. They were workers; she was a quitter. While in Toronto, Carr turned fifty-six; never had she felt so acutely the burden of her wasted years. But there were still a few years left, she told herself, and now she had proof — in the work of Harris, Lismer and the others — that her own ambition had not been futile. "I'm way behind them in draw-ing and in composition and rhythm and planes," she wrote, "but I know inside me what they're after and I feel that per-haps, given a chance, I could get it too."

It was as though a great dam inside her had been bro-ken. Within days of her return to Victoria, Carr was back at work. It was now clear that lack of confidence, as much as economic hardship, had kept her from her painting. Her re-cognition in the East brought no immediate financial benefit; she would have to labour as a landlady for another nine years — scrubbing floors, stoking the furnace, chopping wood and squabbling with her tenants. She bemoaned the way her time and energies were drained, but she could now acknowledge that she often used her household duties as an excuse to avoid the greater challenge of her art. As she wrote in her journal, "It's much easier to dig the garden, clean the basement, paint stairs, than paint to express subtle interior things. I let myself follow the path of least resistance and shirk delving down to the bottom of my soul."

If she needed any further incentive, it was soon to come. When the West Coast exhibition reached Toronto, Harris wrote to tell her that her paintings were impressive, and full of creative life. This was the start of a noble correspondence in which Harris seized every opportunity to encourage her to harder, deeper work. Along with occasional visits from other Eastern artists, it helped sustain her regained confidence. Although she would still complain about her isolation, and about the insensitivity of her fellow Victorians, her link to the artists in Toronto was a guarantee that her work would always find perceptive critics, that she was no longer alone.

In the summer of 1928, Carr made her last great trip up the coast, again reaching the Queen Charlotte Islands and the Naas and Skeena Rivers. This was the most harrowing of all her expeditions. Travelling by fishing boat, she was almost drowned in a torrential storm. At the age of fifty-seven, she was again sleeping in abandoned houses or Indian grave huts, and being tormented by hordes of mosquitoes. But she kept pressing on, for she had heard there were fabulous totem poles in the remote village of Kitwancool. Mounties and other whites warned her that the villagers were hostile and violent, that they used axes to chase out missionaries and other intruders, that it would be folly for a mere woman to tempt their anger. But Carr rode into Kitwancool on the back of a lumber wagon driven by the Chief's son. (She later discovered he was coming straight from jail.) At first the villagers were cold and suspicious, but Carr won them over when she praised the power of their totem poles, and lamented with the elders about the way the art of carving was dying out among the younger Indians. She said she wanted to make pictures of the totem poles so that their young people — and white people — could see how fine they used to be. This convinced the elders; by the end of her visit, Carr was sleeping in the Chief's house and playing with his children. For several days she sketched the totem poles with fierce determination.

From these sketches, Carr produced her most powerful Indian paintings. These were notably different from anything she had done before: her style had become bolder and she was no longer using atmospheric colour in the manner of the French Impressionists. She had clearly absorbed a great deal from the Group of Seven, especially Harris, for she was concentrating on massive and sculptural forms; but the solemn, brooding vision was her own. Capturing the reverence — and the fear — which the natural world had always aroused in the Indian carvers, she showed their totem poles as part of the forest around them, growing right out of the trees, taking on the same forms; as sharing the same mysteries, evoking the same spirits. Dark and ominous, her forest had become engulfing, even menacing. Yet it was starting to draw her in.

What had happened? How can we explain this new authority and passion, suddenly erupting after all the long years of dreary toil and little painting? Carr's journals offer few explicit clues. But it may well have been that she found her new strength and inner vitality, not despite the barren years, but *because* of them. All the scorn and insults — real or imagined — which fed her sense of rejection, all the loneliness and demeaning labour . . . these would have broken anyone of lesser spirit. If she had been less of a rebel, less stubborn and solitary, she would have been distracted from her quest. In that case, she might well have settled for the half-hearted praise of the local arbiters, and become the grand old lady of the Island Arts and Crafts Society. Instead, her hardships drove Carr deeper into herself, in search of a faith that could triumph over all her tribulations. As she wrote a few years later, she was seeking "that vital understanding thing, which must grow and develop and unfold in you yourself before it can come out. That something must be realized and experienced in your own soul before it can possibly be expressed by you." When Carr returned to the forests, she could at last find that "something" in the trees, because she had already sensed it in herself.

The canvases from her 1928 expedition were virtually the last of Carr's Indian paintings. She had seen how the white man and his modern ways were encroaching on the villages, and sapping the confidence of the carvers in their own traditions. The Indians were selling most of their best poles to the museums; since it was no longer based on faith, the new carving was trivial and meaningless. When Harris urged her to abandon the Indian themes, Carr was more than ready to comply. For she had already gone beyond the totem poles, to the verge of the forest itself. Now she was ready to explore that deeper wilderness.

Leaving her tenants to fend for themselves, Carr began the sketching expeditions that would produce her greatest paintings. Several rain forests were fairly accessible from Victoria; she solved the problem of living and working in them with her usual ingenuity. In 1933 she bought an old caravan, and would hire a truck to haul it to places where she could sketch in solitude, often for weeks at a time. It had a bed, a stove and accommodation for her "creatures": the dogs, the birds, the monkey and the white rat who were always with her in the woods, who made her feel less lonely and who helped her, she said, to bridge the gap between herself and the trees, between the human and the natural worlds.

Let us see her now, on the brink of her noblest work, as others saw her. For this, too, became part of the myth. Her caravan was regarded as one of her greatest eccentricities. Proper Victorians were astonished at the idea of a sixty-year-old woman living in a trailer in the woods; with all her animals, and a mentally-retarded boy whom she befriended and who hopped around on the grass, she was once mistaken for a travelling circus. Yet what seemed eccentricity was really self-sufficiency; throughout her life, this most visionary artist was resolutely practical. As a landlady, she repaired her own plumbing and kitchen appliances, as well as doing all the carpentry around the house. During her artistically barren years, she bred and raised hundreds of bobtails and Belgian griffons; often she worked through the night, moulding her pottery and firing it in her home-made kiln. She made her own easels, and sized and stretched her canvases; always short of space, she hung chairs from the ceiling of her studio, each with its own pulley, ready to be swung down if needed for a visitor. To save money, she dressed herself — and her monkey — in clothing that she made from scraps, often appearing in an old army blanket, with a hole cut from the centre for her head, and a length of rope around the waist.

On her sketching trips, Carr would rise at dawn, haul water, chop wood, start a fire and feed herself and her animals. Then, with the animals in tow, she would carry her stool and easel into the woods to begin her day's work. By now she was a squat, dumpy figure who overflowed her stool (and chided herself in her journal about her weight); while her hands were still delicate, her forearms were thick and muscular. Seen like this, with her paint-smeared blanket-dress and her coarse elastic hairnet — not to mention her itinerant menagerie — she was as apparently bohemian as she was apparently eccentric.

Here, again, the myth is over-simplified. For Carr was very much a lady — a Victorian lady — and a profound conservative. Just as she lamented the passing of the old Indian world, with its faith in the power of the totem, so she felt that modern ways were too hectic and distracting; they had broken man's concentration on his inner resources, his spirituality. Although she bought a radio, she found it hateful: "a beastly, mechanized strident thing, all the life whipped out and the cruel hardness of the machine and the new, hard, modern people whipped in." While she had always scorned the affected Englishness of her family and their pompous friends, she was a fervent monarchist who grieved throughout the Abdication crisis ("I cried right from the deep of me"), rejoiced over George VI ("I honour him tremendously"), taught one of her parrots to sing God Save the King, and was flattered when Lady Tweedsmuir, the wife of the Governor-General, came to call, and bought a sketch.

Her prudishness was still formidable. She was disgusted with the amount of sex in D. H. Lawrence and other modern novelists, and repelled by the sight of women in clinging, bare-backed evening dresses; she also pursued a running feud with a neighbour she called "The Nudist" — because he sometimes appeared without a shirt. When other women visited her caravan, she made sure they never saw her bathing. When a man claimed to find erotic symbols in her paintings, she quickly showed him the door.

Yet to call her a puritan is no more accurate than to label her a bohemian or an eccentric. She felt that sex was natural, and that man should be simple and decent about it, like the animals. "Things happen naturally and just *are*," she wrote, "but we — ugh! — we've fouled it all . . . dirty books, filthy cinemas, muck everywhere." When two of her dogs mated, she noted their contentment, and added: "Health and satisfaction are the order of the day."

To Carr the goal was always expression, rather than repression, and what she wanted to convey was intensely spiritual. Although her later paintings were filled with gigantic womb-like and phallic forms, these were not consciously erotic, but the instinctive expression of a divine and fructifying force. She came to see herself as a channel for these transcendent feelings; as she wrote in her journal: "Your job is to keep that channel clear and clean and pure so that which passes through it may be unobstructed, unsullied, undiluted and thus show forth its purity and intention."

She had no doubt about the intention: "It is God in His woods' tabernacle I long to express." She was always telling herself in her journal to work harder and dig deeper, but this meant much more to her than mere technique. What she sought was in herself, as well as in the forest: her deepest, purest, most spiritual response. A painting, she wrote, was more than light and shade, a show of colour or a magnificence of form — "It is a glimpse of God interpreted by the soul."

Going deeper into the woods, she was also going deeper into herself. Sitting on her stool, she would never rush into her sketches; instead she would contemplate the trees, often puffing on one of the home-made cigarettes which she carried in an old tin box, sometimes scribbling her ideas in a notebook. She found it helped to write things down, to describe her central idea: the main feeling that the scene evoked in her. Form and colour and design were important, but secondary: what counted was the intensity of feeling. When she finally began to sketch, she was often so joyful that she would sing to her painting as she worked, usually her favourite canticle: "O, all ye works of the Lord, bless ye the Lord. Praise Him and magnify Him forever."

Her religious feelings were intuitive. With his vitality and his sense of communion with nature, Walt Whitman was her favourite author; she took his *Leaves of Grass* on all her sketching trips. Yet her religious passion is hardly to be defined in terms of Whitman, who seems a shallower artist. Whitman appealed to Carr because of his direct response to the natural world; never a heavy reader, she felt no need for any intellectual framework. Although she dutifully tried to follow Harris and some of the other eastern artists into the realm of theosophy, she finally had to tell them she found it much too cold and remote (and was once tempted to hurl a volume by Madame Blavatsky against the wall). Nor did she require a sectarian faith. "I want Christ's teaching and living," she wrote, "not church dogma and doctrine." Although she occasionally attended Anglican services, she was rarely at ease inside a church. Once she rushed late to a service, only to realize in the midst of the sermon that she was wearing her most bedraggled coat — covered with whitewash and paint, full of holes and with the lining hanging out. So she laughed out loud, and caught the stern eye of the preacher, who clearly thought that she was mocking him.

Carr found that God became static and stuffy when squeezed into a building: "Only out in the open was there room for Him. He was like a great breathing among the trees." Like the great mystics, she felt herself to be part of a divinely-ordered universe. "See God in it all," she told herself, "enter into the life of the trees . . . the God in you responding to the God in them." Perhaps the best word to describe her religious passion is the old theological term *tremendum:* a holy otherness, inspiring awe and worship.

One night about this time she had a dream of greenery. She saw a wooded hillside, an ordinary slope without any particular pattern or design to catch an artist's eye. "But, in my dream that hillside suddenly lived — weighted with sap, burning green in every leaf, every scrap of it vital!" Thrusting and swirling with life, her paintings were now filled with a similar power; if her forests were still solemn and brooding, they were beginning to seem less fearful. Cathedral-like, her trees arched toward the sky, as though striving to transcend their roots; in many of the paintings, shafts of sunlight began to dispel the darkness.

By the early nineteen-thirties, Carr's paintings were gaining greater acceptance in her own community. She was a regular contributor to local exhibitions, one of her canvases was purchased for the provincial Parliament Buildings, and the Victoria Women's Club sent another painting to an international exhibition in Amsterdam. Carr also held her own shows in her studio; on one occasion more than two hundred people came to see her work over a period of six days, and Carr conceded in her journal that most were keenly appreciative, especially the younger ones.

But she was still suspicious of any praise. She hated all newspaper reviews — even favourable ones — and she suspected that many people were only taking notice of her work because it had been praised in the East, not because they really liked it. Although she made occasional trips to Toronto, and often sent paintings to eastern exhibitions, she began to find the critiques and encouragement of the Group of Seven much less crucial. Even in 1927, amid the excitement of her first encounter of the Group, she had felt they had little to teach her about painting the West, which would always be her special subject. In 1934, she decided she had become the best judge of her work, and her most reliable guide to its future direction: "Now I take my own soul as critic." Within another year, she would write with sad resignation that even her close links to Harris had been dissipated. "So be it! One *must* learn that one's own two feet are made to stand on and that one cannot use others as props and crutches. How extraordinarily alone everyone is!"

Although she took pride in her independence, she also despaired at her loneliness. Time and time again in her journal, she would lament her lack of an understanding companion, a kindred spirit. There was no one from her own generation; all her childhood friends were enmeshed with grandchildren and bridge clubs; besides, she added, none of them liked her work. She felt closer to the younger generation, but she recognized the limitations on such friendships: "Twenty can't be expected to tolerate sixty in all things, and sixty gets bored stiff with twenty's eternal love affairs."

As always, she was closest to her sisters. But these were tangled and tormenting bonds, based on blood rather than spiritual affinity. Grudging praise from Alice or Lizzie meant more to Carr than the plaudits of any critic, but she realized they had never appreciated the deepest well-springs of her work: "Neither of them understand the sweat and thought and heartaches that go into painting a picture or writing a story. They want just some surface, sentimental representation." Carr still chafed at the way her sisters carped at her; even in her sixties she felt they treated her as a child.

Often she recalled the loves of her youth. "I have loved three souls passionately," she wrote in her journal. "I have known friendship, jealousy and dreadful hurt." To one of her younger friends, she confided the story of her greatest love, who was lost in the First World War. He had wanted to marry her before he went, but she had been afraid that a wife at home would be too much of a worry for him. Another man had loved her desperately for fifteen years, before she had deliberately killed his love in self-defence. This haunted her; she wondered whether she had also killed something in herself. Pondering the forest and its "inner burstings of growth", she felt she might grasp it better if she had felt the pangs of motherhood in her own body: "Until people have been fathers or mothers they can hardly understand the fullness of life."

Carr's loneliness was real and painful; her descriptions of it go far beyond the mere sentimentality which often mars her writing. But she sensed that marriage would have bored and deadened her; most likely it would also have strangled her art. In old age she recalled her persistent suitor: "He thought I made a great mistake in not marrying him. He ought to be glad I did not; he'd have found me a bitter mouthful and very indigestible, and he would have bored me till my spirit died." At such times Carr recognized that her loneliness was just as necessary as it was self-imposed and that her animals were, in fact, her ideal companions since they were undemanding in their affections and generous with their love, even in her most hateful moods. "B-a-a-a, old sheep, bleating for fellows," she chided herself. "Don't you know better by now?"

Eventually she could even acknowledge that her sense

of artistic rejection was also partly of her own creating. "I have had lots of recognition," she wrote in 1936. "Way over West it has come to me and I have not properly appreciated it. Why? It did not seem to mean much to me. I was wasteful of it, did not follow it up . . . I would not kowtow. I did not push. Praise embarrassed me so that I wanted to hide. You've got to meet success half-way. I wanted it to come all the way, so we never shook hands."

Despite the growing recognition of her work throughout the nineteen-thirties, Carr's life was still onerous. There was little money for art during the Depression, and she made few substantial sales. When bills had to be paid, she sold paintings to her friends for fifteen or twenty dollars. Her financial burdens were somewhat eased in 1936, when she traded her apartment house for a smaller bungalow. She rented the bungalow and moved into a cottage with her animals and her canvases; at sixty-four she was no longer a landlady.

Carr's joy at her new freedom was short-lived. All the years of struggle had begun to tell; in 1937 she suffered the first of several heart attacks. To her despair, her doctors told her she would have to live more quietly; they ruled out any long trips to the forests. There were two consolations: the doctors said that she could still paint, as long as she didn't overtire herself; they also had no objection to her writing.

Carr had been drawn to writing through her practice of making notes before she started sketching; for many years she had also kept her intermittent journal. In 1926 she enrolled in a correspondence course for aspiring authors; later she attended night classes in Victoria: a stolid, grandmotherly figure among her much younger fellow students. For several years she had been working on short stories based on her childhood and her travels among the Indians. These were sent to publishers, who sent them back, or else lost them. Now, with the help of friends, she began to polish and revise them.

This time her success was almost instantaneous. Her friends had some of her stories read on the CBC; then her book of Indian tales, *Klee Wyck,* was published in 1941, gaining critical acclaim and a Governor-General's Award. It was followed in 1942 by *The Book of Small,* based on her childhood, and in 1944 by *The House of All Sorts,* an account of her travails as a landlady. Her autobiography, *Growing Pains,* and her journals, *Hundreds and Thousands,* were published after her death. All the books sold well, and each has remained in print.

Carr had the same approach to writing as to painting: "I tried to be plain, straight, simple and Indian . . . I put my whole soul into them and tried to avoid sentimentality. I went down deep into myself and dug up." Her style was direct and unadorned, but its simplicity was based on discipline and hard work; she spent a great deal of time "peeling" every sentence, stripping away the ambiguous and superfluous words. Carr used words as she used her brush — dramatically. As in her painting, she was always striving for the central idea, for a clean, strong impact.

Yet her books are much lesser achievements than her paintings. Despite her proclaimed intentions, Carr often failed to avoid sentimentality, and rarely dug beneath the surface. She was too often coy, and inclined to self-pity, especially in her childhood stories and her autobiography. Above all she was simplistic in describing events which must have been loaded with deep feeling and complex emotions; very little of this emerged in the telling.

Only in her journals did Carr write with the same passion which she brought to her painting. *Hundreds and Thousands* is a powerful record of her inner turmoil, her loneliness and religious exaltation. Although she always intended that her journals should be published, she wrote in them without artifice or inhibition. Raw, and sometimes contradictory, they are the eloquent outpourings of a tormented, hungry soul.

Her soul hungered to the end. Superficially she might have seemed a contented old lady. During her last years, she took unqualified delight in her new fame as an author. At seventy, Carr no longer felt a need for rejection; she noted with pleasure how her fellow Victorians were entranced with *Klee Wyck* and *The Book of Small* even before the favourable reviews from the East; she cheerfully attended parties and receptions in her honour. She was also gratified when her paintings began to fetch good prices; finally she was free from financial worries.

Yet she was far from resigned to her infirmities, or to

her approaching death. "I am always watching for fear of getting feeble and *passé* in my work," she wrote. "I don't want to trickle out. I want to pour till the pail is empty, the last bit going in a gush, not in drops."

This was the essential Carr, and this, in fact, was how it happened. Despite the warnings of her doctors, she refused to stop painting, and prevailed on friends to drive her to the nearest forests. She knew she still had more to say; when galleries and exhibitions clamoured for her work, she insisted on sending them new canvases, since only these conveyed her truest feelings. For she had embarked, in her last years, on a final quest of the divine force which she felt thrusting in the trees, and in herself.

Carr's last paintings were her greatest and most passionate works. No longer dark and menacing, the brooding forests opened up to fields and beaches, to sea and sky. Some of these paintings were almost all sky: a sky that swirled with energy. In her earlier paintings, the energy had been heavy and threatening, reflecting her own loneliness, rejection and sense of failure. Now the energy became joyful and rhapsodic. After a life of enormous hardship and turmoil, she had found, in herself and in the wilderness, those patterns of divinity which affirmed the unity of all nature. Fusing the spiritual and the sensual, the Apollonian and the Dionysian, she was celebrating the continuous process of life, eternally changing, yet eternally the same. Coming to terms with the wilderness, accepting it within herself and not letting it destroy her, she won a spiritual victory, and entered a world of grace.

Now there would be no question of her trickling out. There were further heart attacks, as well as two strokes; much of her time was spent in hospital, or convalescing at home. But Carr kept on painting. In 1942, at the age of seventy, she undertook her last sketching trip, to the great woods of Mount Douglas, a few miles from Victoria. The forests had called to her again, she wrote, and "the longing was too terrific to subdue." For eight days she lived in a farmer's cottage on the edge of the woods; in a tremendous burst of creative energy, she painted fifteen large oil sketches. These were among her most passionate and celebratory paintings; she was now so certain in her vision that most were completed on the spot, and needed little alteration in the studio. Pouring herself into her work, she expended her energies with reckless extravagance. It ended with another heart attack, this time almost fatal; she was brought back to Victoria on a stretcher.

Carr was confined to bed for most of the next two years, but she refused to stop working. Despite another stroke, she still managed to paint, and finished her autobiography. In early 1945, at the age of seventy-three, she completed and mounted thirty-five oil sketches for an exhibition. Exhausted by the effort, she moved with her typewriter to a nursing home, just across the road from her father's old house. One day later — on 2 March 1945 — she died peacefully in her sleep.

Carr was buried beside her parents and her sisters in the family plot, but she had made sure that part of her would rest forever in the wilderness. Some months before her death, she summoned a younger woman to her bedside. Carr had prepared a trove of personal belongings — broken bits of jewellery, worn books of poetry, old dog collars, faded photographs, a pair of men's gold cuff links and, among many other things, a pile of letters. These were to be packed in boxes, taken to the forest, and buried in an unmarked site. As she told her friend, this was what the Indians did: she had always liked their simple ways.

Scott Symons

On a June evening in 1962, Scott Symons is dining with the Queen Mother at Rideau Hall in Ottawa, in a small company of scholars and artists, most of them older and more prominent. At the age of twenty-eight, however, Symons already seems destined to fill an important role in the Canadian intellectual and cultural community. Powerfully articulate in both languages, he has degrees and diplomas from the University of Toronto, Cambridge and the Sorbonne. Until recently, Symons has been writing for *La Presse* in Montreal, winning a National Newspaper Award for a mammoth series of articles which predicted the Quiet Revolution. Now he is curator of the Canadiana collection at the Royal Ontario Museum, and a recognized authority on North American art and furniture. All his credentials are impeccable: born and raised in the Rosedale heartland of English Canadian civility, Symons has made a respectable marriage, and produced a son; moreover, his wife is wealthy.

Even in such a gathering, Symons compels attention. Short and muscular, with dark brown eyes and a great shock of black hair, he has a smouldering intensity which many find disconcerting. Somehow he conveys an impression that this whole occasion — the glittering banquet, the distinguished company, even the regal presence — is a scene from some larger drama which is still unfolding and which has Scott Symons as protagonist.

After dinner, the Queen Mother asks him when his people came to Canada, and from where. "Two centuries ago, Ma'am, from the Thirteen Colonies, as Loyalists to your Crown," Symons replies. "We are still loyal to your Crown, Ma'am. We are your Majesty's Royal Americans." As he bows, his eyes fill with tears; so do the Queen Mother's.

In March of 1968, Symons and his lover are on the run from the federal police in the mountains of Mexico. During the ensuing years, Symons has been fired from the Museum, and published his first novel; he has been described in Canada's largest newspaper as a "monster", and hounded into exile. Now he has escaped from San Miguel, and its colony of expatriate artists, only hours before the *Federales* threw a road block around the town, and began to interrogate his friends and search their homes. For several weeks, he and his lover will live among the Indians in the mountains, sleeping in their station wagon, never staying more than one night in any place. Chasing the couple, the *Federales* claim to be seeking Symons as the author of an indecent book, and his lover as an illegal entrant. But the real reason is that the lover is a minor, and a male, from a prominent Canadian family. Toronto has spoken to Ottawa, Authority has roused itself, wires have hummed. In a Mexico City hotel room, the parents of the lover wait for the *Federales* to deliver their quarry.

With Scott Symons, we are not only in a realm of violent extremes, we are also dealing with a case of instant mythology. Many Canadian writers of his generation are better known, and more widely read; but few are so publicly outrageous, and few evoke such a strong response. No Canadian writer has been so critical of his country and his people; much of the furor is based upon the sheer scope of Symons' indictment. In three published books, and in scores of lectures and interviews, he has attacked virtually every important aspect of modern Canadian life. ("The Canadian Identity is evil," Symons told an audience at Brock University in 1971. "I am dedicated to the total destruction of the Canadian state.") Moreover, he has *lived* his case, in the course of a remarkable odyssey which has been filled with peril and disaster. In both his life and his writing, Symons has assailed the spiritual and sensual deprivations of our contemporary world, while seeking to lead us back beyond the merely modern, beyond the merely Western, into realms of danger and luminous possibilities.

It is not a path which many want to follow — or see the need to follow. It is not a path which many want even to hear about — especially from Symons. Coming from him, it seems as unnecessary as it was unexpected. This, too, is part of the resentment he arouses. Through breeding, background, marriage and attainment, Symons had all the credentials to become an Establishment figure, a cultural panjandrum. Yet he destroyed it all — his career, his marriage, his respectability. It was hard to understand: his wilful embrace of scandal, poverty and exile; his searing attacks on a society which had given him every opportunity; his despairing talk of suicide and sainthood. Apparently there was no need for any of this to happen.

Hugh Brennan Scott Symons was born in Toronto on 13 July, 1933. He was named by his maternal grandmother, a Brennan from Hamilton, whose family were Irish Presbyterians. Although Symons never knew her, he would find his grandmother embodied in an Ontario Victorian sofa which he described in his furniture book, *Heritage:* "... the Victorian Matriarch in all her dignitarianism ... armed to the teeth with interlocking vetoes ... I admire her and feel some warmth hidden in the grain. But she'd be fiendish to live with unless you wanted to submit to her."

In later years Symons would conclude he had been raised within a matriarchal dynasty, but the influence of his maternal grandfather was just as strong. William Perkins Bull was a roaring, full-bearded lawyer, financier, art patron and author of books on subjects which ranged from church history to birds and flowers. Everything about Perkins Bull was huge, including his appetite for Dickensian feasts. Also from Irish Protestant stock, he was ferociously proud of the British Empire, and was widely known as "The Duke of Rosedale". Imperious in manner, he would stop streetcars on Yonge Street by striding out on the tracks and holding up his cane.

People either loved Perkins Bull, or else dreaded him. There were constant rumours of intrigues and indiscretions: after his death in 1948, a newspaper article noted he had been accused of crimes ranging from forgery and land-swindling through trafficking in drugs to murder. This was hardly true — since Perkins Bull was never charged with any crime — but it reflected the gossip in Toronto when his grandson was growing up: Scott came to hate the tattlers who sneered and whispered within other Rosedale homes.

During the First World War, Perkins Bull had established a hospital for Canadian officers outside London. His daughter Dorothy, the eldest of his seven children, ran the hospital. It was there that she met Harry Symons, who had been piloting a fighter plane in France; they were married shortly after the war.

Here was English and German blood to mix with the Irish strains of the Bulls and the Brennans. Harry Symons was the son of William Limberry Symons who had come to Canada from Devon as a boy. Elegant and gentle, William Symons became an architect who designed the original Union Station and many other important buildings, and founded the Ontario Society of Architects. His wife — Scott's other grandmother — came from a family of Pennsylvania Germans who moved to the Niagara Peninsula as United Empire Loyalists; some died defending their new home in the War of 1812, and are buried at Lundy's Lane. As the product of all these strains, Scott Symons is dark and swarthy. He appears more Celtic than English: there is nothing fair and pink about him, nothing of the WASP.

He was the fifth of seven children (one girl followed by six boys). To support such a family, his father spent most of his life working in real estate. It was not his natural bent. Although he was only five-foot-six, Harry Symons had been a star quarterback, first at Trinity College School, then at the University of Toronto and finally with the Toronto Argonauts. (He was called "The Little Giant".) Sportsman and fighter ace, he was courtly and gallant. His greatest passion was writing: in books such as *Fences* and *Ojibway Melody,* which won the first Stephen Leacock Award, he emerges as a graceful essayist and whimsical humourist, with a strong feeling for his Canadian roots. Like their author in his later years, however, the books are gentle, wistful and even timid. In a seventy-six page letter which he wrote to his mother while on the run in Mexico — but never sent — Symons blamed her for his father's gelding.

Symons grew up in Rosedale: the Rosedale which one grandfather had dominated by his presence and which the other grandfather had partly built. Throughout his child-hood, Rosedale was the heartland of English Canada — with a way of life that was comfortable, cultured and staunchly British. There were books in every room of the Symons' home, even in the kitchen. Sets of Shakespeare, Jane Austen, Dickens, the Romantic poets . . . encyclopaedias, art books, Bibles . . . all of them offering, as Symons later wrote,

> a very specific Presence. Call it — cornily — "the Great Tradition." Because there was, embodied in our homes, a culture whose roots went back to Plato and passed through Christ's World, and through the medieval cathedrals, and the great (and the small) English country homes, and — yes — through Parliament itself, and on through the Cavaliers (and damned few of the dismal Roundheads, thank God. . .the Loyalists left them to rot in New England), and the Battle of the Boyne, and Chippendale Georgian, and Good Queen Vic, and handsome Albert. *That* was all there, in Rosedale, the Rosedale of my child-time. . .

Rosedale, he added, was a library and an ongoing garden party. "It was roses and red wine and The Rubaiyat of Omar Khayyám . . . It was all white ducks and blue blazers and Grenadier crests and ascots, and lithesome ladies in gauze or lace with wide-brimmed hats and pale mien." It was also sumptuous and tangible. The Symons dining room was all ruby: velvet curtains, mahogany panels, a massive chandelier with silk tassels and shelves of cut-glass goblets. At Christmas dinner there would be five glasses before each place, for all the wines and ports and Madeiras, for all the toasts to King and Queen ("God Bless Them!").

This childhood, designed to be a lasting legacy, gave Symons a larger heritage than the Authorized Version. Like Sutherland Brown, Symons always knew there was more to his nation's history than what was described by liberal apologists: an heroic emancipation from the shackles of British rule and a concomitant embrace of a continental destiny. Having absorbed Plutarch's *Lives,* he could only find William Lyon Mackenzie to be a tawdry figure — "for me reality and history did *not* begin in Toronto in the 1820s. There was, quite simply, a bigger reality and — frankly — a deeper one, all imbedded in our Rosedale library." By the age of fifteen, he had read *Pride and Prejudice* a dozen times; he had browsed in Cicero and Gibbon, More and Spenser, Pope and Milton; he had studied Botticelli, Tintoretto, Rubens and Vermeer. His senses had been aroused as much as his intellect. During the Second World War, with no domestic help available, Dorothy Symons had her children clean and polish all the elegant furniture, the rich panelling, the eighteenth-century silver. "Intimate touch with beautiful *objets d'art,"* Symons wrote. "This was my *real* education."

His formal education began at Rosedale Public School, and continued at Trinity College School, Port Hope, where he arrived in 1945 at the age of twelve. By then he was already showing signs of a moody truculence which disturbed his parents. They thought he would benefit from boarding school, from the discipline and the close confinement with other boys. To pay the tuition, his father had to borrow money, and his mother had to sell some of her jewels. These were acceptable sacrifices: with its British public school traditions, TCS was considered the best training ground for a young Rosedale gent — the best place for instilling good manners, a patina of culture, and useful connections.

Symons hated it. He soon concluded that its claims to academic distinction were fraudulent, that its emphasis on Christianity (chapel every evening, and twice on Sundays) was hypocritical, and that its social snobbery was formidable. It was, he later wrote, "a hotbed of affluent philistinism . . . a cultural shell, producing business managers under the guise of producing gentlemen."

At TCS, popularity was won on the playing fields; those who failed to make the team were scorned and pitied. Symons loathed the bashing and bullying; he was also far from a natural athlete. At twelve, he was short and wiry, and weighed only eighty-four pounds. He was more successful in his studies, winning prizes every year and always finishing near the top of his form. But academic success failed to bring popularity, or any sense of fulfilment. Often lonely, Symons found nothing at TCS to correspond with that larger reality which his childhood reading had disclosed. For a time he thought about becoming a writer, but his masters told him that was no way to make a living. He had dabbled in painting, and sung in the school choir, but these also were eventually abandoned. It was as though all his deeper impulses were being throttled.

For most of his five years at TCS, Symons loved another boy. Their affair was consummated — both verbally and carnally — but never as passionately as Symons desired. Yet it was Symons — not his friend — who enforced restraint. It was not that the lovers had been discovered, nor that they lacked opportunity: it was that Symons had felt an overwhelming inner veto. Later he would blame the school, his family and his society for compelling him to suppress his love. He would write that at a crucial moment, when he should have been taking possession of himself — of his eroticism and his spirituality — he had been taught that his body and his desires were dirty. Symons came to see this incident as decisive, and crippling:

> Inside of me I remained eternal thirteen; eternally the boy reaching out to touch but never being allowed to do so . . . except insofar as Mommy and Authority permitted. Allowed to touch only insofar as he had done his duty. Allowed to touch as his reward. And who gave the reward? Mommy — at home. Or his wife — at home, later.

He had been taught that his body was dirty, and that it must be disciplined and developed. So he turned to gymnastics, a form of athletics which suited him because it was solitary and ritualistic, with a touch of grace. During his last two years at TCS, Symons spent long hours in the gym, driving himself with such intensity that he was eventually achieving Olympic exercises. Not for the last time, there was an excess of intensity: practising alone one evening, he flew off the high bar, landed past the mat, and broke his back.

That was the end of TCS for Symons. After a year at the University of Toronto Schools (where there was less emphasis on athletics, and more on studying, writing and debating), he went on to the University itself, entering Trinity College in the autumn of 1951. He studied History, but much of his time was spent on student politics and public speaking. By now he had a way with words — a result of all his reading — and a platform presence which compelled attention. His new flair may have been a legacy from Perkins Bull, but when Symons became a campus leader it was more through will power than natural inclination. For he was still playing the dutiful son, and feeling that his family, and especially his mother, were pushing him to become a public success, pushing him towards politics, or law, or business — all of them acceptable careers, almost the *only* acceptable careers.

He finished Trinity in a blaze of scholarships and medals. But on graduation day there was no response when he was called to receive his rewards. Instead he was at Woodbine race track, selling tickets in the pari-mutuel department. This was one of several jobs he had taken to help pay for further studies, but it wasn't the only reason for his absence. He had come to feel that the honours he had won were fraudulent, that his whole career at Trinity was a sham. Although he still couldn't articulate his discontent, he sensed that something essential was being lost in the struggle for success.

The pressures to be respectable were still at work when Symons arrived at Cambridge in the autumn of 1955, entering King's College on a junior fellowship. His family had suggested that two years of law or economics at Cambridge might be followed by a course of business administration at Harvard. Symons tried both law and economics: they bored him and he soon ended up in English Literature. This was a compromise — since any Cambridge degree would be respectable — and tutors such as F. R. Leavis and Basil Willey often made it seem worthwhile. On weekends and holidays, his Bull relatives took him in hand, and completed his education as a proper gentleman. As he wrote to his family: "I can now enter any home in Europe and feel at ease."

Yet he was *not* at ease. Outwardly he seemed remarkably self-assured for a twenty-three-year-old Canadian. His suits were impeccably tailored, and his manners were elegant. His erudition was increasingly impressive, and he could hold his own in conversation with any of the Cambridge wits. Yet beneath this insouciant facade, he burned with doubts. His family was still pushing him toward the law or public service, but Symons wrote to a friend that "my mind is more than ever set on writing." He had vague plans to tackle a novel, and wondered whether he should start a diary, although this struck him as being too neurotic. He was meant to succeed — but how, and in what? His studies took him deeper into the Great Tradition which he had first encountered in his Toronto library; his emergence as a gentleman made him feel more comfortable than ever in the civilization which derived from that tradition. Yet these struck him as superficial accretions, and external to his deeper needs. More than ever, he felt an impasse in his inner growth. Amid the strongly homosexual atmosphere of King's, he was sometimes attracted to other men: he resisted the temptation. Later, he would conclude that "to sleep with a man was exactly what I did require to grow and to learn and to flower in full" — but at this time, he was still constrained by the old vetoes.

Instead he became engaged. As he later wrote, this was the socially respectable solution for any such dilemma. He had known his fiancée since childhood, and had sometimes taken her to dances. She came from a wealthy Toronto family; now she was also studying abroad. At a time of enormous impasse, Symons fell in love; he sensed that his fiancée was at an impasse, too, and fleeing from her family. In a letter, he described her as exceptionally beautiful, intelligent and cultivated — and also very independent: "She is frankly what Toronto society would term a rebel."

He would be a rebel, too: this became increasingly evident to Symons after he graduated from Cambridge in the spring of 1957 and returned to Toronto to prepare for the wedding. His engagement appeared to be yet another compromise with respectability; in fact it became the opening round in a battle that would continue for decades. The first clash came when he began working as an assistant on the editorial page of *The Telegram*. To Symons, journalism was a way of starting to write, especially since he still had little idea of what he wanted to say. To his family, and even more to his fiancée's parents, a newspaper career was undignified; they argued strongly against it.

His exposure to Cambridge and London had made Symons increasingly sceptical of a community whose highest standards were embodied in a TCS education. In the Toronto living rooms where he and his fiancée were put on almost daily display, he encountered narrow and suspicious elders who were concerned mainly with money and social position, who distrusted intellectual and artistic pursuits, and who became distinctly nervous when the conversation failed to stay within the accustomed bounds of banality. As Symons wrote in a letter: "More and more I feel compelled to muzzle myself in their company."

This growing feeling of alienation was all the more painful because of his nostalgia for the city he had known as a child. From his grandfathers, from the books and furniture in his home, from the rituals of teas and garden parties, Symons had derived a deep attachment to the British tradition — genteel and cultured, conservative and contemplative — which had been legitimately domiciled within English Canada, and especially in Rosedale. His studies had reinforced this allegiance, for he had learned how an elegant society had flourished in Ontario even in early Victorian days, even in the bush, and how the British connection had saved Canada from the inroads of a rude and levelling republicanism.

Now he was seeing the demise of that tradition. On the one hand, he concluded that Toronto (and all English Canada) had been taken over by the rising middle class: a combination of Methodist-Presbyterian Grits and narrow nationalists who were bent on destroying the British connection because it exposed their limitations. On the other hand, he also blamed his own class. Through lack of faith, he later wrote, the people of Rosedale had betrayed their traditions: "When Rosedale ceased to read in its inherited libraries, it lost its own core. And what remained was merely money-with-manners."

Even the manners seemed questionable. Relations between the two families became strained as the wedding day approached. Since his fiancée was an heiress, there were accusations that Symons was only after her wealth. His fiancée's mother made much of the fact that Symons was the grandson of Perkins Bull; she also asked whether he had Jewish blood.

Despite these tensions, the wedding took place on 1 March 1958. Tired of being muzzled, Symons turned the reception into a theatrical performance. Given the chance to speak before the serried ranks of Toronto's High Respectability, he delivered an address on the subject of the city and its spiritual impoverishment that was filled with elegant witticisms and classical allusions which most of his listeners found incomprehensible. But few failed to catch his contempt, especially when he maintained that the bridegroom at such a Toronto society wedding was nothing more than a figment of his mother-in-law's imagination. By now he was a formidable orator who was adept with rolling rhythms, vivid images and sudden bursts of scorn. On his wedding day he used this power lethally, and also mirthfully (for he vastly enjoyed his own performance), against a captive audience whom he was coming to regard as his natural enemies.

This was his first public challenge to his society. While the depth of his discontent was still not apparent (even to himself), while his indictment was still not specific, it was obvious that a battle had been joined. Symons also encouraged his best man, who was somewhat drunk, to deliver a blunter broadside. There were angry mutterings in the audience, and his mother-in-law shouted "Boo-boo-boo!" Sitting in the front row, Harry Symons was one of the few who dared to laugh.

Turning his back on Toronto, Symons now undertook a very different sort of confrontation. Within two months of the wedding, the couple were living in Quebec City, where Symons had accepted a job with *The Chronicle-Telegraph,* an English-language newspaper. (He had been fired by *The Toronto Telegram* after submitting a report on the deterioration of its editorial policy over the previous half century.) The move to Quebec was temporary — since he and his wife were planning further studies in Paris — and it was made deliberately to put some distance between Symons and his in-laws. But it was also a conscious attempt to probe more deeply into the French portion of his Canadian heritage. Soon his interviews, editorials and reviews had gained him an unusual acceptance; an article in *The Globe and Mail* in late 1958 noted that Symons had become one of the few English Canadians ever to make a profound impact upon the proud, suspicious world of French Canadian intellectuals.

By now he was nearly fluent in French; to the *Québecois*, he was also a remarkable curiosity. Here was a Tory from Toronto who not only dared to defend the British tradition in their presence, but who was also steeping himself in their own traditions. Even Maurice Duplessis was impressed. When Symons told the Premier that his grandfather had been a Grand Master of the Orange Lodge, Duplessis roared with laughter at such temerity; thereafter he would refer to Symons as "le petit diable Orange."

The ultimate proof of his acceptance came when Symons was invited to join the St Jean Baptiste Society, the most influential secular body in the province. He was the first non-French Canadian and non-Roman Catholic to be honoured in this way. It was a triumph, he wrote in a letter, "and we are just beginning to realize the potential of our position."

At the age of twenty-six, he was also beginning to sense a role for himself. It would involve writing, it would have something to do with both French and English Canada — above all, it would involve an exploration and a celebration of his dual heritage. In Toronto, he had seen the British part of that heritage as sadly diminished; in the more stimulating atmosphere of Quebec, he found reason to hope that something might be salvaged. First he would go to Paris: this would take him even deeper into the French tradition, and strengthen his potential. Then he would return to continue the struggle which had formally commenced on his wedding day. As he wrote in a letter, he would "carry the warfare into the enemy's territory, forcing him to accept something of my quest for the real." There, in one sentence, were two key images for all that lay ahead — the battle and the quest.

Symons and his wife arrived in Paris in the autumn of 1959, and embarked on an orgy of discovery and learning. There were formal studies at the Sorbonne (where Symons gained diplomas in French literature and grammar) and less formal evenings in the *salon* of Gabriel Marcel, the leading Catholic philosopher, as well as visits to chateaux, cathedrals and wine harvests. Wine had become a major interest — Symons and his wife had used all the cash gifts from the wedding to lay down their own cellar. Symons was stirred by Chartres, where he sensed that he had a basic affinity for the medieval sensibility — a sensibility in which everything was harmoniously linked, with no separation of mind and spirit. And he was strangely moved on a visit to the pre-historic Caves of Lascaux, where the giant beasts on the walls came alive to him in a manner he could hardly comprehend. Here — although he didn't know it at the time — were two components of the vision which he would eventually formulate as his challenge to the modern spirit, and which would take him far beyond his immediate heritage.

At this point, however, his energies were devoted to defending that heritage. In a paper entitled "Canada, Nation-manquée" — which he delivered at Marcel's *salon* — he maintained that Canada's freedom was a myth: in foreseaking their European links, Canadians had embraced the economic and cultural domination of the United States. True independence could be gained only by reviving the English tradition; this was also the only guarantee for the survival of its French counterpart. Symons had begun to propound this thesis in Quebec City; now he was preparing to find a larger audience. In the autumn of 1960, with his wife and new-born son, he left Paris for Montreal, where he had accepted an offer from Jean-Louis Gagnon to join the staff of *La Presse*.

Like his membership in the St Jean Baptiste Society, this offer from one of Quebec's most important editors was further proof of Symons' unusual acceptance by the French Canadian elite: as in Quebec City, he seized the chance to interrogate politicians, intellectuals and artists. Symons saw that Quebec, at the end of the Duplessis era, was entering a period of political and intellectual ferment; in a series of twenty-five articles which took six months to research and write, he investigated the sources of that ferment, and prophesied the future. At a time when English Canada remained largely ignorant of the challenge that was about to be mounted in Quebec, Symons had predicted the Quiet Revolution.

The articles won a National Newspaper Award (at which point Symons was hailed by *The Telegram* as one of its own); they also made him a celebrity in Quebec. In the spring of 1961, *La Presse* sent him on a lengthy tour of the province, to make speeches and appear on radio and television. By then Symons could write in a letter that he had gained his French Canadian citizenship; he was also preparing to return to Toronto.

It was a return that had been long and carefully planned. Before leaving for Paris, Symons had purchased from the rest of his family their fifty-acre farm at Claremont, about thirty miles east of Toronto. (His wife had provided the money, and this had sparked another bitter altercation with his in-laws.) The farm had a small house, a large pond and thousands of trees, as well as countless birds and an occasional deer. While Symons and his wife would live initially in Toronto, they would rebuild the farm house as their eventual home, and as a refuge from the inamicable city.

His strategy was still the same: to explore, celebrate and defend his heritage. But his tactics now took a different turn: in the summer of 1961, Symons joined the Royal Ontario Museum as an assistant curator of its Canadiana collection. Again there had been pressure from his family to forsake journalism, especially since his articles were making him controversial. But Symons also wanted to probe his English Canadian heritage, and he was apprehensive about the direction in which his sensibility was nudging him. As he later wrote: "When journalism became too hot for me — it took me to the verge of revolution, predicting the French Canadian revolution; it took me to the verge of my own voice (and at that very time I became again sensitive to the sexual beauty of men!) — when it became too hot, I backed into what seemed more respectable."

If the job was respectable, it also suited many of his aptitudes and inclinations. Despite his growing reputation as an intellectual, despite his multi-national collection of degrees, despite his burgeoning ability as a writer, despite the diaries he had started to keep in Quebec City (which now amounted to several thousand pages) ... despite all these,

Symons had never been entirely happy with mere ideas, or even mere words. During his childhood, it was the touch of beautiful objects which had excited him as much as any of the books he read; he had always apprehended the world less with his mind than with his eyes, his fingers and (he would soon be adding) his cock.

Nor was he in any way a novice curator. He had grown up amid old Canadian furniture and paintings; in England and France he had sought out their European antecedents. One of his articles for *La Presse* was on "the comparative theologies of Canadian furnitures" — it was illustrated with a page of photographs from his own collection. Since their return to Canada, Symons and his wife had been ranging throughout Ontario and Quebec: their purchases comprised one of the most notable private collections of early Canadian art and artifacts. It included a wealth of French Canadian pine and English Canadian curly maple, glass bowls and barn-roof roosters, two surrealistic paintings by the nineteenth-century Quebec artist Joseph Legaré, as well as a five-foot carved gilt lantern and a twelve-foot Quebec monastery dining table. His home, he wrote, was *"une maison à thèse* . . . it is an argument, a taking-of-consciousness, a synthesis of what we are."

With his Toronto home and his Museum job, he was now outwardly respectable. He was still writing a Montreal newspaper column — this time for *Le Nouveau Journal,* which was in the forefront of the Quiet Revolution — but few in Toronto were aware of his continuing philippics on the two Canadian cultures. His hair was quite long, his conversation was as unpredictable as ever, and any man who wore red velvet smoking jackets and lapels on his waistcoats was clearly a dandy. But these were regarded as tolerable eccentricities. His house in Forest Hill seemed to embody his new respectability: at least from the road, it looked comfortably conformist.

Inside the house, it was a different matter. The sensuous stripes of the maple wood, the flaming Legarés, the barn-roof cocks and crucifixes, a tormented Christ, a den built around his wine cellar, a library with a small but select collection of erotic literature . . . here was passion and reverence, evil and redemption . . . all of it indicating a sensibility that would hardly be constrained by bourgeois conventions. On the surface, Symons later said, his life at this time seemed to have been a long growth into High Gentility, into Highest Conformity. "But underneath there was always an equal step away from conformity into creativity. There was a long slow move away from the world of memo into the world of touch."

During his first three years at the ROM, Symons worked hard to build up its Canadiana collection, and to extend his own knowledge: this led to his appointments as curator, and as an assistant professor of Fine Arts at the University of Toronto. Lectures in the United States extended his reputation, and produced more opportunities: in 1964, he left Toronto on a year's sabbatical which took him, as lecturer and visiting curator, to the University of Pennsylvania, the Henry Francis du Pont Winterthur Museum in Delaware, and the Smithsonian Institution in Washington. The core of one public lecture at the Smithsonian was a comparison — with slides — of French Canadian and New England weathervane roosters. Symons maintained that the French Canadian "cocks" were always full-bodied and orotund, while the American "cocks" were flat and one-dimensional. His audience, who listened in absolute silence, became aware that he was giving a lecture on comparative eroticism.

Ostensibly, he was achieving a growing success. Inwardly, however, Symons was gripped by concerns and passions which would soon compel him to shatter the facade. The first indication was his bitter distress when the Pearson Government replaced the Red Ensign with a new national flag. Like Sutherland Brown, he had come to regard the Canadian political elite as his natural enemies, since they seemed bent on systematically destroying his heritage for the sake of a continental destiny. The new maple leaf banner was dramatic confirmation of their perfidy: to Symons it was a pop-art monstrosity, devoid of all heraldry, tradition and significance. At a time when he was seeking to celebrate a distinctive Canadian civilization, with its specific British, French and American components, he felt that Ottawa had officially slaughtered this reality. "Many intelligent people told me that the flag issue was a small matter," Symons later wrote, "but I knew that it was not; that it put everything into question."

His despair over the flag was the surface manifestation of a deeper discontent. This was not exclusively political, or sexual, or spiritual but a turbulent amalgam of all his thoughts and feelings. He saw his allegiances to the Red Ensign, to Canada, to his family and his wife as one and the same — "all variations of a single loyalty and reality." At the age of thirty-one, he felt that he was in abeyance, since his family, his career, his nation — " all of these, as I had ever understood them, were forever gone."

Increasingly, Symons was engaging in such verbal pyrotechnics: he called them "sensibility syllogisms". Increasingly, he would hold a number of concepts or energies in his mind and keep forming them into new patterns. At different times, different elements from his life would grow luminous — as Good Things, Bad Things or, in some cases (Queen Victoria, feudal values, Rosedale, his family, his wife) as either Good or Bad depending on the context.

This becomes confusing, especially as Symons adopts a terse but elaborate personal vocabulary — a shorthand of his sensibility — so as to impose some order on his tumultuous world. There is always an Enemy but the Enemy will appear in various guises, under various labels. At times it is the Canadian political establishment, with its minions in the civil service, the universities and business. At other times it is the Methodist and Presbyterian traditions ("McCanada"), *or* "the constipated remnants of the Tory Family Compact", *or* "the gliblib media mafia", *or* the Matriarchy, *or* his wife and (later) his lover.

Yet beneath the turbulence, despite the contradictions and inconsistencies, a coherent vision was struggling to be born. Initially this vision would be rooted in Symons' experiences of childhood, TCS, marriage and public life. In each of these, he was starting to find a common element: a denial of his sacramental intuition of the world, a denial of what he would later call "an incarnational mode of being". He sensed that something disastrous had happened to him as a youth; that once he had been forbidden to touch, his mind had been divorced from his emotions, and all inner growth had been blocked. He felt this pattern had continued into adult life — that his family, his wife's family and all the forces of respecta-

bility were bent on curtailing his spiritual and sensual fulfilment. While the Enemy would appear in different forms, it
would always enact the same vetoes: a stern Calvinist suppression of beauty and feeling.

To Symons, this now appeared as the basic Canadian
heresy. It was the same heresy which had destroyed his flag: a
divisive impulse which would treat the flag, or a man's body,
as a mere object, devoid of spiritual essence. Where others
would separate, he felt only unity: flags and furniture, birds
and flesh, prayer and orgasm . . . all were one: "Home-home-
land-wife-work-body-spirit-nature . . . all of these utterly one."
He struggled to express these feelings in his diaries and letters,
but conceded that his presentation was still inarticulate:

> While I have an internal emotional and spiritual and
> carnal coherence, yet I am still possessed of a vast verbal
> and intellectual incoherence. Slowly, slowly, I excavate
> all of this from me. Slowly putting me back together,
> putting all of me into a known articulate unison.

In the midst of this struggle, Symons lost his main link
to the respectable world: while still in the United States, he
was fired by the ROM for insubordination. This was the
result of a prolonged correspondence with the new director
over a minor administrative matter; as in the case of Sutherland Brown and McNaughton, the dispute had a deeper significance than its details would suggest. Just as Brown saw
McNaughton as a cold-blooded technocrat with little feeling
for Canada's British and military traditions, so Symons
regarded the director as an accessory of a "gliblib" political
and cultural Establishment which was conspiring to destroy
his heritage (the Flag), or else to render it harmless as museum
artifacts (the Canadiana Gallery) — treating it not as a reality
to be lived, but as a remembrance to be invoked with mere
nostalgia. He saw the leaders of this Establishment as timid,
second-rate men whose power was based on their ability to
suppress the potency of the culture which they ostensibly represented. Like Carr, he feared their embrace: "So easy to succumb to comfort and respectability," he wrote, "so easy,
provided I could cut one ball off." (Sometime after his firing,
Symons took the director to lunch at the University Club, and

told him he had *no* balls.) Again like Carr, he deliberately exa-
cerbated differences which might have been resolved with a
modicum of tact: something was driving him toward an open
conflict.

He was also being driven toward creativity; even more,
he was being driven toward an attempt to live his sacramental
vision. He had gone as far as he wanted to go as a curator —
at the same time that he was fired by the ROM, he turned
down a permanent job at the Smithsonian. He had seen his
role in religious terms ("I became a kind of priest of the chapel
of Canadiana"), but unlike Bishop White, he could never be
content to turn the Gallery into his cathedral. That would be
too passive, even too furtive. As he wrote to a colleague at the
Gallery:

> I guess I really reached the point at which I had to live
> out, enact, what I believe. I can no longer merely think
> it, or suspect it, or show slides about it, or lecture about
> it. I have got to live my crisis. My crisis is a spiritual one,
> and it is inextricably bound up with the nature of
> Canada.

Here was another of his startling syntheses, but
Symons deeply believed that his personal impasse *did* reflect a
national dilemma, since a nation which proscribed reverence
and tradition, feeling and sentience, was in just as much
trouble as himself, and the root causes were identical. So he
went on the attack — to save his own soul and, as he would
maintain from now on, to resurrect his country and his people.

Symons and his wife were living in the rebuilt farm house at
Claremont, surrounded by all their paintings and furniture:
articulate objects which bespoke his heritage. This would be
his base for his attacks on the Enemy, but for several months
he floundered in searching for a strategy. Partly because of
family pressure, he abandoned a book on Canadian history in
which he had been trying to make his case within a formal,
academic discipline. He made the same case in a play which
was submitted to the Crest Theatre, but was rejected as
unplayable. (In the climactic scene, a driven and unfulfilled

English Canadian achieved beatitude when sodomized by a French Canadian chair.) For a time he contemplated a return to journalism, but he flubbed a try-out with *This Hour Has Seven Days,* the new CBC television program which would become notorious for its iconoclasm. Again he seemed to provoke this rejection: he felt the producers wanted him as comic relief, as a caricature Tory gent who would be outrageous on the air, but who would also be revealed as irrelevant. In the snickers of the stage hands, he heard the mass media's contempt for his traditions, and concluded that he was simply "not viable in journalese". "Now I must go on," he wrote in a letter, "and face up to sheer creativity or live a slow acknowledged death for the next forty years."

He was thirty-two, and he had been married for seven years. Now his marriage was starting to founder under the strain of his compulsions. Three years later, in a massive letter to his wife which was also written on the run in Mexico, and also never sent, he placed the blame on both their families, and especially "those endless spinster aunts and great-aunts and those tyrannical grandmothers and great-grandmothers, whose clenched puritanical Canadian and Scottish cunts vetoed our fulfilment from beyond the very grave." He told his wife she had never acknowledged her sentience, or her need for him. Her family had told her she had hot pants, his family had told him his cock was dirty: "Our families vetoed any sexual fulfilment — any generous, gentle, thoughtful, intimate, compassionate living with ourselves."

Symons felt similar vetoes had led to a national impasse: "At the core of my society lies the power of the woman/the matriarch, and that woman rules by Negative Orgasm, by closing her womanhood." As a result, he wrote, Canadian men were often mere manikins who never grew up, who always remained in thrall to their mothers and their wives. Because they had never taken possession of their manhood, they had betrayed the potent, romantic traditions of English Canada. With his prurient bachelorhood and his crystal-ball communion with his mother, Mackenzie King was an archetypal manikin: to Symons, it was painfully evident that only such a person could have presided over the destruction of the British connection.

In the late autumn of 1965, Symons set out to smash the impasse in his marriage, his creativity and his nation. Leaving the farm, he returned to Montreal where he stayed for three weeks in a small hotel on the edge of La Place d'Armes. During this time — a mere twenty-one days — he wrote his first novel. For five years he had been pouring himself into his diary (it amounted to more than a half-million words), but now he was writing for publication. He had often muted himself in the past, and compromised with respectability. Now he was coming into the open.

Symons threw himself into the task with reckless bravura. Although autobiographical, *Place d'Armes* is not a conventional first novel. Symons was not a Joyce or a Lawrence, looking back on a tormented youth and shaping that torment into art. Instead, he aspired to *live* a novel, and to write it all down, virtually as he lived it. He would actively seek adventures and encounters and then record his reactions to them. For as long as it took, for as long as he could stand the strain, he would set down everything that happened to him, everything that registered in his sensibility. As always he kept a diary (he called it his Combat Journal), but now this diary would become the novel.

The hero of *Place d'Armes* is Hugh Anderson, a young English Canadian who is modelled almost exactly on the author, who is also keeping a journal and writing a novel, and who shares all the author's passions and prejudices:

> I have a nostalgia. For my land, and its people. I'm a romantic. A sin in this era of bleated Canadian positivism. I cry "too little for the sensibility", while all our intellectuals moan "too little for the mind".

The other major character is La Place itself, and especially its Church of Notre Dame. To Hugh, La Place becomes both wife and nation: the novel is the story of his attempt to enter into its heart — "All I want is the right to love my country, my wife, my people, my world." He feels he can do this only by regaining his lost manhood:

> Everything tells me I've been brought up a deaf-dumb paralytic . . . cannot see, hear, touch, move. I can't think

with my balls cut off. There's no substitute for a thoughtful pair of balls.

Like the author, Hugh feels that his impasse is rooted
in the vetoes imposed by his family and his society. Because he
was never allowed as a boy to give himself to the boy he
wanted, he has never since given himself to a woman, "in
revenge for his gelding". Somehow his capacity to love
women — and his capacity to create — are linked to his ability to accept his love for men. He wants to be a fully sentient
man: "I no more want to be homosexual than mere heterosexual." But for Hugh, as for the author, the breakthrough
comes when he sleeps with French Canadian male prostitutes
— "my body is back now."

With his male maidenhead finally smashed, Hugh can
at last abandon himself to La Place, and enter into Notre
Dame to take Holy Communion. At the end, he staggers joyfully from the church, eats the Host in La Place, and turns to
touch, to embrace, the incredulous passersby. They think he is
merely drunk, but Hugh feels he has been reborn.

Although Symons was reclaiming and celebrating his
sexuality, the novel also enacts his conviction that the
national impasse arose in part from English Canada's failure
to partake of its sister tradition. Like Symons, the hero of the
book had fled Toronto to seek deliverance in Montreal; in an
hotel room on the edge of La Place, English and French
Canada come together and rediscover touch. While few readers would accept male prostitutes as agents of redemption, the
homosexual passages are only a small part of the whole. "In a
major sense," Symons would later write, his book was about
"the beauty of historic objects and architecture as against ugly
people." Most of the "ugly people" are English-speaking
Montrealers who are introduced into the narrative mainly to
illustrate the author's indictment of his society, but Symons'
intention was to celebrate as much as to attack. As Hugh
Anderson states at the start of the book, he wants to write "a
novel that glowed with love, with his own love of his community, his nation, his people . . . He wanted to share that love,
and to show that only by that love do people live, really live."

When *Place d'Armes* was published in early 1967, most
of the critics savaged it. They complained about its preten-

tious rhetoric, its lack of form, its feeble characterizations, its repetitious harangues, and its awkward use of tired literary conventions. (As the book progresses, Hugh begins writing a novel about another character, Andrew Harrison, who is little different from Symons and Anderson, and who in turn keeps a journal and begins writing about a character he calls Hugh Anderson. To add to the confusion, the various novels-within-novels and journals-within-journals were printed in five different typefaces.)

All these flaws were a direct result of Symons' hit-or-miss method, his way of pouring himself on to the page with enormous intensity, and a corresponding lack of craftsmanship. (When he rewrote the first draft, it became even more unwieldy.) Yet for many readers, the book's power and honesty transcended its literary faults. Young people especially felt it spoke to them directly — articulating their own discontents and aspirations in a forthright manner they had rarely encountered in any other novel. The editor of a literary publishing house would later state that a large proportion of the manuscripts which he received in the late nineteen-sixties and early nineteen-seventies had been clearly influenced by *Place d'Armes.*

To Symons, his novel was not so much a work of art as a personal testament and a public challenge to his society. He was coming into the open, no longer hiding behind a respectable facade. In describing how he had (as he maintained) reclaimed his manhood and released his sentience, he was also announcing that he was much better armed for the battles which lay ahead.

Now he was preparing for those battles. He felt he had still not fully made his case, or fully lived his case, since he had still not seen his own city in the way that he had at last been able to see La Place. To tackle Toronto — both personally and on paper — would be the next stage in his quest.

Writing in a small cabin on his farm, Symons finished the final draft of *Place d'Armes* in the spring of 1966; it would be nine more months before its publication brought him fully into the open. Within days of delivering the manuscript, he started on his second novel, which was centred on Toronto.

He had returned to the farm because he still hoped his marriage could be salvaged. But now he was spending more time in the city, exploring its buildings and its people, and often staying in a room in a house on Yorkville Avenue.

This was the summer when Yorkville burst into bloom as a haven and parade-ground for the counter-culture, for the hippies and the flower children. Symons moved among them, talked with them in the cafés and often slept with them, both men and women. One evening, his wife's parents gave a lavish party for their daughters. Predictably, the guests included bankers, stock brokers, church dignitaries and the headmaster of TCS. As his contribution, Symons invited a pair of his Yorkville friends. Both were over six feet, splendidly *coiffured,* gorgeously gowned, stunningly beautiful, and very black. It only gradually dawned on the other guests that they were both transvestites.

Symons rejoiced in the openness of the Yorkville youth, in their lack of inhibitions and in their ability to touch. But he was sceptical about their frequent reliance on drugs. (Symons had tried soft drugs from time to time. Like alcohol, they never became essential to him.) More important, he found them equally limited in their total sensibility as the respectable citizens: the "Cubes" or "Blandmen" as he was calling them. He would write:

> The Hip-World is predicated upon "blowing your mind" . . . smashing your mind out of the way of a relaxed sensibility. Which is what acid does. But I was determined to carry my mind with me . . . as a tool and as a partner of my sensibility . . . The Cube-square is schizo: he kills his balls with his brains. The Hip is schizo: he kills his brains with his balls. BUT I WANT MY BALLS AND MY BRAINS WORKING TOGETHER.

This was the message of his new novel, which he was calling *Civic Square.* (The reference was both to Nathan Phillips Square, considered as forming a diptych with La Place d'Armes in Montreal, and to the nature of English Canadian society.) Again he was living his book as he wrote it, and much of its energy derived from the fact that it was literally open-ended: from one day to another, the author never knew what was going to happen. Again, too, the approach was direct and personal. Just as Symons had written *Place d'Armes* in the form of diary entries, so he constructed *Civic Square* as a series of lengthy letters to an imaginary Dear Reader (DR). These letters described the author's encounters with his Toronto-world and its environs. As he ranged from his farm to TCS, to the car races at Mosport, to Rosedale and Yorkville, Symons watched his fellow citizens at dreary work and empty play, often writing them into the book the same day he met them.

Although some of the set pieces are brilliantly achieved, there is little plot to the novel. (Symons would later state that "plots are for novels in which nothing happens.") The first letter states that DR himself is the book's real protagonist, even though he and the author have never met, even though the author doesn't know who DR is. Symons also makes clear that he is after DR's male maidenhead and that their spiritual salvation depends upon their erotic communion: "IF I EVER FIND YOU AND TOUCH THEN WE ARE BOTH BORN!" As he continued writing his book through the winter of 1966 and into the summer of 1967, his pleas to DR became increasingly imperative. In the end, DR seeks out the author in Yorkville, and the book closes with their consummation.

This theme apart, most of the letters to DR are dispatches from the front lines of Symons' battle with the Blandmen. This was now his favourite word for the Enemy: it included all those English Canadians (an overwhelming majority, according to Symons) who were terrified by passion. Symons was also affirming his faith and his joy: in homosexual and heterosexual love, in the birds he watched at the farm, in his embattled Rosedale. Above all, he was affirming the need to touch, to get balls and brains working together, to put body back with spirit — "if this is not achieved, if body is not made holy, then holiness will die further."

Like its predecessor, *Civic Square* is a combination of manifesto and jeremiad. Also like *Place d'Armes,* it is awkward, repetitive and self-indulgent. Friends and editors who read the various drafts had warned Symons that he was in danger of producing a grotesque monstrosity. Symons would listen politely, and go away promising to cut several hundred pages. But instead of trimming the manuscript, he would invariably add more letters.

For Symons, *Civic Square* was not so much a novel as a testament and (quite literally) an offering. It was finally published in late 1969. (It had been delayed, partly because Symons kept writing new letters to DR, and partly because the Old Boys Association of TCS had threatened legal action — this led to a few cuts in the text.) Published in a limited edition of 450 copies, and running to a mammoth 848 pages, it was unbound, and the loose pages were packaged in a large blue box. This was based on the Birks blue box, a recurring symbol in the book: "that perennial present to Brides and Mothers . . . the Toronto Victorian Matriarchal box we're all victims of." To the amazement of his publisher, Symons stood at the printers as the copies were turned out, brandishing a red felt pen, and drawing pictures of birds and flowers and flowering phalli in every copy: his personal gift to the reader. Then he carted one of the boxes (they weighed eight-and-a-half pounds) to a Communion service at St. James' Cathedral, his family's church. He put the box in the offering plate, with a note saying it was his gift to the cathedral, made in memory of his father, who had died seven years earlier, and in recognition of the fact that he had loved his father too late.

At this time Symons had little respect for any attempt to mould him as a conventional novelist. He placed himself in the confessional tradition of the great religious writers such as St. Francis and St. John of the Cross: "a guy opening up and saying these are the difficulties I have in celebrating life." He also put his work in the tradition of Mrs. Moodie and the other letter-writers among the British upper classes in nineteenth-century Canada: "We've rejected that because it seems unCanadian, but . . . this tradition was the vehicle for something fine in being Canadian and it helped me to write."

In many ways Symons is himself a nineteenth-century figure. His modes of discourse are fundamentally Victorian: the sermon (he is always in a pulpit), the essay (his journalism) and, above all, the letter and the diary. Even *Heritage,* his "furniture novel" and his most accomplished work in print to date, recalls Ruskin judging the moral tone of a society by its artifacts. His romanticism, his emphasis on faith and morality, his sense of individual power, his feeling for nature, his crusade against the philistines, his evocation of medieval values in opposition to the ugliness of an industrial age . . . all these are very nineteenth-century concerns. Symons also fails to fit most modern concepts of an artist's role, including Frye's assertion that the writer has matured when the poetic impulse to create overcomes the rhetorical impulse to assert, and Eliot's similar dictum that "the more perfect the artist, the more completely separate in him will be the man who suffers and the mind which creates . . ." In a sense, Symons is *himself* his work of art, painfully and passionately fabricated.

In fact, in the summer of 1967, as he was writing some of the last and most urgent letters to DR, his fictional protagonist, Symons was joined in Yorkville by a handsome, red-headed, seventeen-year-old youth from a prominent Canadian family. With their romance, Symons not only found the ending of his book; he also discovered a mate with whom he felt he could live that sentient and compassionate life which had become his major goal.

By then his marriage was at a total impasse, and the reviews of *Place d'Armes* helped to place it beyond redemption. As Symons later wrote, his first novel was "my absolute and irreparable breach with Respectability and the Canadian Establishment." Most of the critics not only attacked the book for its literary faults; they also emphasized its homosexual passages, and were explicitly offended by the author's broadsides against English Canadian society: most refused to accept Hugh Anderson's claim at the start of the book that he loved his people even more than he hated them. The strongest attack was levelled in *The Toronto Star* by Robert Fulford, one of the foremost Eastern critics. Fulford wrote that Anderson (in other words, Symons) "may well be the most repellent single figure in the recent history of Canadian writing." The hero's problem, Fulford concluded, was that he could not love; "the author's problem is that he can write neither with nor about love." The review was headlined: A Monster From Toronto.

This was the review that rankled the most. As Symons stated in a letter:

It was the voice of the Canadian Queen Grand-Mom, Queen Victoria, speaking via the Canadian Grit Methodist tradition. It was my formal outlawing. From then I could be written off, publicly and in private, as a "monster".

As the companion of a runaway minor, Symons was now especially vulnerable. There were threats from his lover's parents, who also alerted the Morality Squad of the Toronto Police. When his lawyer warned him to leave the country, Symons fled to Mexico. At the age of thirty-four, he was an exile.

His lover was whisked away by his parents to the Bahamas, but he escaped from them in early 1968 and joined Symons in San Miguel, after bribing his way across the border. (His parents had confiscated his passport.) Accepted or at least tolerated by the other expatriates, both began working on novels. Then his lover wrote to his parents, hoping to appease them; instead, the parents appealed to Ottawa, which alerted the Canadian Embassy, and the Mexican police were soon in the hunt. By the time Symons was made aware of the danger, the *Federales* were already in San Miguel, interrogating and threatening some of his friends, as well as brusquely searching their homes. Packing hastily, the fugitives barely escaped before a road block sealed the town. For several weeks, they were on the run, living among the Indians in the mountains, and in small fishing villages on the Pacific coast. Short of funds, and pursued by the *Federales*, they also had to contend with Mexicans who were frequently suspicious and sometimes hostile. (An American girl who joined them for a while was raped and killed by seven soldiers.)

As he retreated deeper into the countryside — and adopted an alias for his mail-drops — Symons assessed his situation in a letter to his lawyer. His arrest and extradition now seemed imminent; he also feared that charges would be laid against him in Canada: "I face the absurd reality of being some mere latter-day Oscar Wilde! — only possible in a still Victorian Canada." If taken to court, he added, his best defence would be insanity:

> But the terrible fact about me . . . is that I am not insane, that underneath all the fol-de-rol, the bravado, the arrogance of panache, and even sometimes the sheer cow-

ard's simpering — underneath all that, I am implacably sane — and I know implacably and to a syllable what I am doing and why . . .

Our case is incredibly simple! Men must be allowed to touch. Men must be allowed their own gentleness as a right, a natural right. Men must control their own maleness, their own cocks. Women must not rule by cock-kill. Women must not rule by killing their own womenhood first, so as to rule cocks by closed-cunt.

He was still writing furiously, even on the run. Increasingly, his diaries and letters take on an embattled tone; increasingly, the pilgrim begins to see himself as insurrectionist. He had already foretold the French Canadian revolution; now, he wrote:

What I am doing, with my male-lover, is the English Canadian revolution. And it is a revolution with a cause . . . the right to love, and to share that love, and to use that love to redeem a hellish Canadian community (a "Scotland of the mind").

In the end, either way I shall win. If I am smashed, by Multi-Mom — by family legal power, or by government, or church or whatever — then I am a martyr hero saint. And my cause marches on. I willingly die for this.

And if I win . . . if I am allowed to love as I shall, and to grow as I need, in my love . . . then thousands and thousands of young men (and women) are released, are freed from the implicit tyranny of feudal parents. Thousands of young people are freed by my example into their own inner life and growth.

This manifesto was part of the letter which Symons wrote to his mother, but never sent. In the same letter, he described his wife as a "complicit member of Multi-Mom" who had allowed herself to be vanquished by her own parents. "I don't know if I'll ever see her again . . . If she wants a divorce she'll get it. I really don't mind." A few days later, he received a letter from his lawyer, enclosing a half-page memo from his wife. She was, indeed, seeking a divorce.

He *did* mind. Hunted and harassed, with hardly any money, and fearful that he would soon be locked up, Symons was plunged by his wife's memo into the deepest despair he had ever known. Even after fleeing Canada, he had continued to hope that he could someday return to the farm — with his lover — and that he and his wife could recreate their marriage. Even now, he refused to relinquish that dream entirely. For two weeks, he burned himself into a single-spaced, 148-page response (which was also never sent). Both tender and terrible, loving and hateful, the letter was partly a plea for his wife to reconsider her decision. But it also was an anatomy of their marriage, and an attack on all the forces which had conspired to wreck it. Symons knew that others were putting all the blame on him, that they saw him as a monster and a deviate, as a corrupter of youth who had abandoned his wife and young son, and as possibly deranged. But if he blamed himself at all, it was only for his cowardice, for his failure to battle sooner and harder.

This letter is an example of how Symons will build a devastating case with hardly any consideration for the other side. It would happen again with his lover, when Symons finally became convinced that he, too, had gone over to the Enemy. At no point, in all the thousands of pages he has written about his family, his wife and his lover, does Symons make any sustained attempt to see himself as they must see him, to present their point of view. Obviously they *have* a point of view, and it does not take much imagination to see Symons through their eyes, or to apprehend their grievances against him. Similarly it is evident that not every member of the political, business and cultural establishment is as narrow, vindictive and spiritually impoverished as Symons portrays them in his novels. It is simply not true that we have, on the one hand, an exclusively vital Symons and, on the other, an exclusively bland and mediocre society. Yet this is what Symons, in his furious pursuit of the hydra-headed Enemy, continually suggests. Even more than Emily Carr, he has a strong compulsion to vilify anyone who refuses to accept the totality of his vision. In his personal relations, he is often much more tolerant and generous than his writing would indicate. Many of his friends would testify that he has been a strong ally in times of crisis; many are men and women who clearly fail to achieve the standards of uncompromising commitment which he advocates publicly. But this hardly mitigates the fact that Symons has often weakened his case by making it so stridently.

For all his anguish while on the run in Mexico, Symons was starting to suspect that his case might be established, and his battle won, some way short of martyrdom. Three days after the memo from his wife, another letter told him that the much-abused *Place d'Armes* had received a $1,000 Beta Sigma Phi Best First Canadian Novel Award. This was a prestigious award — Margaret Laurence and Brian Moore were previous winners — and a further indication that the novel was more important than most of the critics had suggested. It pulled Symons back from the brink: "This letter saved my life . . . I was smack on suicide: absolute."

It was also fortunate for Symons that much of the heat was already off. His lover's parents had left Mexico City and returned to Toronto, frustrated by the ineptitude of the Mexican police, and by their son's adamant refusal to capitulate; moreover, his lover's brother had pilfered his passport from their father's office, and mailed it to him. Within days, the pair had left Mexico without incident and were heading north, so that Symons could receive his award at a ceremony in Toronto. Symons saw all this as a triumph, and a turning-point:

> To cross this border is to accept the conversion that my entire living these past months and progressively years, has preached. It is to accept my own conversion. So that — in another way of saying — I pass from the pangs of professional Martyrdom to the singular life of the practicing Saint . . .
>
> Henceforth, my concern is Grace, Joy, Inner Light . . .

This new sense of triumph barely survived the spring of 1968. In Toronto, Symons received his award, and had a formal encounter with his wife, who had now begun her divorce proceedings (and who told him she had never been more than a figment of his imagination); his lover had several awkward meetings with his parents. Although there was no longer any threat of legal action, both became convinced they could still not live as lovers within their society. By mid-summer, they had settled in northern British Columbia, ten miles beyond the end of the last coastal road, and were finding occasional work as oyster-pickers. By winter, they had moved even further north, near the Alaskan Panhandle. Living in a cabin in the forest, they earned money whenever they could, mainly as lumberjacks.

It was a hard and brutal life. They were bullied by the other lumberjacks, whose idea of manliness was to get drunk and rape Indian women; one winter night, when it was forty below, they lost their way in the woods and almost perished. It was difficult to find work, and they were often without money. On Christmas Day, they were given dinner in a Salvation Army hostel. During this time, Symons' letters and diary entries became increasingly bitter and despairing. They were filled with his sense of exile and betrayal; more and more, they spoke of martyrdom and suicide. ("I must die. I want to give my life for joy.") There were growing strains with his lover: Symons began to complain of his bitchiness and bad faith.

But the letters and diaries were also joyful. Using coloured paper and coloured inks, Symons was filling their pages with swirling drawings of birds and flowers, cocks and crucifixes. Despite the pain and despair, he had a sense that he was bursting through to some new level of ecstatic celebration, both spiritual and sensual: he began to call it his Grace Space. He also saw himself as the forerunner of a "psychic revolution" which would overthrow the rule of Blandman and transform his grey and cruel society. There was a New World aborning in the West, he wrote. "THERE IS A NEW MAN ABORNING IN US ALL."

Symons and his lover left British Columbia in the autumn of 1969, after more than a year in the bush, and came back east. He would still have to endure an even longer and more distant exile; his search for the New Man had only just begun, and would take him to a much older world. None of this was evident to him at the time. He was returning to Toronto for the publication of *Civic Square*, to plan a new book and — as part of an emerging pattern — to make some public sorties against his society, and to preach the psychic revolution.

Because of its bulk, its cost ($17.50) and its limited printing, *Civic Square* made less of an impact than *Place d'Armes*, although some of the reviews were notably more favourable, especially a full-page assessment by Graeme Gibson in *The Globe Magazine*. Symons now regarded both of his books as flawed. Indifferent as he was to conventional literary criticism, he felt that he had muffled himself, especially in *Civic Square*, where he had portrayed the distemper of the city without nailing down its cause. Still not exactly sure of what he had seen, still wanting to protect his mother and his wife, he had failed to identify the Enemy. By calling in the police, his lover's mother had removed any doubts; as he now wrote in a letter: "I'll concede public equality to the North American female provided she confesses and relinquishes her private tyranny . . . the Matriarchate!"

He had other targets (as always, they were all part of the same Enemy): Symons lashed out at them in a rollicking speech at Brock University in early 1970. He told the students he was dedicated to the total destruction of the Canadian state, because the official Canadian Identity was evil. Using Sartre's definition of evil as the move away from the concrete to the abstract, he cited Expo 67 ("the biggest plastic hurdy-gurdy side-show in history") and especially the new flag: "It didn't come out of battle, or passion, or love, or fervour. It came out of Committee." As another move from the flesh-and-blood to the abstract, the Canadian Identity had also been concocted in committee by the power brokers of the Liberal Party, the United Church, the civil service and the academic hierarchy. Since each of these forces had been trammelled by repressed sensuality, the result of their efforts was Blandman: weak of spirit, incapable of touch, joyless and sexless, yet animated by the mechanical energy of an imprisoned eroticism.

Symons told his young audience that *they* were the revolution which would overthrow Blandman's rule. "Toss them out! Jail them!" he thundered:

> Out with all this furtive, obscene, death-dealing puritanism . . . this prurient puritanism that lies at the

base of the Canadian Identity and the Emasculate National Conception. It is time we told these men and these women to come alive, or to die. It is time we told them that we, the young, will no longer pay their psychic and moral dues. They crucify us, to confirm their own failure in faith. Out . . . out . . . OUT! Give them no quarter. They gave you none. They will give you none. It is you . . . or them!

Here again we have Symons as a nineteenth-century figure, a parson in his pulpit roaring against all the wickedness in the world. Aside from the subversive daring of his text, aside from his growing reputation as a peripatetic scandal, he could now hold an audience with the sheer theatricality of his performance. Sometimes scornful and mocking, sometimes indignant and passionate, he had a compelling habit of raising his voice and flicking his left arm backward over his head to emphasize the last phrase of a peroration.

His appearance was equally theatrical; in recent years, it had undergone considerable transformation. *Place d'Armes* had appeared with an Ashley and Crippen photograph on the dust jacket of the author-as-young-aesthete or *fin de siècle* poet: clean-shaven, moody, sensitive, almost langorous. Now his hair was even longer, he had a thick brown beard, and his body had taken on more flesh: he came across as stronger, more substantial and more challenging. In a photograph from this time, he stands with his feet firmly planted and his hands on his hips, confronting the camera with a forceful, mocking stare, looking less like an aesthete than some bawdy Friar Tuck, a swarthy swashbuckler, or Holbein's portrait of the young Henry VIII.

Symons would make many more speeches to students. But he was often much less optimistic about his revolution than his oratory indicated. He did feel he was a Romantic who had paid his dues: "I'm a Romantic who has come clean!" While this was a personal triumph, he felt the cost had been enormous, and that the Enemy had already won the larger battle. In the spring of 1970, his wife gained her divorce, and was given custody of their son — in the years ahead she would consistently deny Symons access to him. As Symons wrote in a letter:

My story with her is the story of what was done by the Matriarchy to the North American Male. You can say that I provoked (convoked) it. You can say that I demanded the full Nemesis of the Male who taunted the Queen to come out clean. I did . . . I got slaughtered. It was the best I could do. It was more than 999,999 out of a million North American men did.

From this point, his letters and diaries are filled with a sense of overwhelming loss — the loss of nation and heritage as well as family — and increasingly the loss is seen as irrevocable. It was in this frame of mind that Symons undertook to research and write an expensive and lavishly illustrated book on early Canadian furniture. "What I want to give you with the text of this book is the definitive ground study in Canadian sensibility," he wrote to his publisher. "It's a kind of swansong for a culture I once loved, and whose memory in me is still warm."

In the spring of 1970, Symons began his pilgrimage into his past. With an advance from his publisher, and grants from three friends, he purchased a truck, camper and twenty-foot trailer: these would be home and studio for himself and his lover. For four months, they ranged through Ontario, Quebec and the Maritimes, tracking down key pieces of furniture in museums, galleries, churches and private homes. This was more than research; as Symons wrote, it was a "personal Odyssey into the heart of early Canadian belief." He felt that furniture was central evidence for any culture: "If we know what our furniture is, then we know who we are, in the profoundest sense — and we cannot escape with a counterfeit identity."

With a pile of notes and photographs, Symons and his lover settled in for a winter of writing at Trout River, a remote Newfoundland fishing village of about one thousand people. Here they were as effectively in exile as they had been in British Columbia or Mexico. They parked their trailer on a hill overlooking the harbour, and staked it down against the wind. Suspicious at first, the villagers came to accept the refugees; Symons and his lover were soon helping them to plant their potatoes, and giving them the use of their truck — in return, they received vegetables, fish, moose steaks, partridge berry pies, knitted clothes and homemade curtains for their camper. Symons taught in the Sunday School, and sang with gusto and pounded his tambourine at Salvation Army services. Scribbling a diary note amid the clashing of cymbals at one of the services, he wrote: "How hard it is. How slow and bumbling I am in my spiritual growing. Perhaps it is best to be here, with these fishermen-peasants, to learn my spiritual A-B-C . . . to learn, not the words, but the *enactment of faith* . . . making my life an Enaction of Faith."

This quest was at the heart of the texts that he was writing. ("Furniture is faith!" he stated in the Introduction.) He finished the book — which was to be called *Heritage* — in the spring of 1971. There were forty-six texts, and they were to accompany photographs by John de Visser. For the first time, Symons had a specific form imposed upon his writing; he responded with essays which were characteristically pungent and passionate, but which were free of the prolixity and self-indulgence that had marred his novels.

The sub-title — "A Romantic Look at Early Canadian Furniture" — was apt. The pieces in the book — the chairs and sofas, the desks and clocks, the altars and tables — are never described as mere objects, but are always alive with a personality of their own, and the personality of the men who made and used them. Symons salutes them, bows to them, strokes them, grapples with them — and sometimes makes love to them: ". . . remember when you first put your arms around me," he begins his ode to a French Canadian Salamander Chair, and then goes on to describe their coupling.

Symons uses the furniture to evoke the earlier cultures of the Maritimes, Quebec and Ontario. He praises the Salamander Chair for her "peasant ebullience" and, at the same time, her "high courtliness", accepting her as the French Canadian *par excellence*. Describing a massive and elegant grandfather clock, he writes that "In 1800, and right on into living memory, culture, quality, physical creativity — these lived together in Canada. Meditation with the hands, and touch with the mind, were not separated in any significant way." In a Nova Scotian pine doorway, he finds "the harmonious fusion of firm yet frolicking folk and dignified responsible squire — the blending at once of the common people and the man of quality: what Thomas Haliburton did with Sam Slick and Squire Poker; and what the Nova Scotians did as a people."

Moving into Ontario, he uses a maple sideboard to refute the Methodist log-cabin myth by demonstrating that there was always another culture in English Canada: "a culture of sophistications, elegances, poise and literacy." In the same way, a teapoy shows that "far from being a nation of squabbling squatters and dominantly dour Scotch, mid-Victorian Canada shows signs of a concern for delicacy of feeling and of personal presence."

Also in Ontario, however, he finds early evidence of the forces which came to dominate and defeat his romantic Tory tradition. A Victorian sofa reminds Symons of the Matriarchy: "She seems to say: 'NOW JUST SIT DOWN PROPERLY.'" With its "lusting asperity", a tiger-maple table embodies the Scotch Presbyterian: "All the flame under the gloss; never gets out. Impasse . . . of national proportions."

In cost and format, *Heritage* was a coffee-table book: rarely has a revolutionary manifesto received such lavish packaging. As Symons wrote in his diary, the book was "utterly seditious". It can best be read in conjunction with his speech at Brock University, with the furniture as living evidence for his case against the Blandmen. In celebrating traditions which the Blandmen had betrayed, *Heritage* is a visual correlative to George Grant's *Lament for a Nation.* (Grant wrote a warm Foreword.) While Symons was just as pessimistic as Grant about the survival of those traditions, he could close his book on a note of personal hope: "My body and my mind and soul were at one," he wrote. "And at the very moment when it was clear that my people had to make their ultimate choice, between faith and cynicism . . . I had renewed my faith — and I rejoiced."

Despite this affirmation, his quest was far from ended. He had taken on the role of revolutionary prophet; everywhere he went, he lived that role without respite. In the most casual gatherings, Symons was a brooding, dark-bearded presence. Devoid of small talk, he was filled with a restless energy that ebbed into exhaustion and despair, but would burst forth again within minutes or hours in a new round of confrontations and celebrations. With tears in his eyes, he once rose to his feet at a dinner party of Toronto literary and publishing luminaries to announce that one of his younger brothers had died that day — and then to deliver a lengthy eulogy which indicted his family and his society for the brother's premature demise.

He had a disturbing knack of sensing the guilts and fears in others — if these were evidence for his case, he would sometimes show no mercy in bringing them into the open. More often he served as a catalyst, rather than a deliberate agent of disruption: it was as though he held up a mirror in which others saw their own frustrations and secret fears. Many found him dangerous, especially when he waded through their marriages, love affairs, friendships and careers.

Faced with such behaviour, many people thought Symons was evil, or mad, or at least enormously egotistical. Yet he was greatly in demand. While many private homes were closed to him, there were signs of a growing recognition that he was important, and far from alone in his concerns. Even more universities were asking him to lecture; there were also television interviews and a grant from the Ontario Arts Council to help finance his next novel. "It is clear I could make a living, a 'career', as a man-of-letters," Symons wrote in the spring of 1971. "And it is perfectly clear that I won't."

Just as he had provoked his firing from the ROM, just as he had wilfully flubbed his test with *Seven Days*, so he now turned his back on the academic and journalistic worlds. Like Carr, he sensed that to compromise with respectability would be to trammel and muffle himself; he had a similar impulse toward the role of embattled visionary. Moreover, he felt it was time for his odyssey to take a new direction. A growing impasse with his lover now convinced him that he had only just begun to identify the full evil in his society, and to formulate an alternative vision.

This was as decisive as the breakup of his marriage, and equally traumatic. Symons took enormous pride in the fact that he and his lover had been together for four years; he saw this as a major triumph over the forces of respectability and repression. Since their time in Mexico, he had hoped that they could embody a new way of being — open and sentient, joyful and compassionate — which would serve as a beacon for thousands of other young Canadians. This was a typically extravagant ambition: it placed a continual strain on their daily life together. In BC, and even more in Trout River, Symons began to suspect that his lover was becoming an apostate — just as much of a bitch-queen as he felt his wife had been, and equally adept at killing all joy and spontaneity.

To Symons, this was an almost unbearable turn of events. After breaking with his wife, he had staked everything on a new life with his lover; now he felt that he had linked his destiny with an even more treacherous creature-victim of the Enemy. As always he saw his personal dilemma as a guide to the national impasse: his lover, he wrote, "IS the Canadian Identity. An Identity predicated upon fear and hate . . . The fact is increasingly clear to me that sado-masochism lies at the very core of our society."

This was a key discovery for Symons: it would reverberate through all his subsequent writing. Although he had little use for the clinical terminology of psychology, he now adopted "sado-masochism" to describe the inevitable result of the split between mind and body which he had long seen as the crux of the Canadian impasse. This split, he felt, drove eroticism down into the body, and spirituality up into the head. Tortured sensuality goes mean, generating negative energy which has to be grounded, like static, in the nearest thing to hand, usually the one we love. The need to give pain, and receive pain, becomes imperative.

Yet Symons was still not able to accept that he had made an irredeemable mistake: he was determined to salvage his dream. This was the challenge: to cure the evil in his lover, and in his society. Above all, it seemed time to find a basis for that new spiritual world of which he had proclaimed himself a herald, and which he and his lover might still enter together.

In the summer of 1971, with *Heritage* at the printers, Symons left his lover in Trout River and took a plane to London. He was exhausted and distraught, but this was more than a holiday. At the age of thirty-eight, he wanted to refresh his European roots, but he also felt he had to go beyond

Europe — in both space and time — in pursuit of his vision. And so he went to Marrakech.

His initial visit to Morocco lasted for only two weeks, but as a new stage in his odyssey it was just as crucial as the three weeks in Montreal which had produced *Place d'Armes*. Later he described it as "a psychic breakthrough — a great philosophical and carnal experience."

Not by chance, Symons had chosen a land which was a haven for Western homosexuals. But he had little sympathy for their lotus-life in Marrakech, and he had always pitied the Gay Queens of the breed, the flagrant and unmanly ones. Symons would say: "I'm homosexual, but not gay" — in Canada, most of the people he liked and respected, both male and female, were heterosexual. (He would often state that certain of his male friends might be regenerated by a homosexual affair, but he never advanced this as a universal panacea.) Just as he could move amongst the young in Yorkville, but refuse to accept their counter-culture as his alternative world, so he could mingle with the gays without losing himself in their *milieu*. Symons felt that both groups were incomplete: each had made an important and honourable break from the bland society, but each lacked that wholeness of mind and body which remained his personal goal. As far back as *Place d'Armes*, he had tried to make this clear:

> A queen drifts by on air . . . leaves me cold. I realize with uncharitable clarity that this is not what I want . . . it is not the homosexual that I want — no, not at all: because there is something decisive missing in these men, some final reality . . . Some capacity to give. Some capacity for compassion. Something to give that has been gutted from them . . .
>
> No — it is not the homosexual I want . . . it is the sentient man. A new *kind* of man. The man who thinks at the end of his fingertips.

Now he sought such a man among the Moroccans. Instead of lingering in the gay bars of Marrakech, he plunged deeper into the countryside, travelling into the Atlas Mountains and encountering — while staying in the palace of a sheikh — a world of elegance and sophistication, physical intimidation and raw violence. (The sheikh was noted for murder. Symons fled his palace on the run.)

He also found an Arab lover, a young man called Kebir: their brief romance was at the heart of Symons' breakthrough. In Kebir, he encountered manliness, simplicity, openness and dignity. He felt as though an awful burden had finally been lifted from him: the burden of uncleanliness and guilt which his mother had imposed, and which his wife and lover had sustained. This was decisive: he had begun *Civic Square* by asserting that "Cocks are beautiful", and the whole novel had described his battle with the forces which denied that verity. Later, in Trout River, he had written in his diary that the fundamental issue in the Western world was not Vietnam, or poverty, but phallic: "the greatest single impoverishment in the world is the Occidental phallus!" Now, on the edge of the Orient, he had found a "permanent phallic carnival". He concluded that "a phallic culture *can* exist — a culture where one has no guilt about one's body."

He would return to Morocco — and stay much longer — for he had only begun to assimilate its impact. Already he sensed that this older, non-Western world was in some way linked to his own traditions, that it offered a means of restoring his authentic roots as a Canadian *and* a basis for that more open, more celebratory existence which he had long quested. Now he wanted to test these new intuitions against the unresolved dilemma he had left behind. So he returned to Canada, and a reunion with his lover.

They were together for nearly another year; in the autumn of 1972, they finally parted. His lover proclaimed that *he* was not homosexual, that it was time (he was then in his early twenties) to finish his education, to settle on some career, even to marry. Symons took this as a betrayal and an enormous defeat. He felt his lover had never given himself fully to their love (any more than his wife had done). Even worse, he was now embracing a counterfeit freedom, a counterfeit respectability and the very counterfeit Canadian Identity against which they had both rebelled. Alone in Mexico, Symons poured out his grief and indignation:

At the very moment my life and works should come to

sweet serene fruition, with the love of my choice — my love fucks us, by fucking my head off (or screwing my heart black and my spirit bleak) . . . and he runs off to hide in the camp of mine enemy, making his new life and career thereby, and I — I am left alone in visual Paradise, in the sun, amidst the flowers whose brilliant red reminds me only of him.

After the break, Symons had returned to San Miguel in the hope of living with a young woman with whom he and his lover had had a mutual affair in the previous year. When he found that she had already moved in with someone else, he felt even more abandoned. It was beginning to seem to him that he would never sustain a love which satisfied all his hungers, and which would also be a paradigm for the New Man whose advent he had long proclaimed. The New Man would have both brains and balls; as Symons now wrote, his marriage had broken up because he had refused to give up his balls, so that his wife had concluded he was sexually insane, while his lover had complained that he was too heavy and too mind-full. "That is, neither of my great loves could sustain the reality of both brains and balls at the same time."

Yet he was still seeking the perfect relationship. After a trip to Mexico City — where he visited the Anthropological Museum, the great Cathedral in the main square and the Gallery of Modern Art — he defined that ideal love by using his sensibility as he had in *Heritage*, to enter into the essence of the buildings and the artifacts.

In the Museum, he felt a dionysian delirium before the Aztec and Mayan sculptures. "It was wondrously pagan . . . great moulded hewn forms, in stone, in wood. Dragons, lizards, giant snakes — forms all larger than life . . . all vehement, all carnal, all dangerous, all blood-thirsty. They made you want to dance up and down, some foot-stamping, thigh-roiling dance of acquiescence, submission and ecstasy. They all reeked of the sun — of a sun which blitzed your eyes open — and which smashed three-dimensional perspective, rather like marijuana."

In the Cathedral, he took Holy Communion and rejoiced in the vaulted splendour and the golden richness of the towering main altar. It was "as though the mind, the

Renaissance mind, the three-dimensional mind, had been taken and squeezed bodily back through Medieval beliefs in some wondrous combination of reason and faith . . . here my mind soared, and my spirit roared . . ."

In the Gallery, he found an exhibition of paintings by Silvio Pardo: "picture after picture of beauteous women — invariably nude, or feeling nude . . . invariably surrounded by flames, or gossamer, or bright webs, or floating lips, or burning bushes, or deep-waving hair . . . Women floating within themselves, all lips and eye and pubescence . . . Women as they must have felt, been, been seen in the Middle Ages . . . a kinduv carnival of silken flesh, dangerous, and spiritual. All of them St Teresa . . . but St Teresa with a cunt! I looked on amazed. Here was woman as I have always *felt* she was, must be, or must well have been. Here was a woman I could understand, respect, celebrate . . . Here was a woman at once princess, nun, mistress . . . and saint."

Describing the experience to a friend, Symons wrote that he had come away from the city with his head reeling — and his heart sore, and rich:

> I said to myself, as I drove back to San Miguel . . . this is what I wanted . . . some combination of the pagan-splendoured life-force of the Indian temple and the Indian dances, along with the Christian prayer, praise and kindness . . .
>
> I wanted first and foremost to live and be the man that was the positives of Aztec Temple and Christian Cathedral . . . I wanted to live this with a man, another man . . . perhaps helping to create the new kind of man that our union was in itself . . . And that kind of man, if he wished, could go and find the Woman of Silvio Pardo, if she wished.

Back in San Miguel, Symons went to a restaurant where the customers were dancing to a modern band, complete with drums and electric guitars. Here, too, he found an embodiment of all that he had sought. The dancing was both gentle and erotic, unrepressed and celebratory: "I was seeing the fluency, the grace, the life-force of the Indian dances . . . plus some gentleness, some mutual physical compassion that was the kindness of the Christian Communion." Yet as he watched the dancers, he also sensed that something was missing:

> As the mod-electric music pounded at my ears, and my mind threatened to dissolve, blow — I knew what was missing. The mind, and all memory of the past, all continuity, all history, all affectionate remembrances and responsibilities . . .
>
> And as I recognized this, I knew what my role was — and always has been . . . the role of link, of missing link, of hyphen, between two worlds. Link between the old and traditional world of mind, memory, culture, manners (yes) — and this new (renewed) world of bodifluency, full flow of feelings and passion, this new world of kindness in the flesh.
>
> My job has been to bring, hold, help the two together.

More fully than ever before, Symons had defined his role — the nature of his quest. With the defection of his lover, however, he felt his personal battle had been lost, and that it was time to go, time to end his life. He felt like "an animal which has been deeply wounded, in the woods, and while it does not die right off, and is not caught by the hunter who has wounded it, yet the animal knows it is sore wounded — and it finds some copse, some haven, to lie down, and it knows it won't come out again." But he insisted that his suicide would be positive — not an act of mere despair. In a letter to the Anglican minister in San Miguel, he said he wanted to *give* his life, to affirm the beliefs for which he had fought, especially the unity of body and spirit. There was nothing negative in this, he added, no spite, no rancour, no hate, no revenge:

> My going is positive. It affirms and sings and celebrates. It affirms my love for a people and a nation and a history and a culture . . . and for a community and a family — and for a lost wife, and for the man I love. Know this, tell them this for me — and be glad, rejoice.

This was close to his nadir: the winter of 1972-73 in San Miguel. Symons was living alone in a small *casa*, and was a source of concern and embarrassment to the resident expatriates. Many felt that he was, indeed, close to suicide. Yet he was also writing, and it was his writing that pulled him through. As always, he was pouring himself into his diaries and letters — pages and pages of them every day — and taking precautions to ensure that they would survive his death, and eventually be published. He told his friends that his wife had threatened to burn his papers, and he often recalled how the wives of Burton, Wilde and Gide had taken vengeance on their husbands in this way. Symons was also at work on two novels: one was an account of his odyssey with his lover, the other was based on his Moroccan experience. Despite his despair, he sensed there was still much to tell, that his testament was not yet complete. As he wrote in a letter: "The blunt (the brutal) fact of the matter is that writing these two novels saved (is saving) my life! Is exorcizing and expiating me, and (I can suspect) an entire culture/nation/people."

Still driving his truck and camper, Symons returned to Toronto in time for Easter. He was nearly forty, with three books to his credit and little else to show for his travails except that great horde of unpublished papers. He had few possessions (the camper was filled mainly with his diaries) and hardly any clothes. As usual he also had little money, and the truck and camper were pledged to cover his debts. His only companion was a black Labrador bitch, who had been with him since Trout River.

Symons had come north to see his lover. He had never fully accepted their parting: now he was hoping they could be reunited. Instead, on Easter Sunday, he was again rejected — even more decisively than before. This drove him back to the brink of suicide. "My death was a matter of time . . . of days, or of weeks," he later wrote. "I had once again placed my life on the line to back my love . . . and it had, once again, been stolen and betrayed . . . I was a murdered man. And I preferred to die true to my faith and love, rather than live as a ghost. It was incredibly clear to me."

Symons had several close friends in Toronto, most of whom were fellow writers: they rallied to help him save himself. Clearly there was part of him that *wanted* to be saved, and was crying out for help — as when Symons told one friend that he had scouted out the location of his suicide: a bridge over the Don Valley. Just as clearly, his spiritual and physical energies were all but spent, and his friends became convinced that he might indeed take his own life.

Every day, Symons seemed to be driven — and driving himself — closer to such a final resolution. He kept his friends on almost constant call; in long, passionate monologues, Symons would pour out his grief and lacerating pain. Yet at the very moment when Symons seemed so grossly impossible, so extravagantly demanding, he also evoked enormous sympathy and compassion. Although his friends led much more conventional lives, Symons generated an overwhelming conviction that he was fighting their battles as well as his own, that his vision was unique and irreplaceable. At the nadir of his life, with a slouching body, a voice that trailed into the merest whisper, and eyes filled with insupportable sadness, Symons was more compelling than ever.

His friends tried in various ways to rescue him, but the breakthrough came only when he was prevailed upon to see a psychoanalyst. Symons went reluctantly to the first appointment — he had long regarded analysts as the evil priests of modern society, as purveyors of a bland and repressed normality — but he was soon returning from the sessions in jubilation. Between them, Symons and the analyst recreated the scenario of the previous six years: as the evidence unfolded, the analyst concluded that Symons was living out a death-wish of his lover's.

As the analyst and Symons came to see it, his lover had tried to transfer on to him all his own hatreds, so that he could escape back into the respectable world, ostensibly cured. But his lover was, in fact, still riddled with the disease of his society: after all the inverted pleasure he had taken in breaking up their love, he still wanted the final satisfaction of being able to say: "Scott died for our love." In short, he was systematically (if unconsciously) driving Symons to suicide.

To Symons, this was a stunning revelation. He rejoiced in being pronounced sane, and in recognizing that much of his blackness and despair were his lover's parting gift, and could now be exorcized. His recovery would be slow and painful — throughout the summer, he was still wracked with sorrow — but he was now seized with a passion for retribution. Under the overall title of *Helmet of Flesh*, his novels were merging into a complex account of all that had happened with his lover, and much else that had happened before: Symons spent most of the summer working on them (while gratefully developing the analyst as a major character). As he later wrote: "Then, as the first shattering agony of pain and loss passed, I turned to the one remaining thing that mattered, to *Helmet of Flesh*. I was absolutely determined that that story should be told! Bluntly, I wanted — no, not revenge — I wanted justice!"

By the autumn, he was whole enough to continue his odyssey. Toronto was the capital of the Blandmen; he felt it was still hostile to his vision. He had been initially refused support by the Canada Council, but a strong and urgent application by several of his friends resulted in a Senior Arts Award. This would pay his way back into exile, and buy him time to write. He would return to North Africa — to work on his novel, and to explore further that older world which had seemed to offer a richer reality than the "psychic void" of Canada. And so, in September 1973, with his pipe, his typewriter and a suitcase filled with manuscript — all his worldly goods — he went back to Morocco.

It was meant to be a six-month visit; instead, Symons stayed in Morocco for two years. Living first in Tangier, then in Marrakech and finally in Essaouira, on the Atlantic coast, he attracted his usual quota of adventures and disasters. At the start, he was nearly murdered in his Tangier hotel. As he wrote in a letter:

> A young Moroccan climbed in through my bedroom window one night, with a large knife. I was naked asleep. We talked, fought, made love ... at the end I sat for about an hour with that carving knife under my naked balls ... while he threatened to cut them off and send them to Golda Meir in Israel.
>
> In the end I kept my balls! He lost a quantity of blood (I wounded him with his own knife), and he made off with my travellers cheques, passport, watch, etc. About two weeks later, I got them all back (I did some amateur

sleuthing) — and the would-be thief-murderer-lover
came back and I took him out to a fine dinner ... And
thereafter, for about two weeks, my testicles became the
talk of Tangier! I was almost proud ...

Shortly after returning to Morocco, Symons was surprised by his own laughter — "I hadn't heard the sound in
months, years." In a letter, he described "the Canadian
Ambassador's wife, in Essaouira, dining on the floor of the
antique shop of one of my Moroccan friends, her back
propped up against a three-foot-tall stone carved phallus, surrounded by Mohammed's young male harem ... and asking
me if I knew anything at all about Moroccan sexual customs
(while she unwittingly kept scratching her straight back
against that very hard phallus!) It was all I could do to prevent myself from *shouting* with laughter!"

Yet there was always an element of peril — a viper in
the bedroom, or a scorpion in the kitchen. In early 1974,
Symons was bitten by a mad dog, and had to take a harrowing series of rabies shots in his belly. For two weeks, he was
wracked with pain and fatigue; more crucially, he was forced
to acknowledge that, for all his returning strength and gaiety,
he was still vulnerable: "Despite my own best efforts, despite
prodigies of work and discipline ... despite whatever psychic
heroism or courage I could muster, I could be knifed down in
a second — in this case by something as absurd as a mad dog!
And this could happen before my work was done."

Impelled by this sense of vulnerability, Symons was
working hard on his novels. This involved hundreds of new
pages (it gradually became apparent that he was dealing with
three separate but connected books), re-explorations of the
Moroccan hinterland (including a return to the sheikh's
palace, where he slept with a knife beside his bed), and a
bulky correspondence with Dennis Lee, his editor in Toronto.
Lee soon noted that a very crucial change was taking place in
the writing. With his first two novels, Symons had been writing directly out of his immediate experience. With his new
trilogy, however, he was no longer pouring his thoughts and
feelings directly on to the page; instead he was looking back in
time, and shaping and pacing his material in a craftsmanlike
manner. Although his protagonist was, as always, himself

(and was again called Hugh Anderson), Symons was at last adopting a sane perspective on his central character; he was also slowly foresaking his obsessive sermonizing and cerebration, as well as creating convincing minor characters. In short, Symons seemed consciously to be fabricating works of art.

While his writing was showing new maturity and discipline, his themes were still the same. Above all, Symons was struggling to assimilate his experiences with his wife and lover, and his whole Canadian society, and to relate these to the new verities he had found, and was now confirming, in Morocco. After a pilgrimage of nearly twenty years — in Canada, Europe, Mexico and North Africa — after three books and more than thirty volumes of diaries and letters — Symons was now setting down his total vision, the resolution of his quest.

He had already celebrated the Great Tradition and its British North American derivation: his own immediate heritage. He had already assailed the Blandmen, the Matriarchy and all their surrogates who had defiled and deposed that tradition in Canada, and substituted a counterfeit identity which was based upon the suppression of joy and touch. After the traumatic events of his last spring and summer in Toronto, he could now describe how this false identity symbolized a particular form of sado-masochistic evil in which Canadians, full of a repressed eroticism, grown hateful and violent, steadily killed the ones they loved. He had prophesized a psychic revolution against the counterfeit identity, and he had seen himself as the missing link between the Great Tradition and the New Man to whom that revolution would give birth.

In search of a spiritual basis for the New Man, Symons was looking back in history — much further back than his immediate traditions. Along the path of his pilgrimage — in Chartres, in Lascaux, in Mexico and finally in Morocco — he had encountered vibrant echoes of older worlds and stronger faiths which might be invoked to redeem the disaster of modernity. Now — in the pages of his novels — he began to put it all together.

Writing to Lee, he described the basic theme of his trilogy, which was also the story of his quest. He said that his hero had fled Canada

a) in a last-ditch effort to divest himself of the "counterfeit Canadian Identity" which is destroying his very psychic-and-nervous system; while

b) restoring, within himself, his never-lost real roots as a Canadian; and

c) entering a deep quest for some new overall reality, which sustains this "restitution" and which allows it to grow.

In Marrakech, he had found his new reality: an older world with an "incarnational mode of being" — a world of touch and passion, of harmony between mind and body. It was there in the dancing of Kebir and the other Moroccan youths; it was also to be found in the total ambience of the sheikh and his palace. It was a world which reminded Symons of the Mexican sun-dances and — most crucially — of the Caves of Lascaux, which he had visited on that long-ago summer in France. In a central passage of the novel, he described an overwhelming mystical vision within the Caves, in which the great beasts on the walls come alive and dance and roar . . .

> . . . a totality of body and being . . . the Cathedral of a world in which man's eye was not yet detached from the object it sees (he "heard" and "felt" the animals before he saw them) . . . the world experienced directly without the mind's intervention . . . in which man and beast and eye and body and being are one and indissoluble . . . whereas Western man has reduced this incarnate world, reduced this endless dance of life to some mere syllogism of mind and manners . . . all reality dying as Western man thought he rose to humanism and, ultimately, to his position as Master of the World. But the World has been crucified in that slow erosive process . . .

> And Marrakech . . . this was another world than the Western world. Marrakech was a world which rooted right back to Lascaux, to the prehistoric caves, to those thundering minotaurs, those aurochs, those phallic-men and hugely fecund women. Marrakech was a sign from another route taken over the past ten thousand years.

Symons had sited his Moroccan world within a tradition which was apparently very different from his own. Since that summer in France, however, he had always felt that Lascaux was part of his heritage. Now he saw the Caves as the essential link between the incarnate world of Morocco and his own Great Tradition. For Lascaux had also led to the other route: the European world which had evolved through medieval cathedrals such as Chartres (which were Lascaux "disembodied", but in which there was still a harmony of vision and being) and then through the Renaissance and the Reformation (during which the harmony was destroyed) and down to the modern world and the modern mind. But the route back to Lascaux was still preserved for modern man, if he only chose to seek it, by taking full possession of his total heritage. As Symons wrote to Lee, the Great Tradition and the new mode of being he had found in Morocco were linked, "and both were accessible to a Canadian in basic possession of his civilization." In other words, his new Moroccan reality *could* sustain the restitution of his authentic Canadian roots — which meant his roots as a citizen of a world still infused with Grace.

Symons was not saying we all must go to Marrakech (and take an Arab lover) in order to restore our authenticity as Canadians. This had been his personal path, and Morocco had provided crucial confirmation of his sacramental vision, as well as a clearer perspective on the repressive evils of his own society. (The contrast between Kebir and his Canadian lover would be a major element in the trilogy.) But Symons is quite distinct from all those Westerners who hurl themselves into sex or drugs, into Eastern religions and often into Eastern lands, seeking some instant nirvana, some immediate panacea for their spiritual impoverishment. For he was still insisting that a Canadian could achieve a wholeness of mind and body only by regaining his own heritage: not the debased culture against which Symons had long contended, but the full romantic traditions of English and French Canada which he had constantly celebrated. Only by restoring his real roots could a Canadian establish an authentic basis for that richer mode of being which Symons had found among the Moroccans, at the end of that other path from Lascaux.

Although he would now define his goal — his "incarnational mode of being" — in terms of Kebir, the sheikh and other Moroccans — he had become that vision himself, and was his own best exemplar. He was still a disturbing and disruptive presence, a ruthless antagonist and a generous but also demanding and often exasperating friend. Increasingly, however, he was joyous, mirthful and positive, an incandescent force. "I'm twice as strong as I've ever been," Symons wrote from Morocco in 1974. "I'm dangerous and beauteous and glad-mad again! I'm a national hazard ... and a national asset!"

He was now in his early forties. His life, he wrote, had been "a long slow battle back to realities which earlier cultures took for granted." In another letter, he assessed himself, and his struggle:

> Presuming that Scott is not simply insane, not simply acting, not simply a belated homosexual on a spree, not simply ... oh, whatever my detractors say about me — then what in God's own name *is* Scott? Because if he is not those negative (and ridiculous) things, then he may just be something positive, fine, strong, brave — he may just be someone who has chosen to stand for the luminous, splendid chivalric, "God-given" things in an otherwise sordid and cynical world ...
>
> Tear aside the trivial ... what has my life been about? Birds, flowers, trees, *objets d'art*, touch ... human, incarnate touch, as celebration (in any mode), spiritual celebration ...
>
> And it's been about this, full time now, for ten years. And it's time people realized it before they finish me off! I'm carrying the ball ... *for them*! I'm trying to say something, tell them something ... with the only thing I have ... my own life.

Symons left Morocco in late 1975. He was returning to Canada with a new lover (a young Canadian who had come to Morocco on his honeymoon) and renewed confidence. His novels needed at least another year of work, but he was convinced that with their publication, people would at last understand the importance of his odyssey, and that his battle might be won. Already, there were signs that people were starting to listen to him, and that he was no longer a total outcast. Under the auspices of the Canadian Ambassador, he had given a lecture at the University of Rabat which received wide newspaper and television coverage. (The government which had once sent police after him was now paying him to talk about Canadian culture.) Symons had more lectures lined up in Canada, and a term as writer-in-residence at Simon Fraser University. But he was still wary of too much respectability; he saw himself as a modern, Rabelaisian warrior-monk, a psychic troubadour who would carry on his battle against the Blandmen. "My morale is strong," he wrote on the eve of his return to Canada. "My vision firm. My intent implacable."

Like the other subjects of this book, Symons has followed a lonely path in search of a more sustaining vision than was offered by his Canadian society. Like the others, he has found his vision in other cultures, and in traditions which modern Canada seeks to denigrate. "After all, you must remember that these foreigners know very little about life." Thus Sarkak in *The White Dawn*. This is what all these six Canadians have said about their own people. Although at odds with their society, they have tried to enrich and redeem that society by sharing their visions with their fellows.

Given the indifference of their compatriots, it is hard to point to any clear-cut triumph — with the exception of Carr's last paintings — which transcends the travail of these lives. Each of these journeys involved loneliness and frustration as much as physical danger and spiritual peril: in the end there is a feeling of enormous waste. Yet nothing is finally lost, since each quest remains exemplary, and points to paths which are still open to us. There is heroism here, and not a little splendour.

NOTES

It took two years to research and write this book. Many people helped me along the way. Their contributions are acknowledged below, under the appropriate chapters. I would also like to thank Shirley Gibson for her valuable suggestions.

Two people deserve special mention. Dennis Lee worked on an early draft of the manuscript; his painstaking comments were a major help. James Polk of The House of Anansi was involved in the project from its inception, and steered me firmly and perceptively to its conclusion. It is customary to state that the faults of any book are the sole responsibility of the author, but I should add that many of its virtues derive from the contributions of these two friends.

INTRODUCTION

For a full discussion of George Grant's ideas, see his three books:

Philosophy in the Mass Age (Toronto: Copp Clark, 1959).
Lament for a Nation: The Defeat of Canadian Nationalism (Toronto: McClelland and Stewart, 1965).
Technology and Empire: Perspectives on North America (Toronto: Anansi, 1969).

For a personal exploration of the same themes, see "Cadence, Country, Silence: Writing in Colonial Space" by Dennis Lee in *Boundary 2* (State University of New York at Binghamton: Vol. III, No. 1, Fall 1974).

BRIGADIER JAMES SUTHERLAND BROWN

I am grateful to Malcolm Sutherland-Brown and Atholl Sutherland Brown, and their families, for providing valuable information and insights on their father, and for permitting me to use personal records and letters. I also received assistance from Araby Lockhart, Diana Mason, John Muggeridge and Maj-Gen George R. Pearkes VC.

The Sutherland Brown Papers in the Douglas Library of Queen's University provided much of the documentary material in this chapter. I am grateful to the archivists at Queen's, and to their colleagues in the Public Archives in Ottawa, and the Directorate of History in the Department of National Defence. The text of Defence Scheme No. 1 is to be found in the former, and Brown's Secret Reports in the latter.

For a discussion of Defence Scheme No. 1, see *In Defence of Canada,* Vol. I, by James Eayrs (University of Toronto Press, 1964), pp 71-85. The same volume deals with Gen McNaughton's work camps on pp 124-148.

Further background on Canadian military strategies is contained in *The Military Problems of Canada,* by C. P. Stacey (Toronto: Ryerson, 1940) and *The Undefended Border: The Myth and the Reality,* also by Stacey (Ottawa: The Canadian Historical Association Booklets, No. 1, 1967).

For discussion of the Loyalist and Tory traditions, see: *The United Empire Loyalists: Men and Myths,* ed. by L.F.S. Upton (Toronto: Copp Clark, 1967); the first chapter of *Canadian Labour in Politics,* by Gad Horowitz (University of Toronto Press, 1968); *The Maple Leaf Forever,* by Ramsay Cook (Toronto: McClelland and Stewart, 1971), especially Chapter Four; and *Towards the Discovery of Canada,* by Donald Creighton (Toronto: Macmillan of Canada, 1972).

Excellent accounts of the Canadian Imperialist tradition are contained in *The Sense of Power:* Studies in the Ideas of Canadian Imperialism 1867-1914, by Carl Berger (University of Toronto Press, 1970), and *Imperialism and Nationalism, 1884-1914,* ed. by Berger (Toronto: Copp Clark, 1969). For a dissenting view by an American writer, first published in 1907, see *The Americanization of Canada,* by E. Moffett (University of Toronto Press, 1972).

For visual and tactile insights into Sutherland Brown's Anglo-Tory world, see *Heritage:* A Romantic Look at Early Canadian Furniture, by Scott Symons, with photographs by John de Visser (Toronto: McClelland and Stewart, 1971).

Relevant essays and articles include:

"The Military Policy of Canada, 1905 to 1924, and Suggestions for the Future" by J. Sutherland Brown (*Canadian Defence Quarterly,* Vol. 1, No. 4, July 1924).

"Anglo-American War Possibilities" by B.K. Sandwell (*Saturday Night,* 15 March 1930).

"Canadian Defence Policy and the American Empire" by Philip Resnick, in *Close the 49th Parallel Etc,* ed. by Ian Lumsden (University of Toronto Press, 1970).

"The Undefended Border" by James Eayrs, in *Canada: A Guide to the Peaceable Kingdom,* ed. by William Kilbourn (Toronto: Macmillan of Canada, 1970).

"Buster Brown Was Not Alone" and "Buster Brown Was Not Alone: A Postscript" by Richard A. Preston, in *Canadian Defence Quarterly,* Vols. III and IV, Spring and Summer 1974.

"The Great Unfinished Task of Col J. Sutherland Brown" by Mark Starowicz, in *Let Us Prey,* ed. by Robert Chodos and Rae Murphy (Toronto: James Lorimer, 1974).

"Two Centuries in the Shadow of Behemoth: The Effect on the Canadian Psyche" by Richard A. Preston (*International Journal,* Vol. XXXI, No. 3, Summer 1976).

BISHOP WILLIAM WHITE

I am grateful to Dr Gordon B. White and Mrs Ronald Perry for discussing their father with me, and permitting me to draw upon his papers in the Thomas Fisher Rare Book Library at the University of Toronto. I was also assisted by Dr Margaret Brown, E.B. Jolliffe, Miss Betty Kingston, the Rev Gordon Taylor and Mrs H.G. Watts.

Dr Lewis C. Walmsley was most helpful. His book *Bishop in Honan:* Mission and Museum in the Life of William

C. White (University of Toronto Press, 1974) is a detailed and authoritative biography from which I have drawn much factual material.

Bishop White's contributions as a curator are described and illustrated in two publications of the Royal Ontario Museum: *The Far Eastern Collection,* by Henry Trubner (1968), and *The Bishop White Gallery* (1969). For an account of the Museum's early days, see *I Brought the Ages Home,* by C.T. Currelly (Toronto: Ryerson, 1956).

There are useful discussions of the missionary impact on China in *The Missionary Enterprise in China and America,* ed. by John K. Fairbank (Harvard University Press, 1974), and *The British in the Far East* by George Woodcock (London: Weidenfeld and Nicolson, 1969), pp 99-110 and 236-7. For a Chinese point of view, see *The Wilting of the Hundred Flowers,* by Mu Fu-sheng (London: Heinemann, 1962), pp 105-110.

JAMES HOUSTON

James and Alice Houston have been more than generous with their help and hospitality. Much of this chapter is based on interviews with Houston.

Among Houston's own works, the following are especially relevant:

> *Eskimo Prints* (Barre, Mass.: Barre Publishers, 1971).
> *Ojibwa Summer* (Barre, Mass.: Barre Publishers, 1972).
> *The White Dawn* (Scarborough: New American Library of Canada, 1972).
> *Ghost Fox* (Toronto: McClelland and Stewart, 1977).

Two basic texts on Eskimo art are:

> *Sculpture of the Eskimo,* by George Swinton (Toronto: McClelland and Stewart, 1972). See pp 123-134 for a discussion of Houston's role.
> *Sculpture/Inuit,* published for the Canadian Eskimo Arts Council (University of Toronto Press, 1971). See pp 52-57 for Houston's essay "To Find Life in the Stone".

For an account by one of the Eskimo artists, see *Pictures*

Out of My Life, by Pitseolak (Toronto: Oxford University Press, 1975).

There are countless books which discuss the impact of the white man on our native peoples, including most of Farley Mowat's many works.

Among the other non-fiction books are:

The Harrowing of Eden: White Attitudes Toward North American Natives, by J.E. Chamberlin (Toronto: Fitzhenry and Whiteside, 1975).

Prison of Grass, by Howard Adams (Toronto: New Press, 1975).

The People's Land: Eskimos and Whites in the Eastern Arctic, by Hugh Brody (Penguin Books, 1975).

Novels on the same theme include:

The Sparrow's Fall, by Fred Bodsworth (New York: New American Library, 1968).

White Eskimo, by Harold Horwood (Toronto: Paper Jacks, 1973).

Riverrun, by Peter Such (Toronto: Clarke, Irwin, 1975).

Two essays on the importance of the North to Canadian nationalism and sensibility are: "The True North Strong and Free" by Carl Berger, and "The Myth of the Land in Canadian Nationalism" by Cole Harris, both in *Nationalism in Canada,* ed. by Peter Russell (Toronto: McGraw-Hill Ryerson, 1966).

See *Survival,* by Margaret Atwood (Toronto: Anansi, 1972) for the roles of nature and native peoples in Canadian literature.

Two of Ralph Connor's most important novels — *Glengarry School Days* and *The Man From Glengarry* — are in the New Canadian Library (Toronto: McClelland and Stewart).

I have also drawn upon "James Houston, the Neglected Hero" by John Ayre (*Saturday Night,* May 1974).

HERBERT NORMAN

Many people gave me information and insights on Herbert Norman. I am especially grateful to his widow, Mrs Irene Norman, his sister, Mrs Grace Miller, and his brother, Dr Howard Norman. Others who provided valuable assistance are: T.A. Bisson, R.B. Bryce, John W. Dower, James Eayrs, Mark Gayn, William L. Holland, John Holmes, George Ignatieff, Alex I. Inglis, Arthur Kilgour, Ross Macdonald, C.E. McGaughey, Genji Okubo, G.A.H. Pearson, Cyril Powles, Edwin O. Reischauer, Kazuyo Sato and Lorie Tarshis. I am also grateful to David Rhydwen, for allowing me to use the library at *The Globe and Mail,* and to A.E. Blanchette and A.F. Hart, successive Directors of the Historical Division of the Department of External Affairs, for making available some of Norman's diplomatic dispatches.

Norman's own books include:

Japan's Emergence as a Modern State (New York: Institute of Pacific Relations, 1940).

Soldier and Peasant in Japan: The Origins of Conscription (New York: Institute of Pacific Relations, 1943).

Ando Shoeki and the Anatomy of Japanese Feudalism (Tokyo: The Asiatic Society of Japan, 1949).

A contemporary anthology is: *Origins of the Modern Japanese State:* Selected Writings of E.H. Norman, ed. by John W. Dower (New York: Pantheon, 1975). Dower's lengthy introduction is especially valuable on Norman's tangled relations with SCAP, his influence on the Japanese, his academic denigration in the United States and his importance as an historian.

Journey to the Frontier: Two Roads to the Spanish Civil War, by Peter Stansky and William Abrahams (New York: Norton, 1970) is a vivid account of John Cornford and the radical movement at Cambridge in the nineteen-thirties.

The Nobility of Failure, by Ivan Morris (New York: Holt Rinehart and Winston, 1975) is an important work on the Japanese tradition of suicide.

Accounts of Norman's political persecution are contained in:

Canada in World Affairs: October 1955 to June 1957, by James Eayrs (Toronto: Oxford University Press, 1959), pp 153-160.

The Things That are Caesar's: The Memoirs of a Canadian Public Servant, by Arnold Heeney (University of Toronto Press, 1972), pp 98, 144-5.

Mike: The Memoirs of the Rt Hon Lester B. Pearson, Vol. Three, 1957-1968, ed. by John A. Munro and Alex I. Inglis (University of Toronto Press, 1975), pp 168-173.

Essays and articles include:

"The Strange Case of Mr Norman" (*U.S. News and World Report,* 26 April 1957). This includes valuable documentation.

"What Kind of Man was Herbert Norman?" by Sidney Katz (*Maclean's,* 28 September 1957). An important article written in the immediate aftermath of Norman's suicide by a journalist who interviewed many of his closest friends and colleagues.

"An Affection for the Lesser Names" by Masao Maruyama (*Pacific Affairs,* Vol. XXX, No. 3, September 1957). An intriguing Japanese view of Norman.

"E.H. Norman and the Task for Japanese History" by Harry D. Harootunian, and "E.H. Norman: Structure and Function in the Meiji State, A Reappraisal" by Bernard S. Silberman (*Pacific Affairs,* Vol. XLI, No. 4, Winter 1968-69).

"E.H. Norman as an Economic Historian" by Kozo Yamamura, and "Political Consciousness in Japan: A Retrospect on E.H. Norman" by David Abosch (*Pacific Affairs,* Vol. XLII, No. 5, Spring 1969).

I have also drawn on the Pearson Papers in the Public Archives of Canada, and on the transcript of "First Person Singular" — the CBC television documentary on the Pearson years.

I should like to thank John K. Emmerson for showing me material from his forthcoming book.

EMILY CARR

Emily Carr's own books are a major source of information on her life and work.

I have drawn upon:

Klee Wyck
The Book of Small
The House of All Sorts
Growing Pains
Hundreds and Thousands
Fresh Seeing

Each of these books is published by Clarke, Irwin, and each remains in print.

Two close friends of Carr have written personal memoirs:

Emily Carr as I Knew Her, by Carol Pearson (Toronto: Clarke, Irwin, 1954).

M.E. - A Portrait of Emily Carr, by Edythe Hembroff-Schleicher (Toronto: Clarke, Irwin, 1969).

Emily Carr, by Doris Shadbolt (Vancouver: J. J. Douglas, 1975) contains reproductions of many of Carr's paintings, a comprehensive bibliography and very useful accounts of Carr's life and work. In her own writings, Carr is often inconsistent in her dates. I have followed Mrs Shadbolt's chronology.

Articles and essays include:

"Emily Carr — An Appreciation" by Ruth Humphrey (*Queen's Quarterly,* No. 65, Summer 1958).

"Emily Carr" by Roy Daniells, in *Our Living Tradition,* 4th series, ed. by Robert L. McDougall (University of Toronto Press, 1962).

"Emily Carr" by William Kilbourn, in *Great Canadians,* The Canadian Centennial Library (Toronto: McClelland and Stewart, 1965).

"Emily Carr" by Flora Hamilton Burns, in *The Clear Spirit:* Twenty Canadian Women and Their Times, ed. by Mary Quayle Innis (University of Toronto Press, 1966).

"A Paste Solitaire in a Steel-Claw Setting: Emily Carr and Her Public" by Maria Tippett *(BC Studies,* No. 20, Winter 1973-74).

See also:

A Canadian Art Movement, by F. B. Housser (Toronto: Macmillan of Canada, 1974). First published in 1926, this is a contemporary account of the origins and early development of the Group of Seven.

"Conclusion to a *Literary History of Canada"* by Northrop Frye, reprinted in *The Bush Garden:* Essays on the Canadian Imagination (Toronto: Anansi, 1971). This chapter includes Frye's discussion of the garrison mentality.

I have also drawn upon the artist's files in the Toronto Central Library, the Art Gallery of Ontario and the Vancouver Art Gallery.

I would like to thank   Doris Shadbolt,   Paul Duval, and Maria Tippett for their assistance.

SCOTT SYMONS

Scott Symons' published books are:

Place d'Armes (Toronto: McClelland and Stewart, 1967).

Civic Square (Toronto: McClelland and Stewart, 1969).

Heritage: A Romantic Look at Early Canadian Furniture, with photographs by John de Visser (Toronto: McClelland and Stewart, 1971).

Forthcoming publications include:

Helmet of Flesh, a trilogy of novels.

I have drawn extensively on Symons' unpublished diaries and letters. Most of these are available for inspection at the library of Trinity College in the University of Toronto.

Symons has evoked his boyhood in "Rosedale ain't what it used to be" *(Toronto Life,* October 1972).

His views on his Canadian heritage were outlined in

"The Meaning of English Canada", an address to the Canadian Centenary Council Symposium, printed in *Continuous Learning*, the Journal of The Canadian Association for Adult Education, Vol. 2, No. 6, Nov.-Dec. 1963.

Symons has discussed his position as a writer in *Eleven Canadian Novelists*, interviewed by Graeme Gibson (Toronto: Anansi, 1973).

His trenchant views on contemporary Canadian literature are expressed in "The Canadian Bestiary: Ongoing Literary Depravity" in *West Coast Review*, Jan-Feb 1977.

Excerpts from *Helmet of Flesh* are contained in *Canadian Fiction Magazine*, Jan-Feb 1977.

I am grateful to Sean Kane, Aaron Klokeid, Dennis Lee and Sandy McCall for their assistance.